Essential App Engine

Essential App Engine

Building High-Performance Java Apps with Google App Engine

Adriaan de Jonge

Addison-Wesley

Upper Saddle River, NJ • Boston • Indianapolis • San Francisco
New York • Toronto • Montreal • London • Munich • Paris • Madrid
Capetown • Sydney • Tokyo • Singapore • Mexico City

Library of Congress Cataloging-in-Publication Data

Jonge, Adriaan de, 1979-
Essential app engine : building high-performance Java apps with Google App engine / Adriaan de Jonge.
p. cm.
Includes index.
ISBN 978-0-321-74263-6 (pbk. : alk. paper)
1. Computer software—Development. 2. Software architecture. 3. Java (Computer program language) 4. Google Apps. I. Title.
QA76.76.D47D425 2012
005.1—dc23

2011030789

ISBN-13: 978-0-321-74263-6
ISBN-10: 0-321-74263-X
Text printed in the United States on recycled paper at RR Donnelley in Crawfordsville, Indiana.
First printing, October 2011

Editor-in-Chief
Mark Taub

Acquisitions Editor
Trina MacDonald

Development Editor
Michael Thurston

Managing Editor
John Fuller

Project Editor
Anna V. Popick

Copy Editor
Carol Lallier

Indexer
Jack Lewis

Proofreader
Kelli Brooks

Technical Reviewers
Joseph Annuzzi
Romin Irani
Alex Moffat

Editorial Assistant
Olivia Basegio

Cover Designer
Gary Adair

Compositor
LaurelTech

❖

To everyone who is chasing their dreams…

❖

Contents at a Glance

Contents

Introduction

A single hype is not enough to change the world. But multiple hypes together can change it as long as they are part of a bigger trend.

This book discusses more than one hyped technology: cloud computing, NoSQL, and HTML5. The technologies in this book combine well with other hyped technologies: functional languages (Scala) and connected devices (iPhone, iPad, Android).

The Internet is changing the world. That is old news, yes, but because it's old news, you may easily overlook the Internet's ongoing dynamics and influences. A good indicator that you are missing the cybership is if you are still stuck on Spring and Hibernate. Frameworks solving yesterday's problems are blocking the way to handle tomorrow's challenges.

The Google App Engine is a perfect fit with current Internet trends. Reading this book gives you a head start with upcoming technologies. This Introduction describes how both the App Engine and this book fit in the current trends.

Analyzing Internet Trends

To analyze the current Internet trends, you need to take a few steps back in time and see what has happened in the past two decades.

Starting in the Nineties

Let's start with the early 1990s. At first, the World Wide Web was used mostly to serve static HTML pages. The best way to serve a dynamic web application was to configure a `/cgi-bin` directory connecting to Perl scripts or binary programs that redirected the output to the web visitor. Web applications were nowhere near as mature as classic office applications. By the late nineties, though, developers were incorporating best practices from classic office automation into web applications, and the Internet soared with the dot-com bubble.

Switching to the New Millennium

In the early 2000s, web programmers realized that a Model-View-Controller pattern was not such a bad idea after all. And around 2005, Asynchronous JavaScript and XML (AJAX) helped make web applications more interactive. By 2008, web applications and office applications were on the same maturity level, sharing many of the same technologies, such as SQL databases and heavy application servers. Some UI libraries even tried to mimic classic Windows interfaces, with the ultimate goal of bringing a not-so-user-friendly interface concept into the browser.

Analyzing Current Developments

Right now, you can see the start of a trend in which Internet technology surpasses the maturity level of classic office automation. The frontrunners in Internet technology are critically investigating all parts of their systems and analyzing their designs for fit with the requirements of the current Internet environment. New technologies are being developed from scratch with the Internet's scalability requirements as a first priority.

It won't be long until office automation will have trouble keeping up with Internet technologies. That is the point where office automation will start adopting the best practices from the Internet instead of the other way around.

Replacing SQL Databases with NoSQL

Relational databases are one of the most widely used technologies in classic office automation. They are mature, well standardized, taught in most schools and universities, and available in all sizes. However, they were designed at a time when storage was still expensive, the number of users was limited to the number of employees in a single company, and the focus of their use was on transaction processing.

Relational databases do not scale well. They were designed as central storages operating efficiently enough to handle most of their work alone. In larger environments, their capabilities can be expanded using horizontally or vertically distributed databases or load-balanced setups that replicate data among multiple machines. Usually this functionality requires expensive software, machinery, and specialized knowledge, though, so at the end of the day, relational databases are still limited.

Switching to NoSQL with the Google App Engine Datastore

A common characteristic of NoSQL databases is high scalability. NoSQL databases are designed specifically with the requirements of the Internet in mind. To serve millions of visitors around the world in a few hundred milliseconds, you need functionality beyond that of relational databases. If you do not need to serve that many visitors, you may still consider relational databases because of their consistency and transactional integrity. You should choose NoSQL only if the advantages match your requirements.

Google App Engine offers the datastore as NoSQL storage. It allows you to store entities, each with a set of key-value pairs. A value can also consist of an array of values. Benefits of the App Engine offering are that you need not worry about system administration, and its APIs easily integrate with the rest of the platform.

When you start working with the App Engine datastore, you discover that NoSQL databases have additional advantages over the classic SQL offerings. The APIs are less awkward to use than JDBC APIs.

Moving Away from Object Relational Mapping

Object relational mapping has always been painful. Doing the mapping yourself is so cumbersome that it scares developers into using heavy and code-intensive frameworks like Hibernate, Java Data Objects (JDO), and the Java Persistence API (JPA). Choosing not to map relational structures to objects is virtually impossible. It would imply keeping JDBC connections open longer than necessary.

NoSQL databases relieve you from the burden of object relational mapping. If you insist, you can still map your datastore's structures to Java objects. This does not always make sense though. This book shows many examples of datastore entities being directly passed to an HTML template. The result is clean, simple, and efficient code.

Considering Alternative NoSQL Solutions

Examples of other NoSQL databases are Amazon SimpleDB, Riak, Voldemort, Microsoft Trinity, Hadoop, Cassandra, CouchDB, MongoDB, Kyoto Cabinet, Hypertable, GraphDB, Redis, Google Pregel, and Google BigTable (the underlying platform of the App Engine's datastore). Each of these products has its own characteristics. Some are key-value storages, graph storages, document storages, or variants of these structures.

After reading this book and practicing with App Engine datastore, you should investigate the various NoSQL initiatives for your work on platforms other than the App Engine. Many of the advantages of the datastore on the App Engine platform can also be found outside the App Engine. This is all part of a larger trend, after all.

Computing in the Cloud

Cloud computing changes the way you write your applications. Classic enterprise applications usually optimize performance by taking a performance hit at startup time. If your application is restarted only once every few months, that can be an acceptable strategy. However, on some cloud platforms, including Google App Engine, your applications may be started and stopped multiple times an hour. This means that you should optimize your application to start up extremely fast, which may require throwing out all heavyweight frameworks, like Spring or Grails.

Maintaining Systems in the Cloud

Hosting applications in the cloud means hosting without worrying about the underlying infrastructure. In all cloud offerings, you pay only for what you use. This is especially interesting if your site experiences sudden high spikes in visitors. In classic setups, you require a machine park that is standing still most of the time, waiting for the exceptional spike when it really needs to work.

The advantage of the App Engine over other cloud initiatives is that it scales automatically. You need not give orders to start up additional instances of your application. If you are worried about controlling your budget, you can set a maximum on your every day expenses. This helps you prevent bankruptcy after a distributed denial-of-service (DDOS) attack.

The App Engine does not expose details of the underlying operating system to its users. Cloud services like Amazon Elastic Compute Cloud (EC2) and Microsoft Azure let users maintain their own instance of an operating system. This is a trade-off between freedom and maintenance costs.

The App Engine could be characterized as a software developer's cloud platform, whereas EC2 could be characterized as a system administrator's cloud platform. Microsoft Azure is most interesting if your company is already running on a full Microsoft stack. It fits best with the .Net developer community, although it must be mentioned that Microsoft also targets Java developers with its Azure platform.

Make an informed decision about which platform you'll use before you start developing, because some lock-in is involved. Don't choose the App Engine just because it's Google or because you liked the cover of this book. Choose it because you want a well-integrated platform that relieves you from the burden of system administration and automatically scales to sudden changes in demand even while you sleep.

Connecting with Other Cloud Offerings

You can also consider cloud computing from a nontechnical perspective. When managers discuss cloud computing, they are usually talking about Google Apps rather than Google App Engine. Google Apps includes Google Docs, Gmail, Google Calendar, and Google Sites for Business. The App Engine is just a technical platform on which software vendors can host their applications. Managers may not be interested in such hosting. They are interested in the applications.

The Google Apps Marketplace helps software vendors sell applications that integrate well with Google Apps. The Google App Engine is the ideal platform for hosting applications that integrate with Google Apps. Hosting in Google's cloud may also help when selling your application to customers who already use Google Apps.

Adopting HTML5

HTML4 and XHTML1 have ruled the world for a long time. Now it is time to move on. The World Wide Web made a shift from serving documents to serving web applications. And even though documents will probably be served until the end of time, the real technical challenge is in serving user-friendly web applications.

Web interfaces are more easily understood by the average user than classic Windows interfaces. In operating systems, you can see a trend toward simplifying client-side interfaces to work similarly to web interfaces. Smart phones show similar advancements. Smart phone vendors are trying to keep up with the simplicity of Apple's iPhone.

HTML4 and XHTML1 have some limitations that quickly become awkward when using them to offer web applications. A lack of descriptive HTML element names is just a minor flaw that leads to overly complicated Cascading Style Sheet (CSS) files. HTML5 fixes this problem. More interesting are the additional JavaScript APIs offered with the HTML5 specification.

Using HTML5 offers many benefits. For example, consider the File Chooser dialog when uploading a file. HTML5 allows you to drag and drop files into your browser. You can try this by adding an attachment in Gmail using drag and drop. Another example is the use of cookies or heavy server-side sessions. HTML5 offers session storage, local storage, and IndexedDB to store about 5MB of data on the client for later reuse. HTML5 allows you to make drawings on the client side using the Canvas.

Finally, the support for HTML5 on mobile and connected devices is better than you might expect. Some of the features of HTML5 are particularly useful on handheld devices. The lack of Flash support on iPhone and iPad is well compensated by HTML5. And possibly one of the most interesting features of HTML5 on a mobile device is the ability to ask for the user's location. If the user allows it, you can use it to customize search results to the things most relevant in that particular area.

Discussing Trends Out of Scope for This Book

Essential App Engine: Building High-Performance Java Apps with Google App Engine discusses some of the latest trends in cloud computing with NoSQL and HTML5. Some related trends are beyond the scope of this book, but with some additional reading, you can combine these trends with the technologies discussed here.

Serving Apps on Connected Devices

The examples in this book assume that the visitors are accessing the application using a web browser or a mobile browser. All examples target HTML, CSS, and JavaScript.

In addition to browsers, applications are increasingly served through platform-specific applications running on the iPhone, iPad, Android, Windows Phone, or BlackBerry. Numerous books on developing applications for these platforms are available.

From an App Engine perspective, requests from mobile applications are in many ways similar to AJAX requests made from browsers. You can serve JSON (JavaScript Object Notation) strings over a RESTful interface, providing the same data in a format that is easily read by the applications.

Moving to New JVM Languages

Java has been called the Cobol of the 21st century. Without arguing against that, the examples in this book are nevertheless in Java. A seeming trend away from the Java language does not necessarily imply moving away from the Java Virtual Machine (JVM). Most popular new languages like Scala and Clojure compile to JVM bytecode.

At this point, the Java language is still the largest language on the JVM platform. Despite its growing popularity, Scala has nowhere near the user base of Java yet. And even for those who are interested in other JVM languages, the Java language itself serves well as the lingua franca of JVM languages. This book demonstrates the Google App Engine API in a language-neutral way, independent of the heavy Java framework. Code examples in this book easily translate to Scala, Clojure, Groovy, JRuby, or Jython.

This Book's Target Audience

Essential App Engine is written for software developers and software architects.

For *software developers*, this book provides a hands-on approach to developing applications for the Google App Engine. It contains many simple, standalone code examples that demonstrate the concepts without distractions of unrelated code and frameworks. Software developers can modify the examples to use as working code, realizing their applications.

Software architects can read this book to get a general overview of the characteristics of the App Engine platform. In addition to the code examples, this book provides in-depth background knowledge of how the App Engine datastore differs from classic relational databases. It covers how you should change your design to get the best performance out of it. In addition, this book provides many pointers on how to change the way you design web applications to optimize their performance when hosted in the cloud.

Overview of This Book

This book contains twenty chapters divided into five parts. The order of the parts is consistent with a software development project that follows a design-first approach. You can read the chapters in a different order, though: Chapters are cross-referenced when more detailed background knowledge is desirable.

- **Part I, "An App Engine Overview,"** introduces you to the basics of the App Engine. It presents a discussion of performance characteristics and a practical guide to setting up your development environment so that you can continually address performance.
- **Part II, "Application Design Essentials,"** discusses all configuration options in the App Engine platform. It provides a design philosophy for modeling your data, targeting the Google App Engine datastore. And it discusses general technical design choices you should make before you start developing for the App Engine, such as whether or not to use Java Server Pages.
- **Part III, "User Interface Design Essentials,"** focuses on modern browser technology rather than on the App Engine itself. HTML5 and CSS3 are great companions when developing web applications in the cloud. The added possibilities in the browser help relieve the server from a lot of work and memory usage, ultimately lowering your usage costs while leveraging a responsive and user-friendly application to your client. In addition to discussion of HTML5 and CSS3, Part III provides an elaborate explanation of how to use JavaScript and AJAX to continue programming on the client side.
- **Part IV, "Using Common App Engine APIs,"** contains everything you need to know about the App Engine APIs. This includes the datastore, the Blobstore, the

Mail API, task scheduling, memory cache, URL retrieval, web application security, and XMPP messaging.

- **Part V, "Application Deployment,"** discusses how to improve your development process, optimize the quality of your web application, and sell it to potential customers.

The Essential App Engine Blog

Google provides frequent updates to the App Engine, adding new features and APIs, in response to popular demand. To keep you up to date, a companion website to this book, the Essential App Engine blog, is available at www.essentialappengine.com.

Check this website for the latest updates, the source code for this book, and additional code examples!

Acknowledgments

Writing a book is impossible without a strong and reliable support team.

First, I'd like to thank everybody at Addison-Wesley for all their help and support. I owe special thanks to the following people:

- Trina MacDonald, for helping me through the process, providing practical tips on project planning, being my conscience for keeping the schedule, and knowing when to be patient and impatient at exactly the right times.
- Michael Thurston, for the thorough and detailed feedback on all texts and structure.
- Olivia Basegio, for all the work behind the scenes, keeping things running flawlessly at all times.
- The technical editors Joseph Annuzzi, Romin Irani, and Alex Moffat, each with their own specific area of interest and expertise. This book was greatly improved thanks to all their feedback, suggestions, and ideas, both high-level and in great detail.
- Carol Lallier, for making great improvements in the text while copy editing.

I'd like to thank everybody at ANWB who showed interest in the writing process of this book. You can hardly imagine the positive effect of your involvement.

Last but not least, great thanks go to all my family and friends. Thank you, first, simply for being my family and friends. And thank you for bearing with me throughout the process of writing this book—even if it sometimes meant I spent less time with you.

About the Author

Adriaan de Jonge is an online specialist in the Netherlands. He has worked in several roles: researcher, consultant, software architect, and author. He is not planning to settle down in a single role any time soon.

His areas of interest are Internet, gadgets, buzzwords, programming languages, and datastores—almost anything as long as it is new, lightweight, and challenging food for thought.

Adriaan works for ANWB, the Dutch association for tourism, traffic, and roadside assistance.

PART I

An App Engine Overview

Chapter 1

Setting Up a Development Environment

Before you start developing for the Google App Engine, you must set up tools to help you in the process. This chapter starts with the default tools in Eclipse in their most basic setup. At the end of the chapter are some pointers on how to deploy your application from the command line without using Eclipse.

Working with Eclipse Tools

The App Engine restricts developers from using certain APIs. To overcome some of the limitations, services are offered allowing you to implement functionality regardless of the restrictions. When writing code, you want to make sure, early in the process, that you do not violate restrictions. Also, you want to be able to work with the App Engine services in the earliest possible stage.

Google provides tools to simulate the App Engine environment on your own computer. Both the restrictions and the App Engine services are mimicked on a local Jetty server. By default, these tools are provided as a Software Development Toolkit (SDK) you can access from the command line.

Most Java developers prefer integrated development environments (IDEs) like Eclipse, NetBeans, or IntelliJ IDEA to write their code in the most efficient way. To help Java developers, Google provides a plugin for the Eclipse IDE.

> **Registering Your Application**
>
> Before you start installing Eclipse development tools, go to http://appengine.google.com and register an identifier for your application. Remember the identifier http://<your-identifier>.appspot.com for later in this chapter. It may take some time to find an unused name. Keep in mind that you can always change the name to your own domain name later on.
>
> When you register an App Engine application for the first time, Google may ask for additional information such as a mobile number that needs to be verified using an SMS (Short Message Service).

Installing Plugins in Eclipse

Use a recent version of Eclipse, and check that you have a clean installation without any plugins installed. Figure 1.1 shows Eclipse in a clean installation.

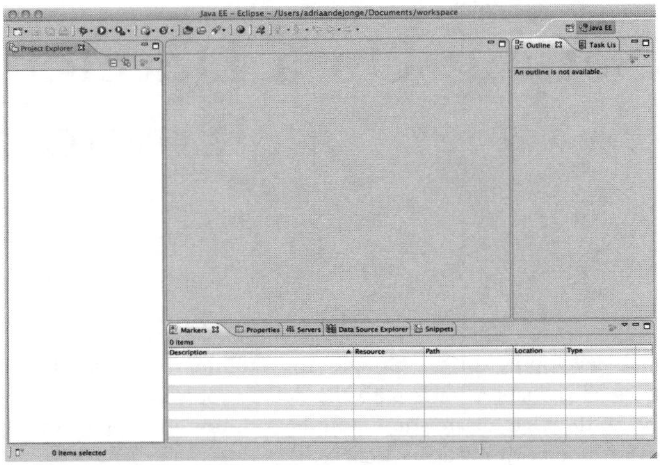

Figure 1.1 Starting with a clean Eclipse window without plugins installed.

Eclipse allows you to install plugins in the application. Most likely you have done this before. The only difficulty is that the Eclipse developers change the installation dialogs relatively often when new versions of Eclipse are released.

At the time of writing, Eclipse version 3.6 has separate dialogs for installing new software and updating existing plugins. You can find both under the Help menu, as shown in Figure 1.2.

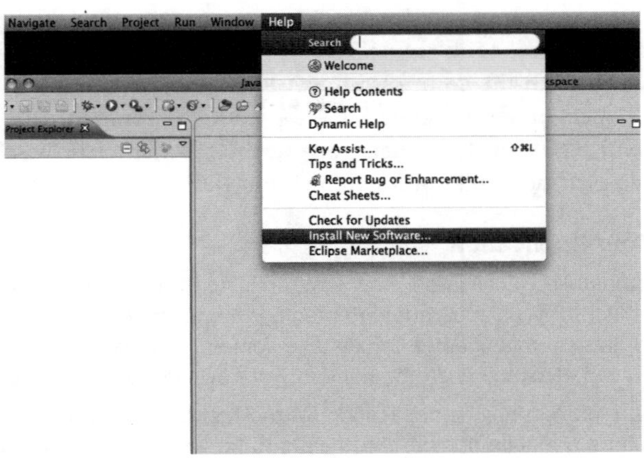

Figure 1.2 Selecting the menu item for installing new software.

The installation dialog may contain a list of existing software repositories from which you can download new plugins. Most likely, the repository for installing the App Engine tools for Eclipse is not there yet.

The repository path you need to enter depends on your Eclipse version. You can find the most recent repository paths on Google's website: http://code.google.com/appengine/docs/java/tools/eclipse.html. Make sure you select the repository corresponding with your version of Eclipse. The example installs the plugin in Eclipse 3.6.

After entering the current repository path, click the Add button, as shown in Figure 1.3.

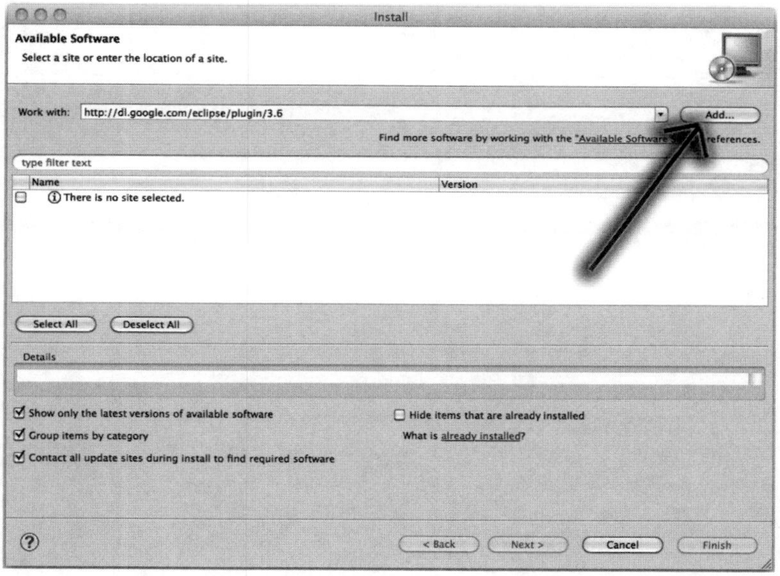

Figure 1.3 The install new software dialog before adding the Google App Engine repository.

Once you click the Add button, Eclipse asks you to provide a name for this repository. You can choose a name that is logical to you. In Figure 1.4, it is named GAE after Google App Engine. In some cases, it might be wise to stress the version number in the name.

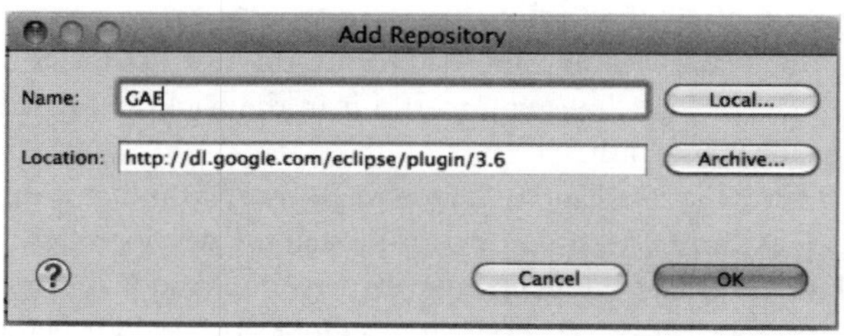

Figure 1.4 Adding the App Engine repository to the software install dialog.

After adding the repository and storing it, you can install new software from this repository. From the list of new software to install, choose only the modules you really need. For example, the repository also lists the Google Web Toolkit (GWT) modules. It is better to keep your IDE as clean and light as possible. Eclipse is currently heavy enough as it is out of the box. A cleaner installation of Eclipse is more responsive and performs better. Figure 1.5 shows only the module that is absolutely necessary to work with the Google App Engine within Eclipse.

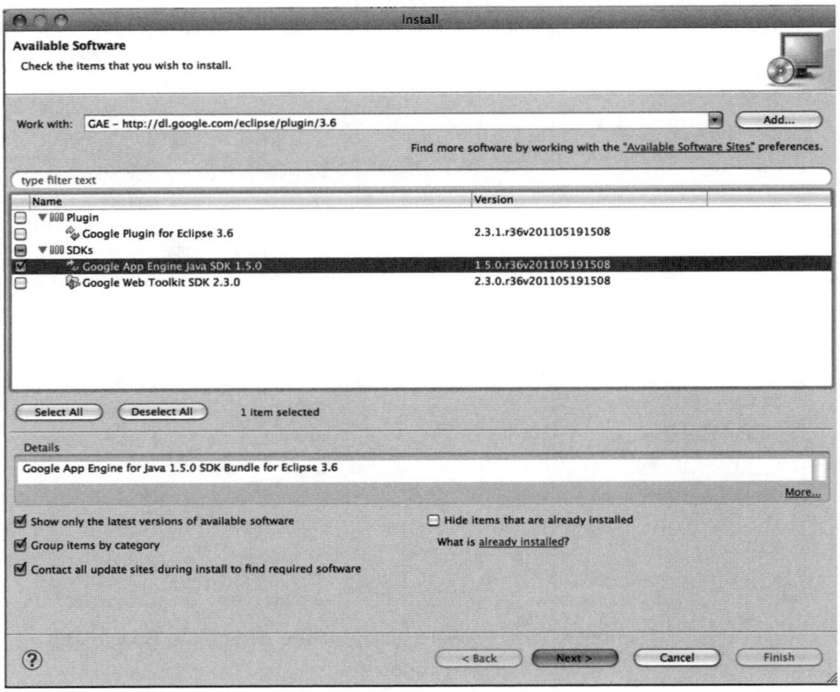

Figure 1.5 Selecting the only necessary module for installation.

A standard procedure in Eclipse is to ask the user to agree with the software license before installation. Read the licenses careful before you agree with them. Figure 1.6 shows the agreement with all the licenses.

The installation may take several minutes. During the installation, you see the progress indicator. Although the dialog allows you to run it in the background, in practice you might want to wait for it to finish.

At some point during the installation, Eclipse might warn you that it cannot confirm the authenticity of Google's certificate. If you want to install the development tools, you have no choice but to click OK. Perhaps the Eclipse developers should add an extra button named "This is not really OK, but I have no choice, so continue anyway." Or perhaps the developers considered such a message but found the text too long for a small button.

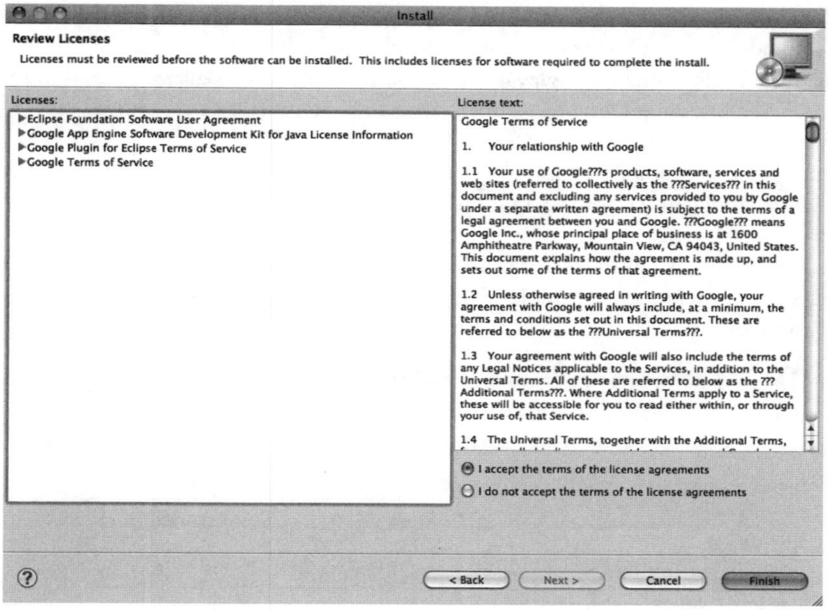

Figure 1.6 Accepting the software license.

After the installation finishes, Eclipse asks whether you want to restart Eclipse. Although the software may work without an Eclipse restart, your safest bet is to restart it. If your installation is sufficiently clean, restarting does not take too long.

Starting a New App Engine Project

When the newly started Eclipse instance shows on your screen, you'll find a few extra buttons in the toolbar that weren't shown in Figure 1.1. The new blue button allows you to create a new Google App Engine project, as shown in Figure 1.7.

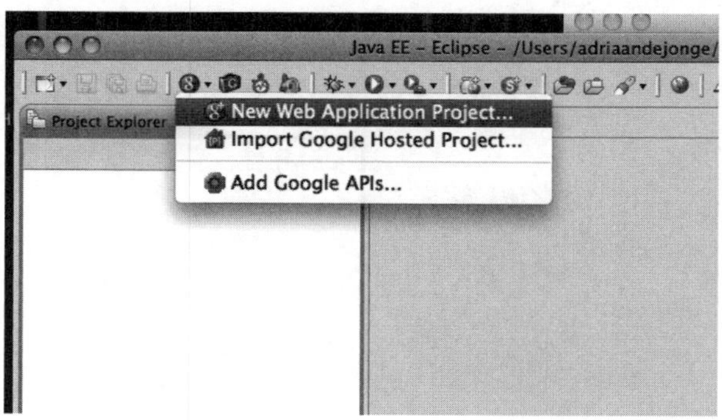

Figure 1.7 Starting a new web application project.

When you click the blue button, a dialog opens with a simple wizard to set up a new project. In addition to choosing a name, you select whether or not you want to use Google Web Toolkit. The examples in this book do not use Google Web Toolkit. Instead, Part III, "User Interface Design Essentials," provides pointers on the optimal use of browser technologies HTML5, CSS3, and JavaScript.

Figure 1.8 provides an example for naming the application. At this point, your project name can be independent of the application identifier you chose at the beginning of this chapter.

After the dialog is completed, the App Engine plugins generate a little basic code to get you started. Included is a simple Hello World servlet that you can execute to see that everything works. Figure 1.9 shows the resulting Eclipse screen.

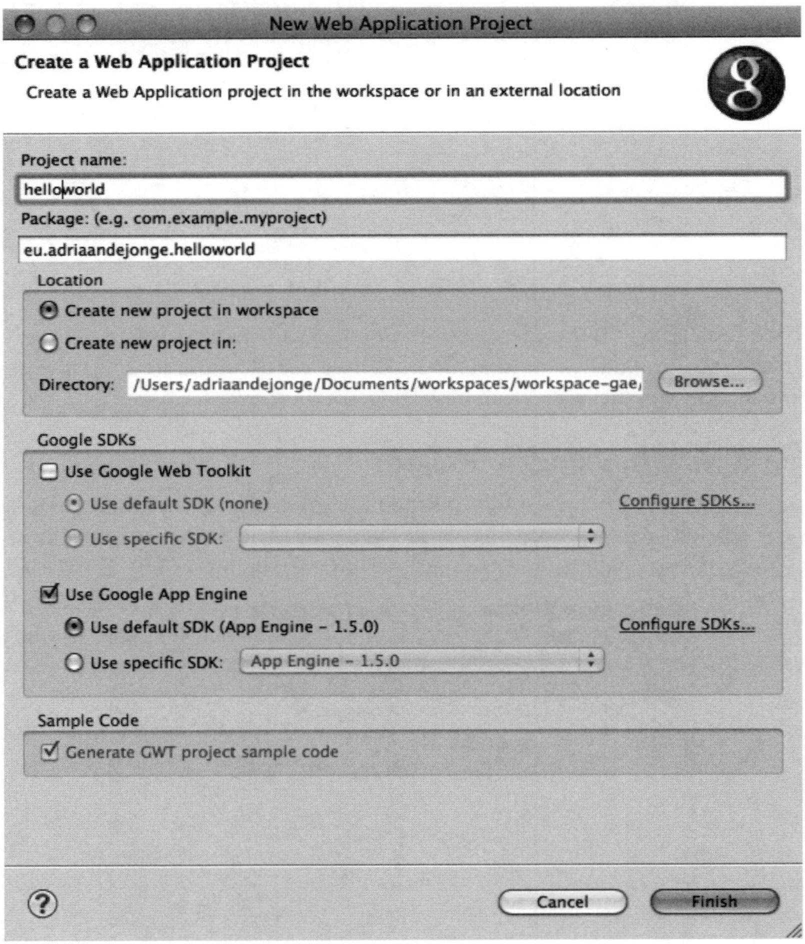

Figure 1.8 Typing a name for the new project.

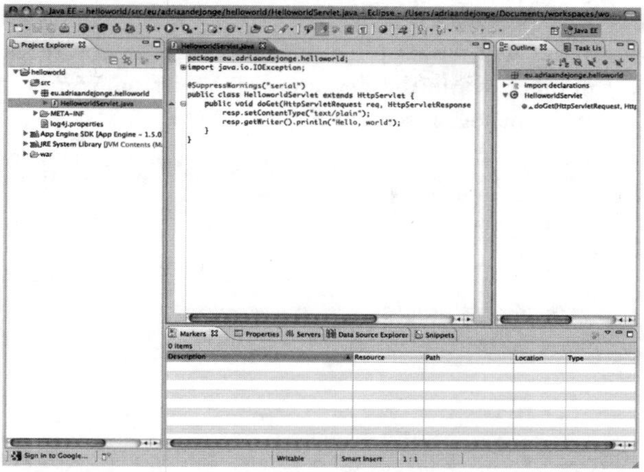

Figure 1.9 The Eclipse screen after generating the new project including a servlet.

Starting the Development Server

Before uploading the code to Google, you want to check that everything works on your development server. Starting the development server is similar to starting a regular program in Eclipse. As Figure 1.10 shows, you can select the right-click menu Run As and choose the Web Application next to the blue g.

Figure 1.10 Starting the local development server.

You can see that the server started in the Console view. Any messages written to System.err and System.out will show up here during development. If you did not explicitly configure a port number to run the development server on, you can find the current value at the bottom of the dialog, as seen in Figure 1.11.

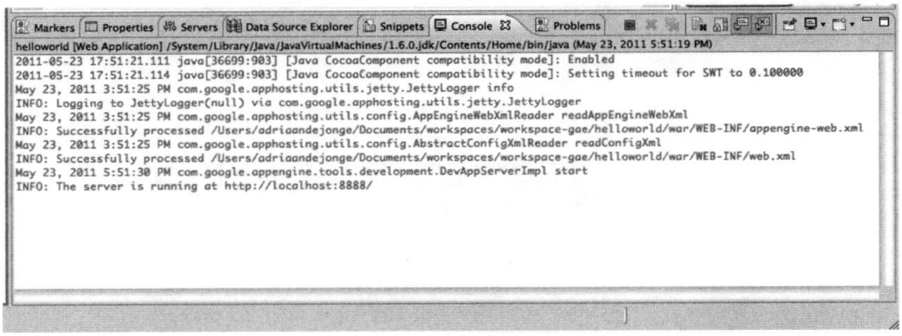

Figure 1.11 Viewing the Console window after starting the development server.

The more interesting output of the application is in the browser. If you open the URL shown at the bottom of the Console view, you get a list of available servlets similar to the screen shown in Figure 1.12.

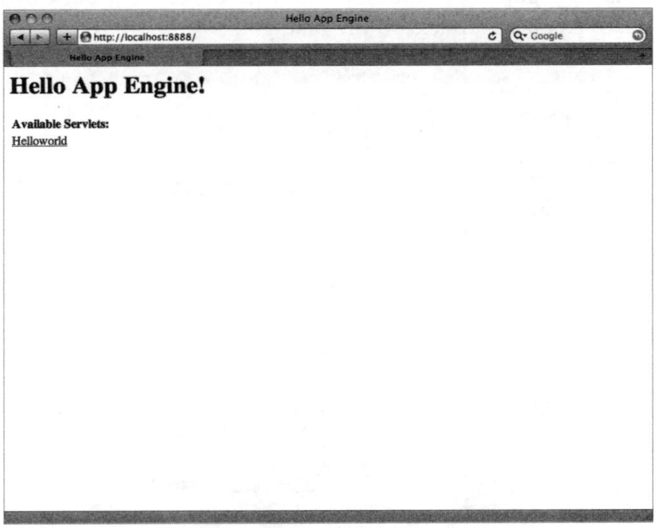

Figure 1.12 Viewing a list of available servlets.

Although you will be tweaking and tuning your web.xml file soon, at this point you can see the default output under the default URL by clicking on the link in the last screen. The result should not be too surprising: "Hello, world" as seen in Figure 1.13.

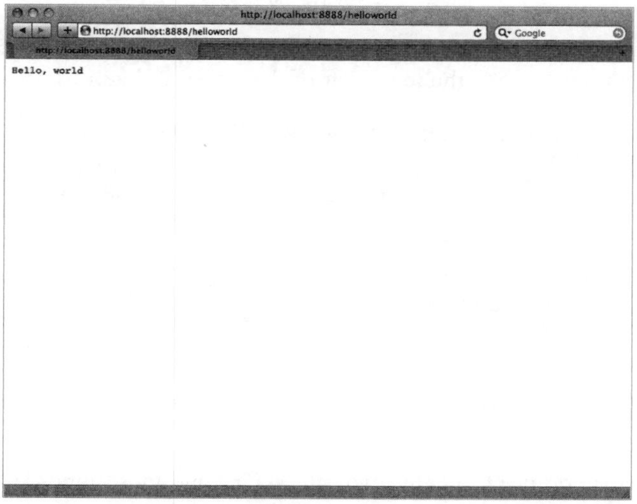

Figure 1.13 Viewing the actual servlet on the development server.

Deploying to the Online App Engine

Running the application on the local development server is a good step, although it is still an emulation of the real App Engine environment. The real work starts when you upload your application to the online App Engine environment. At this point, you have not yet configured the application identifier that you created at the beginning of this chapter. Let's find out what happens when you load the application. Click the toolbar button shown in Figure 1.14 to start the deployment process.

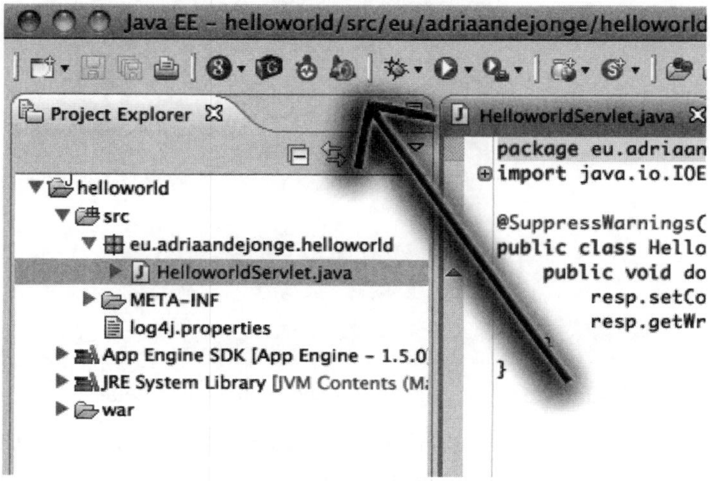

Figure 1.14 Launching application deployment from the Eclipse toolbar.

As expected, the deployment dialog provides an error message. Fortunately, the dialog makes it easy to fix the error directly by providing a link to the dialog where you can enter the project's settings. See the lower left of the screen in Figure 1.15.

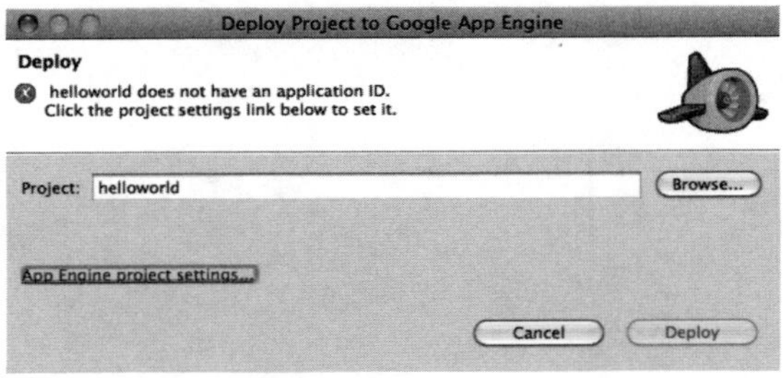

Figure 1.15 Finding out what configuration is missing before deploying the app.

To fix the error, you need to enter two values. First and most important, you must provide the application identifier you created earlier in this chapter. Second, you need to add a version. The App Engine management console allows you to have multiple versions of the software uploaded at the same time and to switch versions any time you like. In addition, you can start each of the versions separately without switching the default entry. Figure 1.16 shows the Hello World application configured as version 2.

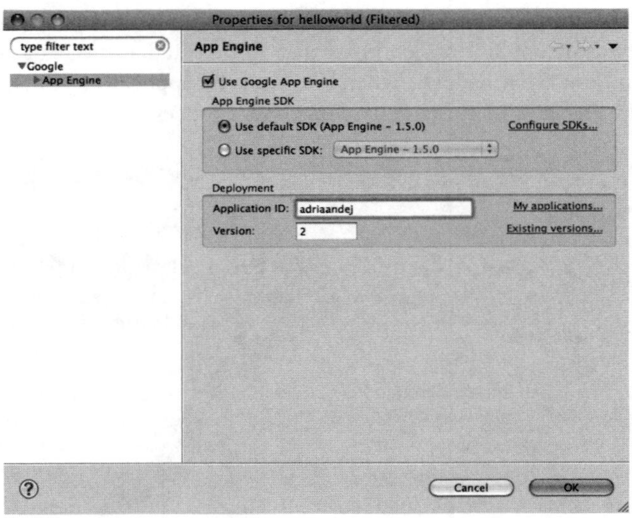

Figure 1.16 Adding the missing configuration details.

After saving the configuration parameters, you return to the deployment dialog. Instead of an error message, it shows you are ready to deploy your application and summarizes the configuration you entered; see Figure 1.17. You can click the Deploy button now!

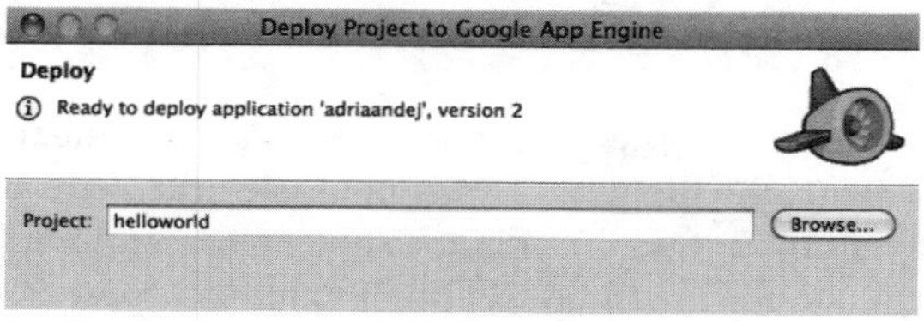

Figure 1.17 Checking that the configuration is now ready for deploying the application.

After you click the Deploy button, Google wants to authenticate you as the owner of the App Engine instance. It asks you to authorize Eclipse to upload the application on your behalf with a dialog similar to those in Chapter 16, "Securing a Web Application Using Google Accounts, OpenID, and OAuth." As shown in Figure 1.18, simply click Grant Access to proceed.

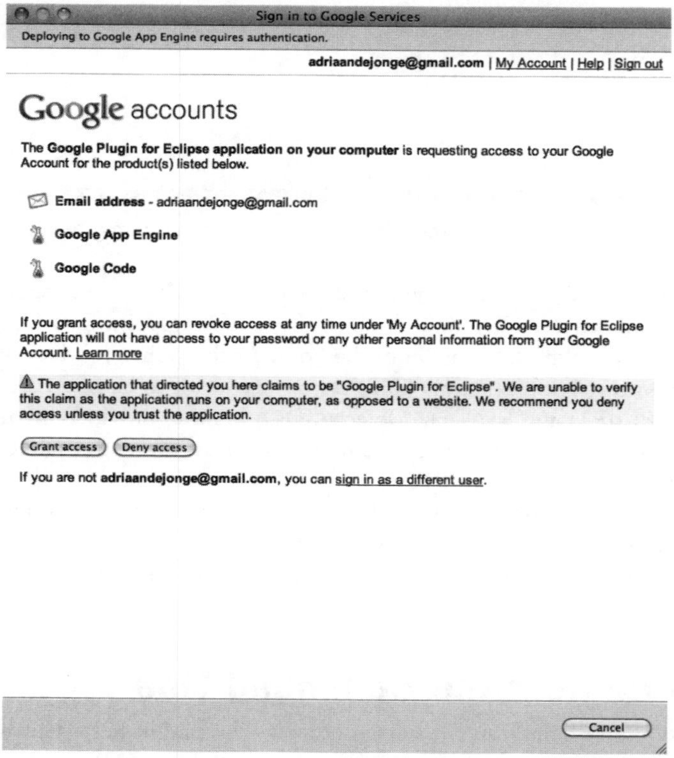

Figure 1.18 Granting access to deploy the application using your Google account.

After you finish deploying your application, you can return to your web browser and see if the application works.

Open http://<version>.<app-id>.appspot.com/ to go to your newly deployed web application without switching the default version in the management console. If you do switch the default version, or if you configured the deployment descriptor to overwrite the existing default version, you can go to http://<app-id>.appspot.com/. Figure 1.19 shows the resulting browser screen.

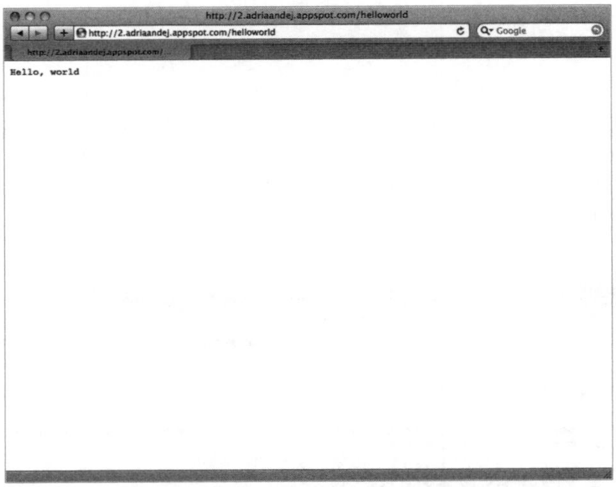

Figure 1.19 The resulting servlet seen online from a browser.

Congratulations! You are now the proud owner of a Hello World application running on Google's infrastructure! This is a clean and basic starting point for adding further functionality, as you will do throughout the book. At this point, you have minimal overhead to worry about. The only libraries you may want to clean up are the Java Persistence API (JPA) and Java Data Objects (JDO) libraries provided by default. Chapter 10, "Storing Data in the Datastore and Blobstore," explains how to use the low-level APIs without the overhead of JPA or JDO.

The Eclipse plugin does not like it if you throw out its libraries, though. This may not be the first thing to worry about when you start developing for the App Engine. You can throw them out later when you start deploying a really clean web application from the command line.

Deploying from the Command Line

The Eclipse plugin helps you get started quickly. The plugin helps you with some common tasks, such as configuring the default Java archive (JAR) files to be deployed with your application. At some point, when you want full control over each JAR to be deployed with your web application, you need to throw out the Eclipse plugin or separate your production deployment process from your development process.

You may have other reasons not to use the Eclipse plugins. Perhaps you are used to working with NetBeans or IntelliJ IDEA instead of Eclipse. Although the commercial version of IDEA provides App Engine tools, the community edition does not. If you use the community edition of IDEA or NetBeans, you must connect to the App Engine yourself.

To work from the command line, download the App Engine SDK for Java from Google: http://code.google.com/appengine/downloads.html.

The command-line tools allow you to deploy a directory that is set up in the same structure as a web archive (WAR) file except that an additional file, appengine-web.xml, is required in the WEB-INF directory. You can find this file in the project you created in Eclipse. More information on this file can be found in Chapter 3, "Understanding the Anatomy of a Google App Engine Application."

Starting the Development Server Command Line

Before you can start the development server, you need to build your web application. For a simple build process that allows you to also compile from the command line, you should set up your project using Ant or Maven.

To start the development server from the command line, use the following command:

```
/<app-engine-sdk-home>/bin/dev_appserver.sh -port=8085 <webapp-folder>
```

Port 8085 can be any other port available on your computer.

Deploying to the App Engine Command Line

Once you confirm that your application works in the development server, you can deploy it to the App Engine with the following command:

```
/<app-engine-sdk-home>/bin/appcfg.sh update <webapp-folder>
```

When you start this process for the first time, it asks you for your Google login name and password. If you haven't used the tool in a while, you are asked for your credentials again.

In case something goes wrong during the deployment process, the next time you try to deploy the application, it may ask you to roll back your previous transaction. In this case, you can use the following command:

```
/<app-engine-sdk-home>/bin/appcfg.sh rollback <webapp-folder>
```

On Windows environments, you replace the forward slashes with backslashes and the .sh extensions with .bat extensions. Apart from that, the tools work similarly.

Summary

In this chapter, you set up the basics for working with the App Engine. The easiest development environment is a clean Eclipse installation with a minimum number of App Engine plugins. However, once you are up to speed with the App Engine, you may want more control over your web application and stop using the App Engine plugins altogether. If, for example, you want to throw out the JPA and JDO libraries or work with your favorite non-Eclipse IDE, your best approach is to switch to the command-line tools provided by the App Engine SDK.

Chapter 2

Improving App Engine Performance

Throughout this book, a lot of attention is given to performance optimization. By improving performance, you get the added benefit of lowering the usage costs of your application when you surpass the App Engine's free quota. This chapter explains performance characteristics specific to the Google App Engine environment. It starts by discussing the process of starting and stopping instances in the cloud. The cost of starting an instance is demonstrated by showing the performance of a servlet using a third-party library compared to the performance of a plain vanilla servlet. This chapter also offers pointers for minimizing and, where possible, avoiding cold startups. Finally, it provides a high-level overview of performance-related topics you can find in other chapters in this book.

Performing in the Cloud

One of the unique selling points of cloud computing over traditional hosting is high scalability and flexibility when responding to changes in the demand of your application. The pricing model of cloud computing is especially convenient if you experience sudden high spikes in the number of visitors on a regular basis.

In the cloud, you pay for what you use. On the App Engine, this means that if your traffic is usually below Google's free daily quota and you have only incidental traffic spikes, you pay only for the computing power used during the days with high spikes. The advantage of cloud computing over having a physical machine park capable of handling high-traffic spikes is that you are not paying for machines that remain idle except during a traffic spike.

This flexibility also introduces a new challenge that might not be apparent at first sight. Responding to changes in demand means starting and stopping instances multiple times per hour. The time necessary to respond to a change in demand is directly related to the time necessary to start your web application. This means that your web application does not necessarily become flexible and scalable simply because it is deployed on the App Engine. You need to optimize your application to get the most out of the specific circumstances of running on the Google App Engine.

Comparing the App Engine to Traditional Web Applications

Whereas the lifetime of a typical App Engine instance is measured in minutes and hours, the lifetime of a traditional web application instance is measured in weeks or months. *Traditional web application* here means a web application running on a physical machine that you maintain yourself rather than an application running in the cloud.

One of the most common approaches to optimizing the performance of a traditional web application is to take a performance hit on startup of the instance. For example, if you load a lot of classes and data into memory during startup, you can save loading time while processing the actual user requests because starting and stopping an application instance is unrelated to handling a request.

Taking a performance hit during the startup of a new instance is not such a good idea, though, if a website visitor is waiting while your application is starting. You may lose a visitor every time a new instance is started.

In addition, the scalability requirements of the App Engine ask for different storage strategies. Most traditional web applications are based on relational databases. Strategies for optimal usage of a relational database can sometimes be catastrophic when applied to NoSQL storages like the Google App Engine datastore.

As a result, web application frameworks originally designed for use with software stacks can lead to bad results when used on the App Engine without consideration.

Optimizing Payments for Resources

On the App Engine, you pay for the resources you use. This means that optimizing your application to use fewer resources also leads to cost reductions.

On the App Engine, some resources are more expensive than others. The optimal usage versus cost ratio depends on the characteristics of your application. How much data do you store? How much traffic is generated by your visitors? How is the traffic distributed over the total data set? How much data processing is involved? How is the number of visitors distributed over time?

When you consider these questions and look at the current pricing tables on Google's site, you quickly find that you may have an optimization challenge. Take a look on http://code.google.com/appengine/docs/billing.html for more information.

Although there is no silver bullet for an optimal cost reduction, this book aims to give you the most control over the performance and costs of your web application.

Measuring the Cost of Class Loading

Every library or framework you introduce brings lots of additional classes to load at startup. For this reason, this book introduces only three third-party JARs to help with the code examples: Commons FileUpload, StringTemplate, and ANTLR. Commons FileUpload is used to process form submits with files as content. StringTemplate is used as a template language to generate output for the visitors, and it can also be used to generate text for an e-mail. ANTLR stands for Another Tool for Language Recognition and is a dependency of StringTemplate.

To show you the cost of class loading, this chapter investigates the startup time of the App Engine instance with StringTemplate and without StringTemplate. In addition, there is a startup time comparison between a web.xml file of roughly 400 lines and a web.xml of 21 lines.

Timing a Servlet That Contains a Library

Listing 2.1 shows a very simple servlet that processes a template using the StringTemplate framework and shows "Hello, World" in the browser window.

Listing 2.1 **Writing Hello World with StringTemplate**

```
01 package com.appspot.template;
02
03 import java.io.IOException;
04
05 import javax.servlet.ServletException;
06 import javax.servlet.http.HttpServlet;
07 import javax.servlet.http.HttpServletRequest;
08 import javax.servlet.http.HttpServletResponse;
09
10 import org.antlr.stringtemplate.StringTemplate;
11 import org.antlr.stringtemplate.StringTemplateGroup;
12
13 public class StringTemplateServlet extends HttpServlet {
14
15   protected void doGet(HttpServletRequest request,
16                        HttpServletResponse response)
17         throws ServletException, IOException {
18     long startTime = System.currentTimeMillis();
19
20     StringTemplateGroup group = new StringTemplateGroup("xhtml",
21         "WEB-INF/templates/xhtml");
22     StringTemplate hello = group.getInstanceOf("hello-world");
23     hello.setAttribute("name", "World");
24     response.getWriter().write(hello.toString());
25
26     long diff = System.currentTimeMillis() - startTime;
27     response.getWriter().write("time: " + diff);
28
29   }
30 }
```

Lines 18 and 26 process the timer, while the code loading the StringTemplate and ANTLR JARs are on lines 20 through 24.

Writing the resulting time at the bottom of the HTML (line 27) is not really elegant, but it works sufficiently for the simple timer required in this example.

Line 22 refers to an external file with an HTML template. This template is shown in Listing 2.2.

Listing 2.2 **Setting Up the HTML Template for StringTemplate**

```
01 <html>
02   <head>
03     <title>Test</title>
04   </head>
05   <body>
06     Hello, $name$ from a file!
07   </body>
08 </html>
```

Line 6 processes the attribute provided in line 23 of Listing 2.1. The rest of the HTML template should not require any explanation. The resulting screen just after a new instance is launched is displayed in Figure 2.1.

Reloading the same servlet when the instance is already started is a lot faster. Processing the StringTemplate takes 10 to 15 milliseconds on subsequent requests.

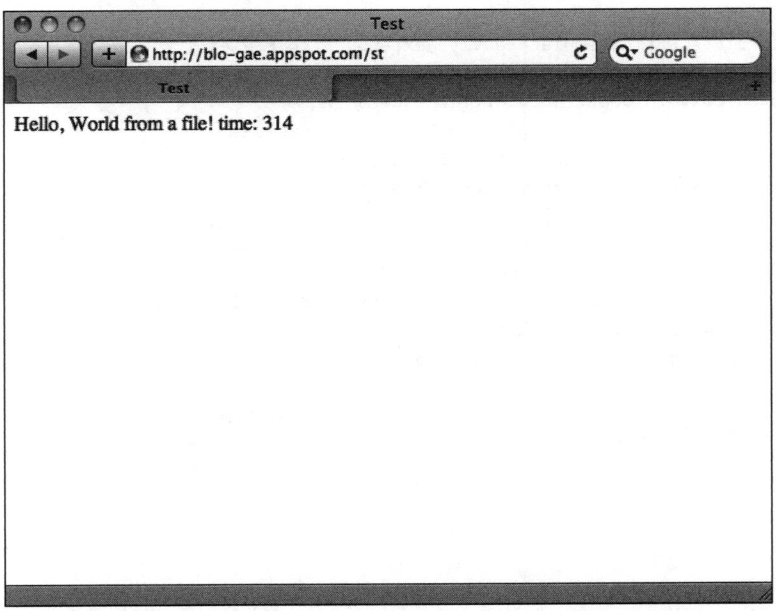

Figure 2.1 Displaying the resulting time in the browser screen with StringTemplate.

Timing a Servlet That Does Not Contain a Library

Writing Hello World to a browser screen is simple enough to do without a library like StringTemplate. If you modify the code to write Hello World directly to the browser, you get a servlet as shown in Listing 2.3.

Listing 2.3 **Writing Hello World without StringTemplate**

```
01 package com.appspot.template;
02
03 import java.io.IOException;
04
05 import javax.servlet.ServletException;
06 import javax.servlet.http.HttpServlet;
07 import javax.servlet.http.HttpServletRequest;
08 import javax.servlet.http.HttpServletResponse;
09
10 public class StringTemplateServlet extends HttpServlet {
11
12   protected void doGet(HttpServletRequest request,
13                        HttpServletResponse response)
14         throws ServletException, IOException {
15
16     long startTime = System.currentTimeMillis();
17
18     response.getWriter().write("Hello World without ST! ");
19
20     long diff = System.currentTimeMillis() - startTime;
21     response.getWriter().write("time: " + diff);
22
23   }
24 }
```

The only difference is in line 18. To avoid wasting too much code, the HTML is left out. Seven short lines of HTML do not have a significant influence on the loading time: they account for less than a millisecond.

Figure 2.2 shows the browser window loading the servlet from Listing 2.3 while starting a new instance. The decrease in loading time is substantial!

If loading the StringTemplate library increases the loading time of a new App Engine instance by 300 milliseconds, then why not switch to FreeMarker, Velocity, or Java Server Pages (JSP), you might ask. Or perhaps you know another template engine not mentioned here. You are encouraged to investigate and find out for yourself which library has the most efficient loading times on cold startup.

For any other library or framework you'd like to introduce, you should first investigate what the effect is on the total load time. Adding an additional JAR is always a big step.

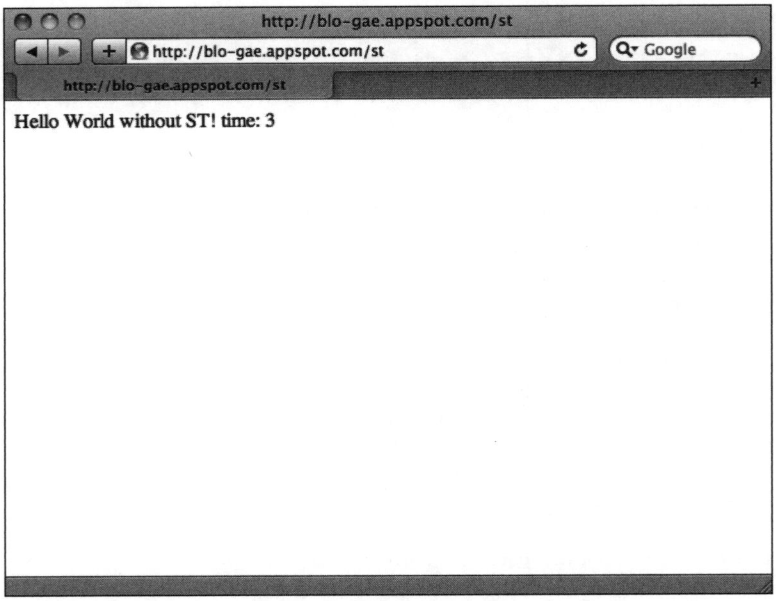

Figure 2.2 Displaying the resulting time in the browser screen without StringTemplate.

Reducing the Size of web.xml

Explicit changes like adding JARs are relatively simple to manage. More tricky is making changes more gradually over time. For example, this book is full of servlets. As servlets were added, the web.xml file grew. At the end of the writing, the web.xml file contained more than 400 lines of configuration setting up all the examples demonstrated in the book.

The number of servlets declared in web.xml has a significant influence on the class loading time. To test the difference, the web.xml was reduced to minimal size, as shown in Listing 2.4. Just a single servlet is included—the servlet from Listings 2.1 and 2.3.

Listing 2.4 **Reducing web.xml to an Absolute Minimum**

```
<?xml version="1.0" encoding="utf-8"?>
<web-app xmlns:xsi="http://www.w3.org/2001/XMLSchema-instance"
      xmlns="http://java.sun.com/xml/ns/javaee"
      xmlns:web="http://java.sun.com/xml/ns/javaee/web-app_2_5.xsd"
      xsi:schemaLocation="http://java.sun.com/xml/ns/javaee
           http://java.sun.com/xml/ns/javaee/web-app_2_5.xsd"
      version="2.5">

```

Listing 2.4 **Reducing web.xml to an Absolute Minimum (Continued)**

```
    <!-- Template -->
    <servlet>
      <servlet-name>StringTemplateServlet</servlet-name>
      <servlet-class>
         com.appspot.template.StringTemplateServlet
      </servlet-class>
    </servlet>
    <servlet-mapping>
      <servlet-name>StringTemplateServlet</servlet-name>
      <url-pattern>/st</url-pattern>
    </servlet-mapping>

</web-app>
```

Take a look at the log files before and after the web.xml size reduction. Figure 2.3 shows the difference in CPU usage for both scenarios.

As you can see, the difference in load time on cold startup is significant. This is an indication that you should be careful with the number of servlets you declare in a web application. On the other hand, one very large servlet is unlikely to perform much better

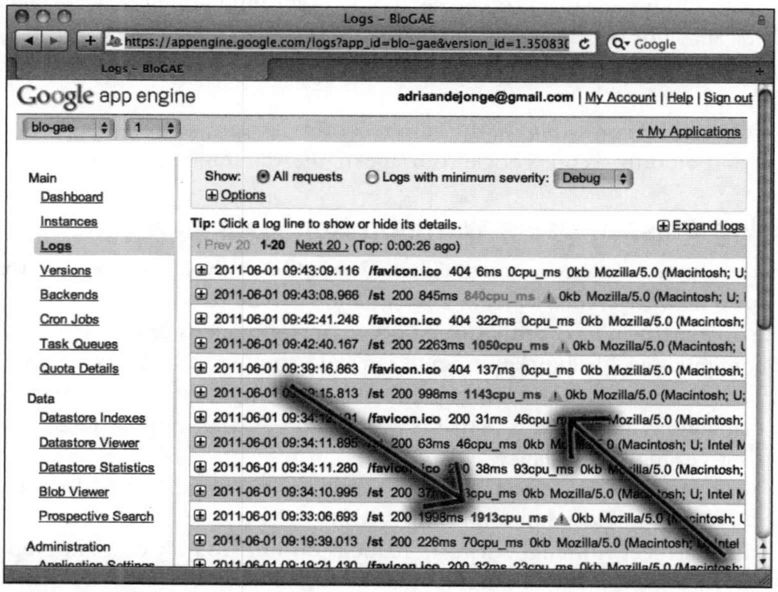

Figure 2.3 Displaying the logged CPU times before and after a web.xml reduction.

than several smaller ones, so you must consider the trade-off. How do you divide your code over a number of servlets with the least class loading overhead? Again, there is no silver bullet for doing so. The important thing is that you think about this trade-off in your specific situation.

Avoiding Cold Startups

In the early days of the Google App Engine, any request could lead to a new instance being launched. For applications with low traffic, there was a high risk of long response times on the first request by a visitor, especially if the application was not optimized for fast cold startups.

Only high-traffic applications with a relative constant load could serve a large percentage of users without confronting them with longer response times. But even those would lose a few visitors with instance starts and stops.

Later, Google added new features for paying customers that help avoid longer response times. It should be noted that these strategies may fail when the application experiences very sudden spikes in traffic.

Reserving Instances with Always On

Paying customers can hire instances that are never turned off. This solves the problem of low-traffic applications, where almost every visit leads to an instance being launched.

The Always On instances are supplemented with dynamic instances when the demand exceeds the capabilities of the available Always On instances. This means that just switching to Always On does not completely fix the problem with long responses on cold startups.

Always On can be configured in the admin console, as described in Google's documentation on http://code.google.com/appengine/docs/adminconsole/instances.html.

Preloading Classes Using Warm-Up Requests

When at least one instance is running, either Always On or dynamic instances, the App Engine can sometimes predict when a new instance will be required.

As long as you haven't explicitly turned off warm-up requests in the appengine-web.xml configuration file, the App Engine can send a request to /_ah/warmup sometime before a new instance is required. You can configure your own servlet to listen on that address and make sure that classes and other data are preloaded before a visitor starts accessing that instance.

Warm-up requests do not work when no instances are running. They do not add much value for low-traffic applications unless Always On is used.

Even with instances running, warm-up requests do not always work. The App Engine is not always capable of predicting traffic in advance.

More information on warm-up requests is found on http://code.google.com/appengine/docs/adminconsole/instances.html.

Handling Concurrent Requests with Thread-Safe Mode

By default, an instance handles only a single request at a time. If an instance takes long to respond and there are other requests at the same time, the App Engine launches additional instances to handle the rest of the traffic.

In some cases, loading new instances can be avoided by allowing concurrent requests. This requires you to develop thread-safe servlets. More information on thread-safe mode is found on http://code.google.com/appengine/docs/java/config/appconfig.html.

Handling Memory Intensive Requests with Backends

In addition to Always On instances, you can purchase, for a higher fee, specialized instances that are optimized for handling requests of a backend nature—that is, requests that require longer than 30 seconds to finish. Another characteristic of backend applications is higher memory consumption.

More information on backend instances can be found on Google's website at http://code.google.com/appengine/docs/java/backends/.

Improving Performance in General

The subtitle of this book is *Building High-Performance Java Apps with Google App Engine* because this book focuses on performance optimization more than do other books. This section provides a general overview of possibilities for performance optimization.

Optimizing Your Data Model for Performance

If you model your data for the App Engine datastore the same way you model your data for a relational database, you can be certain that you will run into performance problems at some point. The way the App Engine datastore divides data over multiple machines in the cloud is fundamentally different from the way a relational database stores data on disk. In many cases, you need to do the exact opposite of what you are used to doing. For example, you need to denormalize your data instead of normalizing it.

Because you can store arrays of data, there is less need of relationships between tables, although you should be cautious if you feel the need to index the array, because the size of your total index may explode.

You should consider the need for transactions before you set up your data model. Transactions require entity groups, and larger entity groups may harm scalability.

Chapter 4, "Data Modeling for the Google App Engine Datastore," presents a detailed discussion of datastore characteristics. Using the APIs is demonstrated in Chapter 10, "Storing Data in the Datastore and Blobstore."

Avoiding Redundant Processing Using Cache

Many time-consuming tasks are done repeatedly for subsequent requests—think of tasks that require gathering data or processing intensive calculations. The same processing might be repeated for a single visitor or for multiple visitors.

Proper caching can help avoid repetitive processes. This book explains both fine-grained caching using memcache and page-level caching on the Internet. See Chapter 14, "Optimizing Performance Using the Memory Cache," for in-depth information.

Postponing Long-Running Tasks Using the Task Queue

In many cases, high responsiveness is more important than high performance. Responding quickly to a visitor's request can sometimes be done by postponing the actual work. As long as the visitor can trust that the work will be done eventually, he or she will be pleased with the quick response.

The Task Queue API can be used in multiple ways. You can preschedule tasks at regular intervals, or you can post tasks to the queue on demand. Both methods can help improve performance and responsiveness.

Details on Task Queue are discussed in Chapter 12, "Running Background Work with the Task Queue API and Cron."

Improving Page Load Performance in the Browser

A high-performing server is practically useless if the page loading in the browser ruins the total response time. For example, if your HTML is full of useless elements, classes, and IDs, your Cascading Style Sheet (CSS) file beats the size of an average phone book, and you reach a megabyte of JavaScript files, all server-side efforts are lost. You could make it even worse by adding one or more Flash files in your page. But then you are clearly working in the wrong direction.

With HTML5 and CSS3, you hardly need Flash anymore except, perhaps, for an incidental video player being used until HTML5 videos are sufficiently mature. The newly added elements in HTML5 may help you downsize your CSS files. The less specific your CSS file, the easier it is to maintain.

The way you load your JavaScript has a large impact on the page load time. Loading JavaScript unobtrusively at the bottom of the page allows the rest of the page to render before the JavaScript is interpreted. This improves the responsiveness to the visitor.

Part III, "User Interface Design Essentials," covers HTML5, CSS3, JavaScript, and AJAX, providing details on browser optimization from a technical perspective.

Working with Asynchronous APIs

Page loading generally does not entail heavy data processing. Mostly it consists of waiting for services such as the datastore to respond. If you know in advance that you need to make multiple backend requests and the backend requests are independent of each other, you can work with asynchronous APIs.

One of the most important asynchronous APIs is described in Chapter 10, "Storing Data in the Datastore and Blobstore."

Optimizing Your Application before Deployment

Some performance optimizations are a result of planning and designing. The more effective performance improvements usually result from careful experimentation and measurements.

You can profile calls to Google's backend services using AppStats. Most of the overhead in an average App Engine application is in the backend calls. If you do a lot of heavy lifting in your own code, you are encouraged to profile this code and optimize where possible.

AppStats is explained in Chapter 19, "Assuring Quality Using Measuring Tools."

Summary

Cloud solutions, and specifically the Google App Engine, are designed for scalability and flexible usage from scratch. However, in the case of the Google App Engine, this design may mean that some classic performance optimization strategies are counterproductive. This chapter focused on cold startup time and why you should avoid cold startups when possible. It also discussed the overhead of frameworks and libraries—also to be avoided when possible. The end of this chapter presented a few performance questions with cross references to the chapters where you can find the answers.

PART II

Application Design Essentials

Chapter 3

Understanding the Anatomy of a Google App Engine Application

This chapter explains the structure of a typical App Engine application, the way the files are organized before they are deployed, and where the files reside after deployment. The chapter starts with an overview of the servers running the application. Next, it provides an outline of the files involved in a deployment package, with special attention given to the configuration files—every configuration file is discussed. This chapter ends with the configuration parameters that are set in the Admin Panel.

Uploading Files for Dynamic Deployment

When you upload your application, it is not directly deployed as an application instance. Instead, the application is stored on a server from which it can be dynamically deployed when necessary.

Deployment is necessary when a request is received by one of the frontends. In this context, the *frontend* is the web server that accepts incoming requests before passing them to an application server instance.

On the basis of data from the App Master, the frontend decides whether the request should pass to a static file server or to one of the application servers running the App. Figure 3.1 provides an overview of the servers involved in this process.

Google scales applications by dynamically starting and stopping application servers according to the current number of requests. Applications respond not only to the size of the load but also to the origin of the load.

If your application becomes popular in Japan, for example, Google starts machines in (or near) Japan. If your application becomes popular in Germany, application servers are started over there.

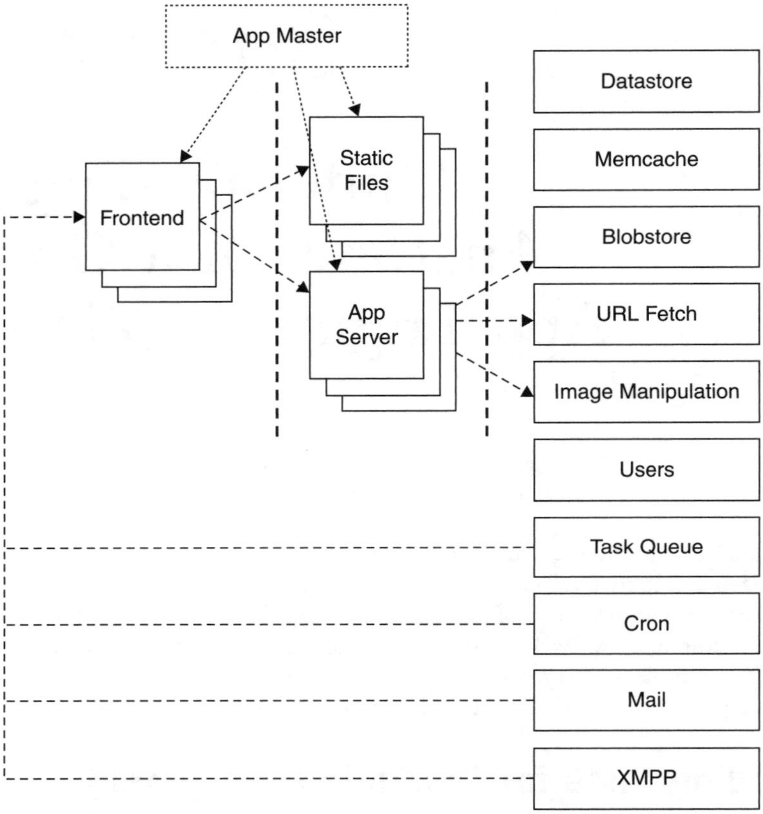

Figure 3.1 An overview of the App Engine application servers and services.

When thinking about the performance of your App Engine applications, remember that all Google services are running on remote servers. Invoking one of the services always involves communication overhead.

Figure 3.1 also points out how the App Engine architecture is modeled with the philosophy that *everything is an HTTP request*—at least, all requests sent to the App Engine instances are done using HTTP.

Simple Mail Transfer Protocol (SMTP), Extensible Messaging and Presence Protocol (XMPP), Task Queue orders, and cron jobs are all translated into HTTP requests that are routed through the frontend. This use of HTTP simplifies both the implementation of request handlers and the scalability of the App Engine. Scaling your instances for large numbers of incoming e-mails works exactly the same way as scaling instances for large numbers of web visitors.

Setting Up the Directory Structure

To install an application to the App Engine, you provide a web application structured similar to the web archive (WAR) files you usually deploy to application servers like Tomcat or Jetty. However, the App Engine does not accept WAR files, and some extra configuration files are necessary.

Instead of a WAR file, the App Engine deployment tool expects a folder with an expanded version of a WAR file. After compilation, a typical App Engine application has a file structure similar to the following:

/my-app/
  /any-file-directly-accessible
  /WEB-INF
    /appengine-generated/
      /datastore-indexes-auto.xml
    /classes/ (*)
      /your-package-top-level/
        /and-so-forth/
    /lib/ (*)
      /jar-one-you-need.jar
      /jar-two-you-need.jar
      /appengine-api-1.5.1.jar
      /appengine-api-labs-1.5.1.jar
    /any-file-hidden
    /appengine-web.xml (*)
    /cron.xml
  /datastore-indexes.xml
    /dos.xml
    /logging.properties
    /queue.xml
    /web.xml (*)

The files with marked (*) are mandatory for the application to run. Files printed in **bold** will have the exact names displayed in this listing. The files printed in regular font are example file names that are likely to be different for every application.

> **Note**
>
> Strictly speaking, the /classes/ and /lib/ folders are not required for the application to run. For example, you could create a web application containing a single Java Server Pages (JSP) file that does not use any of Google's services. But under most normal circumstances, they are necessary.
>
> Of course, you could also bundle your classes into your own Java archive (JAR) and include them in the /lib/ folder. The division between /classes/ and /lib/ makes a nice, natural separation between actual program code and provided libraries, though.

If you compare the list of libraries in this overview to the usual list of libraries included by Google's development tools, it may seem rather short. You may be accustomed to seeing libraries for Java Data Objects (JDO), Java Persistence API (JPA), DataNucleus, Java Specification Request (JSR) 107 and perhaps others. If you do not use these libraries, you do not need to include them in your web application. This book does not advocate using these additional libraries and therefore does not include them.

Using Google's default development tools, like the Eclipse plugin, it takes effort to get rid of the libraries you do not want to include. You can delete them, but they keep coming back. The best way to deal with this problem is to quit using the Eclipse development tools and start using the command-line SDK. The simple command-line tools are sufficient for any task as long as you know how to compile a Java web application.

After you switch to the command-line tools, you have more control over the files you want to include in your application. If you use the command-line tools as demonstrated at the end of Chapter 1, "Setting Up a Development Environment," and provide a directory structure similar to the preceding example, you can leave out all libraries you do not wish to include.

You may want to include appengine-api-x.y.z.jar (where x.y.z is the most recent version) at all times. It is hard to do anything useful without it.

To help you generate directory structures in the right format, you can use build tools like Maven and Ant, perhaps with the Ivy plugin for Ant. Using such build tools gives you the power to compile your code into the desired file structure from the command line, regardless of which integrated development environment (IDE) you use to write your code. Once you also start using the command-line deployment tools for the App Engine, this independence makes it easier to switch from Eclipse to NetBeans or IntelliJ IDEA if you wish.

Specifying Deployment Parameters

Using the file appengine-web.xml, you can specify configuration parameters specific to the Google App Engine. Most of the parameters in this file are optional. If you do not provide them, the App Engine falls back to default values.

Identifying the Application

The first two elements, `application` and `version`, are mandatory; they are required to tell Google the identity of the application you are deploying. An example of these parameters is shown in Listing 3.1. During deployment, the tool asks for your e-mail address and password and checks whether you have permissions to update the web application. Setting these permissions is discussed at the end of this chapter.

Listing 3.1 **Specifying appengine-web.xml**

```
<?xml version="1.0" encoding="utf-8"?>
<appengine-web-app xmlns="http://appengine.google.com/ns/1.0">
  <application>blo-gae</application>
  <version>1</version>
```

Listing 3.1 **Specifying appengine-web.xml (Continued)**

```
05
06    <static-files>
07      <include path="/**.jpg" expiration="6h"/>
08      <exclude path="/resources/**.xml"/>
09    </static-files>
10
11    <resource-files>
12      <include path="/**.xml"/>
13      <exclude path="/static/**.jpg"/>
14    </resource-files>
15
16    <!-- Configure java.util.logging -->
17    <system-properties>
18      <property name="blog.production-version" value="true"/>
19      <property name="java.util.logging.config.file"
20                value="WEB-INF/logging.properties"/>
21    </system-properties>
22
23    <env-variables>
24      <env-var name="LANGUAGE" value="EN"/>
25    </env-variables>
26
27    <ssl-enabled>false</ssl-enabled>
28
29    <sessions-enabled>true</sessions-enabled>
30
31    <user-permissions>
32      <permission class="com.unknown.CustomPermission"
33                  name="custom-name" actions="read"/>
34    </user-permissions>
35
36    <public-root>/my</public-root>
37
38    <inbound-services>
39      <service>mail</service>
40    </inbound-services>
41
42    <precompilation-enabled>true</precompilation-enabled>
43
44</appengine-web-app>
```

Separating Static Files and Resources

The `static-files` and `resource-files` elements on lines 6 through 14 refer to the high-level overview discussed earlier in the chapter. If you do not specify these elements, all files except /WEB-INF/* are copied to both the static file servers and the application servers. This means they take up twice as much space as your application needs, and you may run out of quota earlier than expected.

The /WEB-INF folder and everything under it are treated as resource files by default. For every other file, you should determine if they are ever read programmatically on the server side. If not, exclude them from the resource files and include them only in the static files.

Conversely, if you have files outside the /WEB-INF folder that are never read directly from the browser and serve only as input for the program running on the server side, you may consider excluding them from the static files. Perhaps it would be even better to move these files to the /WEB-INF folder to ensure they can never be read elsewhere.

Configuring System Properties and Log Files

Using the appengine-web.xml file, you can specify system properties. An interesting use of system properties is to specify where the logging.properties file can be found. Using this configuration file, you can adjust the minimum severity level for messages to be included in the logs.

You can use the `env-variables` element to specify environment variables. There is no direct use that is specific to the App Engine. However, in general, it is easy to read environment variables in Java using `System.getProperty()`.

Setting Sessions

By default, Google App Engine applications are 100 percent stateless and do not support sessions. By switching the sessions-enabled element to true, you can use the `HttpSession` class from the `Servlet` interface.

Be careful when you turn this switch, though! The underlying implementation uses both the datastore and memcache. Apart from quota usage, you should mind the performance characteristics of reading and writing cache data.

This means you need to watch both the overhead of communicating with external services and the possible additional overhead of object serialization. All objects added to the session should implement `java.lang.Serializable`. Some warnings on using this interface are given in Chapter 14, "Optimizing Performance Using the Memory Cache."

Securing the Application

At the time of writing, the Google App Engine supports Secure Sockets Layer (SSL) connections only when the applications are run on the default appspot domain. When running on a custom domain, you cannot (yet) use SSL. Google is working to change this in the near future. For the latest status, you can check Google's roadmap at http://code.google.com/appengine/docs/roadmap.html.

Right now, when you are running your application on an appspot domain, you can require all URLs to be secured with HTTPS using the `ssl-enabled` element. You can choose to make all URLs secured or all URLs unsecured; you cannot make some secured and others unsecured.

For specific Java libraries that provide third-party permission classes, you can configure permissions using the `user-permissions` element. You may need this option for some Java frameworks. In the remainder of this book, you will not need this option.

In addition to being able to include and exclude files from the static file server, you can use another parameter—the `public-root` element—to restrict access to static files. This element does not change the location of static files or the URL used to access them. Rather, it tells the application that any folder other than the one specified cannot be reached on the static file server. For example, if you put the value `/static` in this element, static files starting with `/other` cannot be reached. Static files under `/static/sublevel/something-else` are accessible.

Configuring Services

The overview provided in Figure 3.1 shows four services that access the frontend to invoke actions on the application servers: Task Queue, cron, Mail, and XMPP. Only Mail and XMPP need to be specifically turned on in the appengine-web.xml.

The difference between XMPP, Mail, and the others is that XMPP and Mail are *inbound services*, responding to non-HTTP requests from the outside world. You can turn them on by providing the values `mail` and/or `xmpp_message` in the `inbound-services` element, as shown in Listing 3.1, line 39.

> **Disabling Precompilation**
>
> For performance reasons, the Google App Engine precompiles bytecode before your application is run. In most cases, you do not notice the precompilation feature running in the background. There is at least one scenario in which you may consider turning it off: if you need to use signed JARs, precompilation breaks the signature. In this case, you should set the `precompilation-enabled` element to false.

Specifying Repeating Tasks

You can use the cron.xml file to schedule tasks. The cron service invokes tasks by firing an HTTP request to the frontend servers. Listing 3.2 provides an example of a cron.xml configuration file. More details on how this configuration file works are provided in Chapter 12, "Running Background Work with the Task Queue API and Cron."

Listing 3.2 **Specifying cron.xml**

```
<?xml version="1.0" encoding="UTF-8"?>
<cronentries>
  <cron>
    <url>/tasks/cron/mail</url>
    <description>Send a spam mail…</description>
    <schedule>every 2 minutes</schedule>
  </cron>
  <cron>
    <url>/tasks/cron/read-rss</url>
    <description>Read RSS feed…</description>
    <schedule>every day 22:00</schedule>
    <timezone>Africa/Johannesburg</timezone>
  </cron>
</cronentries>
```

Specifying Datastore Indexes

In the file outline at the beginning of this chapter, you find two files starting with the name datastore-indexes: one is datastore-indexes.xml, the other is datastore-indexes-auto.xml.

The datastore-indexes.xml file is used to specify which properties for which entities should be indexes in order to optimize query performance for the datastore.

The datastore-indexes-auto.xml in the /WEB-INF/appengine-generated folder is created by the development server. It can cooperate with the other datastore-indexes.xml file as long as the `autoGenerate` attribute is set to true. Otherwise, the datastore-indexes.xml file is used and the datastore-indexes-auto.xml is ignored. Listing 3.3 shows a datastore-indexes-auto.xml file that allows automatic additions to be provided by the development server in the datastore-indexes-auto.xml file.

Listing 3.3 **Specifying datastore-indexes.xml**

```
<?xml version="1.0" encoding="utf-8"?>
<datastore-indexes
  autoGenerate="true">
    <datastore-index kind="BlogPost" ancestor="false">
        <property name="title" direction="asc" />
        <property name="entry-date" direction="desc" />
    </datastore-index>

    <datastore-index kind="User" ancestor="false">
        <property name="name" direction="asc" />
    </datastore-index>
</datastore-indexes>
```

Chapter 4, "Data Modeling for the Google App Engine Datastore," provides more background information on the workings of indexes.

Blacklisting IP Ranges

To prevent abuse of your application, you may want to restrict access on the basis of IP ranges. You can put an IP address or a range of IP addresses on the blacklist using a file called dos.xml, where dos stands for denial of service.

Listing 3.4 provides an example that blocks both one specific IP address in the IPv4 range and a subnet. The subnet is specified using Classless Interdomain Routing (CIDR) notation. A full explanation of CIDR is beyond the scope of this book, but you can find many resources on the Internet explaining the concept.

Listing 3.4 **Specifying dos.xml**

```
<?xml version="1.0" encoding="UTF-8"?>
<blacklistentries>
  <blacklist>
```

Listing 3.4 **Specifying dos.xml (Continued)**

```
    <subnet>170.224.225.27</subnet>
    <description>One specific address</description>
  </blacklist>
  <blacklist>
    <subnet>170.224.225.0/24</subnet>
    <description>A full subnet</description>
  </blacklist>
</blacklistentries>
```

Configuring Log Levels

Listing 3.1 contains a reference to the logging.properties file. In this file, you can specify the minimum severity of a log message to appear in the log files. The example in Listing 3.5 logs all messages with minimum severity `INFO` regardless of the package or class.

Listing 3.5 **Specifying logging.properties**

```
#logging.properties
# Set the default logging level for all loggers to INFO
.level = INFO
```

Other log levels are trace, debug, warning, error, and fatal. You can set different log levels to different application parts by specifying package names or full class names before `.level`. This is the standard `java.util.logging` configuration mechanism.

Configuring Task Queues

If you do not provide a queues.xml file, there is always one default task queue with a throughput of five tasks every second. To provide additional separate task queues with different rates, you can add a queues.xml file, as Listing 3.6 does. Chapter 12 provides the details on the configuration and use of task queues.

Listing 3.6 **Specifying queues.xml**

```
<?xml version="1.0" encoding="utf-8"?>
<queue-entries>
    <queue>
      <name>mail-queue</name>
      <rate>2000/d</rate>
    </queue>
    <queue>
      <name>second-mail-queue</name>
      <rate>8/m</rate>
    </queue>
</queue-entries>
```

Securing URLs

Most configuration files you have seen so far are specific for the App Engine and have no function if you try to deploy your application on a different servlet container. Part of the App Engine configuration works exactly the same as all standard servlet containers. This part is in the only remaining configuration file: web.xml. This file does not require much explanation.

However, one part of this file should be mentioned: restricting access to URLs to logged-on users is done using web.xml. Listing 3.7 provides an excerpt of web.xml containing a URL with restricted access.

Listing 3.7 **Specifying web.xml**

```
<?xml version="1.0" encoding="utf-8"?>
<web-app xmlns:xsi="http://www.w3.org/2001/XMLSchema-instance"
    xmlns="http://java.sun.com/xml/ns/javaee"
     xmlns:web="http://java.sun.com/xml/ns/javaee/web-app_2_5.xsd"
    xsi:schemaLocation="http://java.sun.com/xml/ns/javaee
http://java.sun.com/xml/ns/javaee/web-app_2_5.xsd"
    version="2.5">

    <!-- […] -->

    <servlet>
        <servlet-name>ReceiveMailServlet</servlet-name>
        <servlet-class>com.appspot.mail.[…]</servlet-class>
    </servlet>
    <servlet-mapping>
    <servlet-name>ReceiveMailServlet</servlet-name>
        <url-pattern>/_ah/mail/*</url-pattern>
    </servlet-mapping>

    <!-- […] -->

    <security-constraint>
      <web-resource-collection>
        <web-resource-name>receive-mail-url</web-resource-name>
        <url-pattern>/_ah/mail/*</url-pattern>
      </web-resource-collection>
      <auth-constraint>
        <role-name>admin</role-name>
      </auth-constraint>
    </security-constraint>

    <!-- […] -->

</web-app>
```

Line 28 provides the role-name `admin`. There are only two possible values here: `*` or `admin`. The value `admin` means that only registered developers of the application or the system itself can access the URL. The value `*` means that anyone who is logged on can access the URL.

Configuring the Administration Panel

Most of the configuration of the Google App Engine takes place in configuration files you provide when you upload the application. A small part of the configuration is done in the Administration panel. For most configuration options in the Administration panel, it is clear why they were not in the configuration files. The easiest way to explain this without getting stuck in a philosophical debate is that it is done for practical reasons. The Administration panel is sufficiently minimalistic.

Setting Application Basics

In the Application Settings screen, you can set a few basic parameters, such as the application name, the cookie expiration time, and the way users can authenticate. You can add a custom domain to the application or disable and delete the application if you want to stop providing services. Figure 3.2 gives the overview.

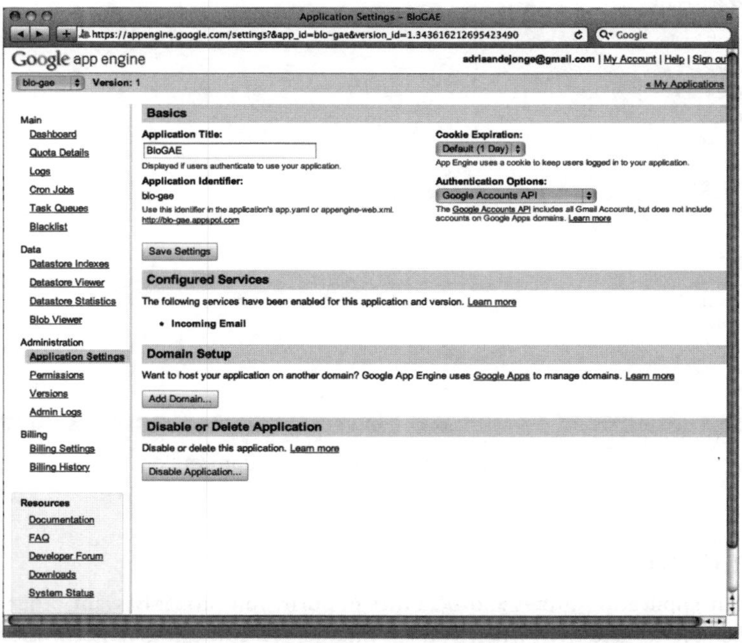

Figure 3.2 Specifying the application title, domain, and authentication mechanism.

Setting the Current Version

In Listing 3.1, you were able to set a `version` element. Using the Administration panel shown in Figure 3.3, you can switch versions. This allows you to prepare for an upgrade and control when it goes live. It also allows you to roll back a version in case of unexpected trouble. Keep in mind that only a single version of the datastore is running regardless of the application versions. Data access should be written with backward and forward compatibility in mind.

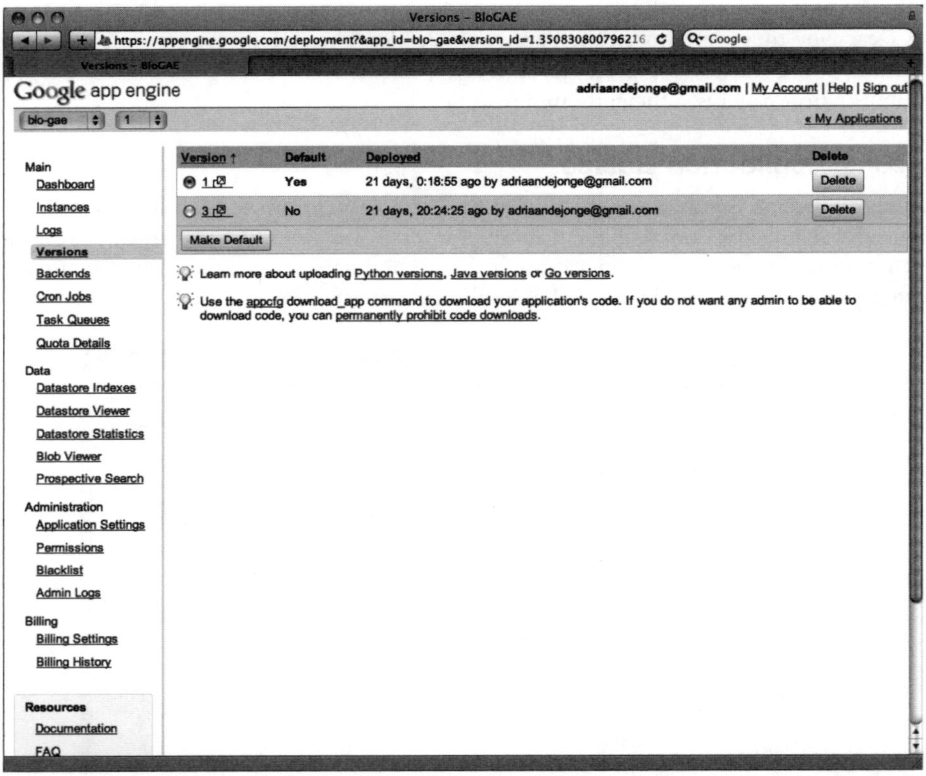

Figure 3.3 Setting the application version.

Adding Users

When your application grows and becomes popular, you probably want other people you trust to be able to take over when you are unavailable. You can give permission to other people with Google accounts to upload new versions of the application and manage the applications using the Dashboard. See Figure 3.4.

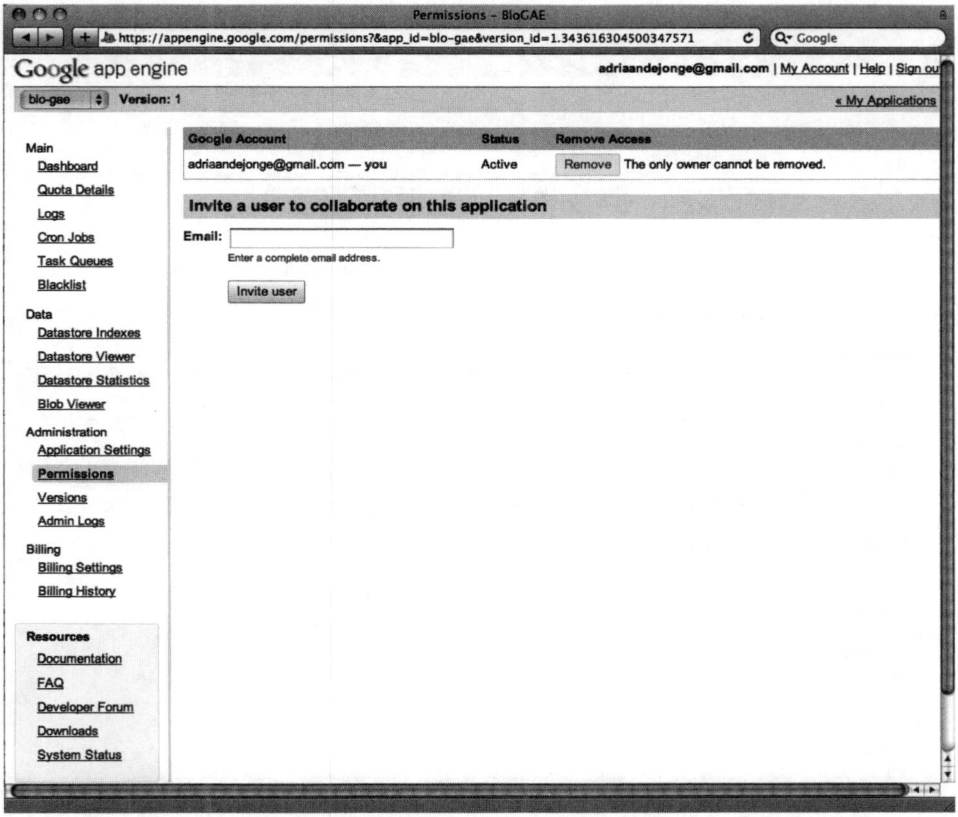

Figure 3.4 Inviting additional users for system maintenance.

Enabling Billing

When your application becomes popular, you may run out of free Google resources. If you have a clever business model behind your application, this should not be a big problem. You can pay Google to consume additional server resources and plan on which resources you want to spend your money, as shown in Figure 3.5.

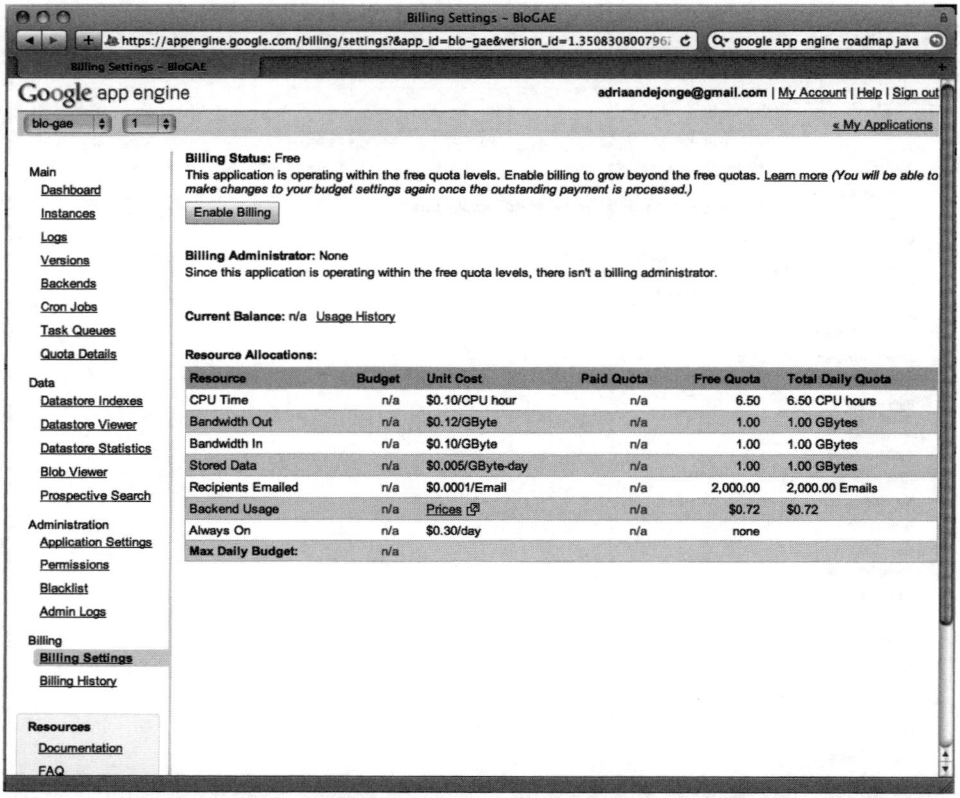

Figure 3.5 Configuring the App Engine to exceed daily quota by enabling billing.

Summary

Now that you have read this chapter, you should have a good idea of how a Java App Engine application is set up. This chapter started with a high-level overview of how the App Engine servers cooperate and where your application fits in. As it turns out, your application is separated over application servers and static file servers. Where your files are located depends on your configuration. If you don't pay attention, all static files go to both servers and consume twice the space they need from your quota. The remainder of this chapter outlined all other App Engine configuration files.

Chapter 4

Data Modeling for the Google App Engine Datastore

This chapter provides a conceptual overview of using the Google App Engine datastore. In Chapter 10, "Storing Data in the Datastore and Blobstore," you'll read how to actually implement the code to do everything that is described here. At this point, the focus is on the concepts behind this code. The goal of this chapter is to understand why the App Engine datastore performs well if you use it as intended and why it does not perform well if you treat it without consideration. This chapter points out some fundamental differences of thinking about data in comparison to relational databases. Next, it explains the questions you should ask yourself while modeling data. Finally, it discusses the ways to interact with the data and the performance characteristics.

Moving Away from Relational Storage

Most developers have a lot of experience programming to relational databases. You likely know some basics such as normalization, joins, and the way transactions work.

If you want to work with the Google datastore and make it perform well, you should forget everything you have learned from relational databases. The App Engine datastore is designed and optimized for completely different usage scenarios and performance characteristics than relational storages offer. The things you should do to take advantage of this may seem counterintuitive at first.

The App Engine datastore is based on Google's BigTable, which is Google's storage system used for Gmail, Google Maps, YouTube, and many other services. This system is designed to scale across thousands of machines and perform well under circumstances typical for a dynamic Internet application.

Denormalizing Data

Conventional wisdom says that duplication is a bad thing and normalization is a good thing. Although under some circumstances this is true, you should not think too dogmatically about duplication.

Whether you are talking about data or source code, the main reason to avoid duplication is to simplify maintenance. In some cases, there is a trade-off, however. Simplifying maintenance means making it more efficient to write data. Making it more efficient to write data may inadvertently make it inefficient to read data. The question is whether you are making the right choice when doing so.

In many web applications, data is usually read several thousands of times more than it is written. Gaining efficiency in writing data may not compensate for inefficiency in reading that same data.

Your application is more likely to benefit from optimizing data reading even if data writing becomes very inefficient. In many cases, you can write data in a background process on the task queue while the visitor is not waiting for a server request to return. Chapter 12, "Running Background Work with the Task Queue API and Cron," covers this topic in more detail.

When using the App Engine datastore, it is more efficient to read a single, larger entity than to read multiple smaller, related entities containing the same data. Therefore, to model data for the App Engine datastore, you should do exactly the opposite of what you are used to doing: you should denormalize data and accept duplication of data when it speeds up the reading process.

> **Considering High Replication**
>
> When storing data in the App Engine datastore, Google offers two modes for data replication in the cloud: *master/slave* and *high replication*. Master/slave improves writing speed, while high replication improves availability and reliability. At the time of writing, Google charges a higher fee for high replication. In addition, Google switched the default storage mechanism from master/slave to high replication. Consider changing this setting if your user requirements favor fast writes over availability.

Aggregating Data without Joins

In normal relational databases, reading from a normalized database is relatively efficient because of the ability to perform join operations. The App Engine datastore does not support the join operation.

You may think you'll miss the join operation, but remember the "Denormalizing Data" section you just read. If you denormalize well, you don't need the join operation—or at least you don't need it frequently.

And that's fortunate because join operations are very inefficient given the design of the App Engine datastore. Every entity in your datastore—whether entities of different kinds or of the same kind—may be stored on a different machine. Performing a join divided over multiple machines would be extremely inefficient.

You may still be worrying about disk space. Stop worrying; disk space is cheap. At the time of writing, storing a gigabyte of data is 15 cents per month, and CPU time is 10 cents per hour!

Designing Schemaless Data

Separating entities over many machines gives you scalability. Scalability is a broad subject. Mostly it means that you have the ability to use large numbers of machines to handle large numbers of users.

Scalability may also mean that you store the data of your Japanese users on servers in or near Japan, while your American users read their data from U.S. servers. Google's datastore automatically distributes the data to the optimal servers.

One of the reasons the datastore can handle data automatically is that it does not require a fixed data schema up front. Not requiring such a schema also means that it does not enforce a schema.

Enforcing schemas is a responsibility of the web application. Updating or rolling back versions of your web application does not affect the datastore. This is why you should always think about backward and forward compatibility of application versions when it comes to upgrade strategies.

Modeling Data

The worst way to learn something is to be told what *not* to do. Up to this point, this chapter told you *not* to normalize data, perform join operations, or design schemas. The reason for this introduction is to stress that data modeling for the App Engine datastore requires a completely different mind set.

If you look at the datastore with the mind set of never having used any type of data storage before, and if you think about the performance consequences of every choice you make, it is not difficult to achieve good results.

Designing at a Micro Level

Let's start with the basic ingredients of a data model. The basic entry point to access data is an *entity*. An entity can distinguish itself from a different entity by its *kind*. An entity can have one or more *properties*. A property has a *name* and a *value* of a certain *type*. Figure 4.1

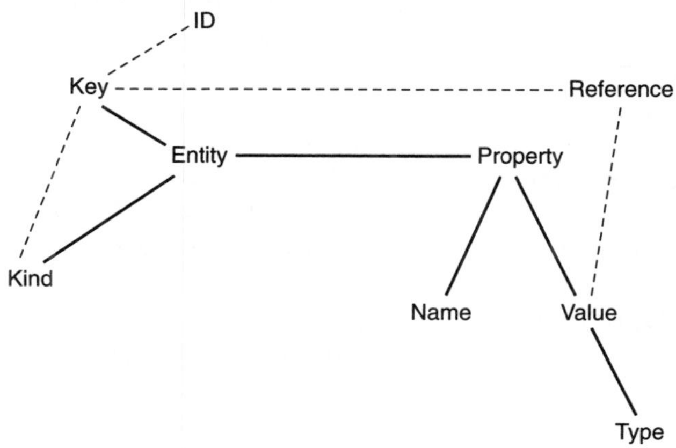

Figure 4.1 The entity concept.

illustrates these concepts. You can read the solid line as *has one or more* and the dashed line as *references*.

Because the datastore is schemaless, two entities of the same kind can have a property with the same name but with values of a different type. Also, one entity can have a multivalued property, where different values have different types.

Table 4.1 gives an overview of the possible property types.

Table 4.1 **Datastore Property Types and Their Meanings**

Type	Description
`java.lang.String`	Text, less than 500 characters, indexed
`cgaa.datastore.ShortBlob(cgaa = com.google.appengine.api)`	Byte array, less than 500 bytes, indexed
`java.lang.Boolean`	False or true
`java.lang.Long (Short/Integer)`	Discrete numeric value
`java.lang.Double (Float)`	Floating-point value
`java.util.Date`	Date/time
`cgaa.users.User`	Google user, identified by e-mail address
`cgaa.datastore.Text`	Long text, more than 500 characters, not indexed
`cgaa.datastore.Blob`	Byte array, over 500 bytes, not indexed
`cgaa.datastore.Key`	Key reference to other entity
`cgaa.datastore.Category`	Text signifying a category
`cgaa.datastore.Email`	Text signifying an e-mail address
`cgaa.datastore.GeoPt`	Object with latitude/longitude
`cgaa.datastore.IMHandle`	Text signifying instant messaging address
`cgaa.datastore.Link`	Text signifying URL
`cgaa.datastore.PhoneNumber`	Text signifying phone number
`cgaa.datastore.PostalAddress`	Text signifying postal address
`cgaa.datastore.Rating`	Numeric value signifying a user rating

The special text classes, such as `Email` and `PhoneNumber`, do not do much more than signify which kind of content they contain. They do not perform validation on the content you enter in them. Especially for `PhoneNumber` and `PostalAddress`, these values differ too much from country to country to validate them well.

Choosing Properties

Most of the properties speak for themselves. You know you need a `Date` object if you want to store a date and/or time. However, when you have longer text and you want to be able to search it, should you store it in a `String` or `Text`?

The first question is, Do you want a long text to be indexed? Indexes cost space and therefore money. You could also consider using Google Custom Search (a JavaScript widget on your site) for full-text searches. Native support for full-text search is on the roadmap for future releases of the App Engine. In this case simpler searches can use the smaller `String` fields.

A second solution is to store longer texts in `Text` objects and store keywords from the text in `String` objects. This may require some manual action from your users to recognize the keywords.

A third solution is to split longer texts over multiple indexed `String` fields. Even though this might work, you should not do it. In general, trying to use tools for purposes they were not meant for has its downsides. In this case, your indexes could end up requiring a lot of storage space. Indexes are further discussed later in this chapter.

The choice is easier in the case of byte arrays. If you have less than 500 bytes and you are sure you will not exceed this limit, use a `ShortBlob`. Between 500 bytes and 1MB, use the `Blob`. For more than 1MB, use the Google Blobstore described in Chapter 10.

Separating Entities

You have already read about denormalizing your data. You have seen the way properties can be modeled and how they can have multiple values. The next question is, When is something a separate entity, and when is it not?

Given that our gut instinct will not work properly for a while, because we're still inclined to think in terms of relational databases when it comes to data storage, here is some advice that will help (at least temporarily): keep the content of your entities as close as possible to the content you view in screens.

I know what you're thinking: data model and view should be separated! And of course you are right. In the end, you do not want a one-on-one tight coupling of views and data. Why not? Well, mostly because you want to be able to create multiple views on the same data.

Remember, this is temporary advice you can use as training wheels to gain experience. After a while, you'll make informed decisions against this rule, and you know why you make these decisions. In the meantime, it bears repeating: keep the content of your entities as close as possible to the content of your screens.

For example, in many applications you have both a list view and a detail view. Usually, the list items are excerpts from the items in the detail view, so modeling logically, you would have one kind of entity, the same for both the list view and the detail view.

Will it work? Definitely! Will it perform? That depends on the number of details in the details view. If you have a list view summarizing four or five properties of the entity and retrieve these properties for the current page of 10 items, you are downloading about 50 properties from the datastore. But you might also be downloading more than 500 properties if the detail view contains that many details.

Remember: when you retrieve an entity from the datastore, all properties are fetched. This includes all the properties you are not viewing. In a list view, you are retrieving multiple entities, so the number of properties quickly increases. In a detail view, you view only a single entity (assuming a simple detail view) and the number of properties remains limited. Figure 4.2 proposes a more efficient data model that copies the values for the list summary into separate entities.

Figure 4.2 A data model with list view entities referring to detail view entities.

The conclusion you can draw is this: if your detail view has many properties, it might be wise to create separate entities, especially for the list view. If these list view entities contain only a summary of the real entities, you save a lot of data transfer between the datastore and the App Engine when building list view pages.

Creating and Maintaining Relationships among Entities

An entity can create a relationship to another entity by adding a property with a *key* as a value. A key contains both an identifier and the kind of entity, so you have everything needed to reference a specific entity in a single object.

In addition to a kind and ID, a key can have a *parent*. Parent-child relationships are relevant only in the context of transactions, discussed later in this chapter. For now, all you have to remember is that you should avoid parent-child relationships when you do not strictly need them!

Entities can have many other relationships with other entities. The main question is, If A and B are related, should A refer to B, should B refer to A, or should both refer to each other?

The answer to this question depends on circumstances. All three options will work, but they may not be as efficient as you would like. You must consider two things: How many times do you want to refer from A to B or B to A while reading? How many times do you want to refer from A to B or B to A while writing?

Figure 4.3 illustrates the simplest data model, involving two entities and a reference.

Let's start with reading data from this data model. Assume that A refers to B using the property `b-reference`, but B does not refer to A.

Figure 4.3 Relationship between A and B.

If we already have A and we also want to retrieve B, we can simply retrieve entity B by using its key, which is stored in A as a reference.

However, if we already have B and we also want to retrieve A, we need to create a query and ask for all items B that have a property `b-reference` containing a key referring to our current B. This process requires an index to perform well.

Although there is nothing wrong with an incidental query, you should start rethinking the direction of the relationship if a query is executed frequently.

Maintaining One-to-Many and Many-to-Many Relationships

More likely than not, relationships are between one entity and multiple other entities or between multiple entities and multiple other entities, which adds a level of complexity to the optimization challenge. The rules of thumb for many-to-many relationships, however, might simplify things.

Let's start with the one-to-many relationships. Assume entity A has a relationship with B1, B2, and B3. Keep the reading and writing optimization question in mind and consider a multivalued property in A to refer to all three B entities. Figure 4.4 illustrates A referring to three B entities.

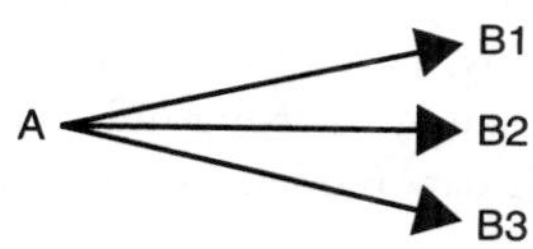

Figure 4.4 Entity A referring to B1, B2, and B3.

Now assume entity A has a relationship with B1 through B238. This is easy: let all B entities refer to entity A, even if an additional query is required while reading. Figure 4.5 illustrates 238 B entities referring to a single A entity.

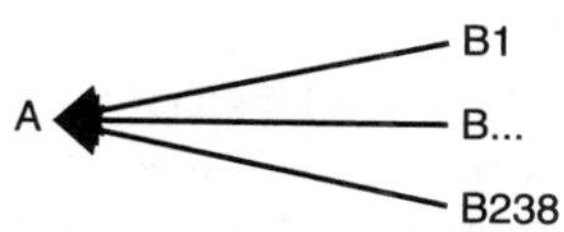

Figure 4.5 Entities B1 through B238 referring to A.

What about many-to-many relationships? Assume entity A1 has a relationship with B1 through B5. Entity A2 has a relationship with B2 and B3. Entity A3 has a relationship with B3 through B238. Figure 4.6 displays 238 B entities referring to three A entities.

In many-to-many relationships, you should count the number of relationships from every entity. In our example, of the A entities, A3 has the most connections: 236. Of the B entities, B3 leads with three connections.

If, on average, an A refers to n B's and a B refers to m A's, you should initially consider keeping a reference in A to B if m is greater than n.

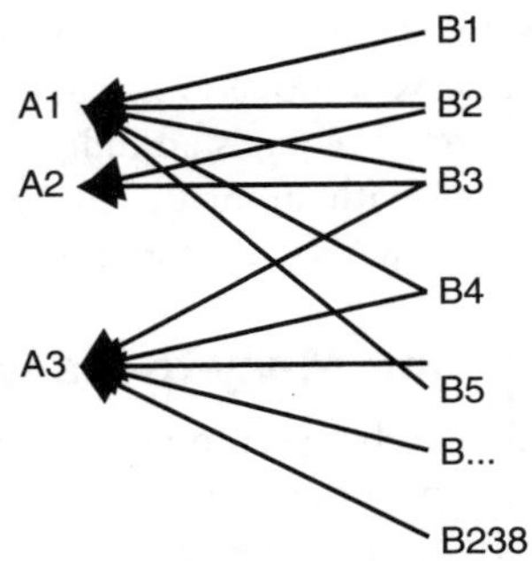

Figure 4.6 Many-to-many relationships.

With the information given in this example, you should consider letting B refer to A instead of the other way around. Please keep in mind that this is not exact science. Data may change over time. Will A always have more references to B, or is this an incidental or temporary situation because you are just starting up? As long as you are continually investigating and optimizing your data model, you can avoid running into performance problems.

Working with Data

After modeling data, you probably want to use it to make modifications, query efficiently, and perform read actions. Read actions are simple and do not require much discussion in this chapter. However, modifying may involve transactions, and queries may involve indexes.

Performing Transactions

As mentioned earlier, parent-child relationships should be avoided when they are not strictly required because of transactions. Why should they be avoided?

The App Engine datastore recognizes a general concept of transactions. This concept is different from what you are used to, though. The datastore is set up to spread entities over many machines and perform well under very heavy and distributed loads. The concept of transactions contradicts with this kind of scalability.

Still, you want to ensure integrity and consistency between data parts divided over multiple related entities while making changes. The datastore provides a transaction mechanism based on exactly that premise: *related* entities.

In the datastore, you can define parent-child relationships. By defining a parent-child relationship, you implicitly define an *entity group*. Every entity, directly or indirectly descending from the same parent, belongs to the same entity group. Tree structures of entities belonging to the same entity group are kept together on the same machine instead of being spread over multiple machines.

These tree structures can consist of entities of different kinds. Multiple entities of the same kind may be divided over multiple entity groups. A single entity can only be a member of a single entity group. Figure 4.7 illustrates two entity groups with one group containing mixed element types.

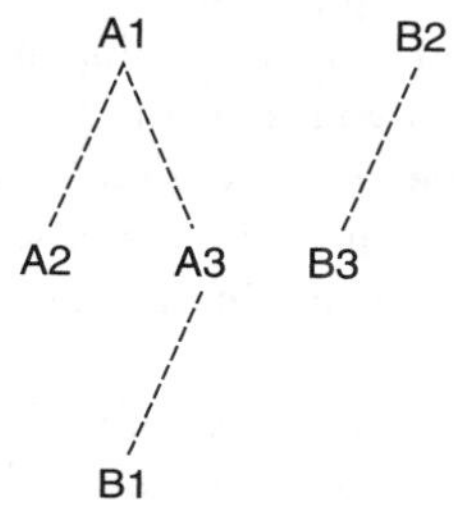

Figure 4.7 Entities A1, A2, and A3 and B1, B2, and B3 in entity groups.

With this concept, you can have multiple concurrent transactions in different entity groups without transactions interfering with each other. Within the entity group, the principle of a transaction remains unchanged. Either all changes fail or all changes succeed.

Performing Queries

A query on the App Engine datastore is a lot simpler than a query on a relational database. Always keep in mind that performing a query is more expensive than retrieving an entity by its key if you have access to it.

You can query for all entities of a certain kind, filter them by a certain property, sort them by the same or a different property (or multiple properties), and limit the size of the query to a subset, possibly with an offset to introduce paging mechanisms.

In addition, you can query entities regardless of their kind. In this case, though, you cannot sort or filter on anything other than their key value. Such a query may be used to retrieve all entities in a single entity group.

In certain cases, it may be most efficient to only retrieve entity keys as a query outcome instead of retrieving full entities. The query API allows you to specify whether or not to retrieve full entities.

Creating Indexes

Most databases use indexes, regardless of whether they are relational, native XML, object, column, or other.

> **Note**
>
> I prefer the plural form *indices* over *indexes*. However, Google uses the *indexes* in its configuration file names. Therefore, this book sticks with indexes.

The purpose of an index is to speed up a query. The App Engine has a clever mechanism built in to the development server that automatically determines which indexes should be created based on usage patterns it sees when you run the application. As a result, it generates a configuration file, containing the required index definitions, that can be used in production.

Not all queries require an index. Simple equality and inequality filters without sorting can be used without an index. Even though creating an index may be advantageous, the index becomes necessary only when you start sorting.

Despite the automatically generated index configuration, it is better to keep control over this file. Sometimes automatic generation is not sufficient: consider sort orders in both directions on a single property or mixing equality and inequality filters over multiple properties.

The more tricky part of indexing is the use of multivalued properties. When indexing only a single multivalued property for an entity kind, this is not much of a problem. Every property value leads to a separate row in the index.

However, if you want to index multiple multivalued properties for a single entity kind, you should be careful. A row is added to the index for every possible combination of two multivalued property values, so the size of the index can quickly explode.

Upgrading When the Datastore Is Involved

When you switch to a new version of the software you deploy on Google App Engine, the datastore behind it remains unchanged. As long as you are switching from an older version of your application to a newer version, and as long as you are only extending your previous data model with new properties and entities, most of the transition will go relatively smooth.

However, when for some unexpected reason you need to roll back your application to the old version, you should be sure that your data model was designed to tolerate that scenario. Especially when switching back to the new version again, you should not assume that the new properties and entities are there for data created between rollback and reinstallation of the new version.

It becomes more difficult when you need to change existing properties—for example, if you change the name or type of a property or if you move a property to a different entity kind.

One thing that may help is the use of *update tasks* and perhaps *downgrade tasks*. However, such tasks take time to execute and could mean extra downtime.

If it is possible to do so, the most failsafe method is to support both data models for a while and write the properties under two names or in two entities. Then, when you are certain that the new version works 100 percent correctly, you remove backwards compatibility and delete the old properties.

Summary

This chapter emphasized the differences between modeling data for relational databases and modeling data for the Google App Engine datastore and explained normalization, join operations, and schemas from a datastore standpoint. Next, the chapter introduced the properties you can use for an entity, focusing on the key for referring to different entities and the use of multivalued properties. After reviewing some pointers for separating entities, the chapter explained references between entities. The direction of references greatly depends on your application's demands. This chapter ended with a discussion of transactions, queries, indexes, and data migration—important tools for working with the data model. From this chapter, you can conclude that the performance of your web application greatly depends on the choices you make while modeling the data.

Chapter 5

Designing Your Application

Before you start building your application, you must think about the technical design and do some planning. In the code examples in this book, the process of building a weblog application is a recurring theme. This chapter discusses the design of such an example application. It starts with a brief overview of the functional requirements, then looks at technical choices specific for this example: frameworks and libraries. The last part of the chapter translates the functional requirements to a data model and a URL structure.

Gathering Requirements

This book is not the first tutorial to explain a platform by building a weblog. For example, when the Ruby on Rails platform was first introduced in 2005, the website featured a screenshot demonstrating how to build a weblog in 20 minutes. Later, it reduced the demonstration to a 15-minute video. A weblog is a nice application for providing explanation: it is small enough to cover in a limited amount of time, simple to understand, and yet powerful enough to be useful when it is finished.

The weblog you build in this book does nothing spectacular: it will take you more than 20 minutes to build, and it will require more than 20 lines of code. However, the example won't take 20 seconds on the first cold request, and it won't require you to upload 20MB of frameworks and libraries—not by far. That's pretty awesome but not necessarily spectacular.

The weblog is a basic application: a homepage containing the most recent posts and links to older posts and a rudimentary interface for content administration. It does have a few special features, though, to show you some of the functionality you can build into your applications.

When writing a weblog that is a bit more advanced than a typical weblog, you can introduce new features such as the functionality to write *series* of posts in which each post is self-contained but relates to other posts. Such a weblog must allow easy navigation to earlier and later posts. To enable easy navigation, the weblog needs a table of contents covering more than one post, and one post can be part of only a single series. The table of contents *must* have links to all the other posts in the series, and it *must* contain their titles. The table of contents should also have an overview of the subheaders within the post. These subheaders might contain links to their respective anchors.

A series might contain several recurring subjects, and the weblog *must* be able to use *tags* to group posts on certain subjects. However, tags are not always clear, so the user should be able to provide description texts for the tag, which should be displayed when the user's mouse rolls over on the tag.

Apart from that, the weblog requires only simple formatting. A solution like BBCode or Wiki markup should be sufficient for most of the typing the user will do.

Choosing a Toolkit

Many developers start their development with a prefabricated framework, such as Struts, Spring MVC, Spring Roo, Grails, Wicket, or Seam. The rationale for choosing a framework is not always clear. Some choose a framework they are familiar with. Others choose a framework they want to take for a test drive.

Choosing a Framework

Chapter 2, "Improving App Engine Performance," mentioned that loading a framework has a considerable performance penalty for the first request at cold startup. So instead of asking which framework you should choose, consider whether you need a framework at all.

Defending the Choice for a Framework

Most framework authors take the time to justify the existence of yet another framework, generally naming the flaws of other frameworks. The stories usually involve a quest for a framework that solves a specific problem. When their quest fails, the authors finally give up and write their own solutions. These new solutions are shared with the rest of the world so other people can have the same benefits.

This is the business case for using frameworks: using frameworks saves time, because most of the code is already there, you only have to fill in the blanks. If you know how to use a framework well, you can do a lot of things with a lot less code. The better you understand the inner workings of a framework, the more you can do with it.

Well-known frameworks are on the résumés of many Java developers. This means that if you start using these frameworks, you can easily extend your team with new developers, and they need little or no training to get up to speed.

Frameworks add a level of abstraction, making it easier to switch the underlying technology, such as the data storage you use. You can also switch implementations of interfaces without changing the rest of the code.

Some parts of software applications are more difficult than others. Take object-relational mapping as an example. Using a framework can take the harder parts of software development out of your hands.

The final reason for using frameworks is that you learn how other people solve the same problems you have in new ways.

Working without Frameworks

Now imagine a world without frameworks. Consider some of the reasons you might miss them.

Would you miss frameworks because they save time and use less code, as the previous section claims? Most of a software developer's time is spent thinking about how to solve problems, not about how to code the solution. If development is time consuming because of repetitive coding and duplication of logic, should you switch to a framework? Or should you rethink your own solution design? Sometimes a framework makes coding so easy that you forget to think about the actual problem, and by limiting your thinking, you may be overlooking other—better—solutions.

Although you can save time by using a framework designed for a specific purpose, you're likely to use additional time solving problems the framework was not designed for. Most frameworks force you into certain boundaries—hence the name "framework"—and boundaries are also limiting.

Would you miss listing a framework on your résumé or seeing it on the résumé of developers you are hiring? You may think that having a large number of frameworks on your résumé makes you a *senior* developer. However, knowing lots of frameworks often means you have skimmed the surface of all of them but know none of them well. With a framework mind set, you may tend to look for prefabricated solutions instead of thinking about the actual problem.

Would you miss the abstraction level that frameworks add to your system? You may be perfectly comfortable not to concern yourself with the inner workings of a system. This layered way of thinking about systems is what you probably learned in college: the OSI network stack resolves certain problems, layer by layer, and each layer adds a level of abstraction.

The Java platform was set up with the same design philosophy. It abstracts away from the operating system and memory management. Although useful, this abstraction is actually one step too far. Despite the abstraction, you have to think about both the underlying operating system and memory management. You cannot just do whatever you want and expect it to work without problems.

Most of the abstraction introduced by frameworks does more harm than good. For example, look at what data goes in and out of the database and what remains in memory in a typical Hibernate solution. All of the inner workings you comfortably disregard actually cost you in terms of performance and system resource usage.

Many framework abstractions assume relational databases under the hood. They also assume that the system keeps running indefinitely. Both assumptions are false on the Google App Engine. Chapter 4, "Data Modeling for the Google App Engine Datastore," explained that in many cases you should do exactly the opposite of what you are used to doing when you are modeling for the App Engine datastore.

Would you miss the ease of use of a framework that eliminates the difficult parts of programming? Of course, some things you just don't want to program yourself. Would you write your own XML parser? Perhaps you can, but you won't. However, you do not need a full framework to parse XML. You need only a small library. The same holds true for some other very specific requirements, which we discuss later in this chapter.

Would you miss any other aspect of using frameworks? Perhaps writing code of a declarative nature takes more effort without a framework. It depends on your style of coding, but at the end of the day, Java is not a declarative language. The point is, frameworks add only a small amount of declarativeness but at high cost in terms of system resource usage. If you are looking for declarativeness, domain-specific languages may be a more appropriate solution for you, but that is a whole different book.

Frameworks have their upsides and downsides. Even if you are willing to give up using them, it won't happen overnight. But with time and thought, you'll find that working without frameworks and making your own design choices puts the fun back in programming!

Choosing a Template Engine

There are many ways to generate texts to output from a servlet. You can hardcode strings in a servlet or use Java Server Pages (JSP), Velocity, or FreeMarker templates, XSLT transformations, or libraries such as StringTemplate.

Hardcoding strings in a servlet may be efficient in terms of system performance, but they are not easily maintainable. Their flexibility is also questionable, although a clever object model may help out.

Using JSP is hardly better than hardcoding strings in a servlet. It saves you some boilerplate code, but underneath, JSP is translated to inefficient servlets after all. Maintainability is hardly better: JSP still must be compiled, only later in the process. And its flexibility is worse: the possibilities for clever object models are more limited.

Using Velocity and FreeMarker templates is better in terms of flexibility: both libraries can work with templates loaded from sources other than the web application code base. However, both libraries are somewhat large.

The StringTemplate library is a bit large, but it provides a powerful yet simple template engine in return. It is powerful in terms of flexibility: you can apply templates to the outcome of templates. The output of a template is a string. You can use this output as one of the inputs for a different template. It is simple in terms of both code and usage and requires only a few basic language constructs.

The examples in this book use StringTemplate to generate HTML. An added benefit of template engines like Velocity, FreeMarker, and StringTemplate over JSP is that they allow you to use them for channels other than HTTP responses, such as for the content of an e-mail that needs to be sent.

Before you start developing your own application for the App Engine, you should make a similar assessment for yourself. Find out the resource use of your own favorite library on the App Engine. Create a table comparing pros and cons of each choice.

Choosing Libraries

At this point, we have thrown out all frameworks and fallen back to plain vanilla servlets. To be more specific, the App Engine currently supports the servlet 2.5 specification. If you look closely, you can see that using a servlet allows you to follow Model-View-

Controller (MVC) patterns without using additional framework layers. Even though the classes don't follow an MVC naming convention, the servlet specification does not stop you from distinguishing between models, views, and controllers yourself.

In the previous section, we chose to use StringTemplate for the example weblog application. StringTemplate requires you to include two libraries: ANTLR and StringTemplate. ANTLR is a *parser generator*—a way to let you create your own languages for specific purposes. StringTemplate is a library that uses ANTLR in a clever way to create a template language, and it does not work without the ANTLR library.

Google ships several libraries with default App Engine applications when you use Google's Eclipse plugins. You should throw out most of them but keep the App Engine API and the labs version of the App Engine API. If you don't plan to use the Google Services, you could even throw these libraries out, but your platform would be a bit limited.

You do not need Java Data Objects (JDO), Java Persistence API (JPA), DataNucleus, Java Specification Request (JSR) 107, or anything else included with the default distribution. The remainder of this book shows that you can work very well without them. Removing them should improve cold startup time, because the system has fewer classes to scan.

One last library needs to be added to the stack: Apache Commons File Upload. This library helps you extract uploaded files from multipart MIME (Multipurpose Internet Mail Extensions) requests. Working without this library leads to cumbersome code, so the functionality of the library is worth the overhead. Of course, if you do not require file uploads, you can leave the library out.

In the weblog example, you use Commons File Upload to upload images and attachments that belong to a blog post. An alternative would be to store images and attachments on external servers and provide links to them. If it does not interfere with the usability for the blog author, this may be a simple way to reduce resource usage on the App Engine.

Now you have your full and thin stack to work with. It may seem a bit crude and rigid, but you'll find that a thin stack is sufficient for performing common tasks without writing too much code. And in the end, it helps you keep your code running fast and efficiently.

Making Design Choices

Our design choices so far have been general: the libraries we chose can be reused for almost any application that fits the same profile. There are also some application-specific choices to make.

As Figure 5.1 shows, the example requires only a basic and rudimentary weblog with a list of posts and a menu bar.

The most important choices for the design of this weblog are the data model and the URL structure. The data model must be in line with the recommendations from Chapter 4 for performance optimization. The URL structure should be simple and descriptive, and it should allow for additional JavaScript to enrich the application.

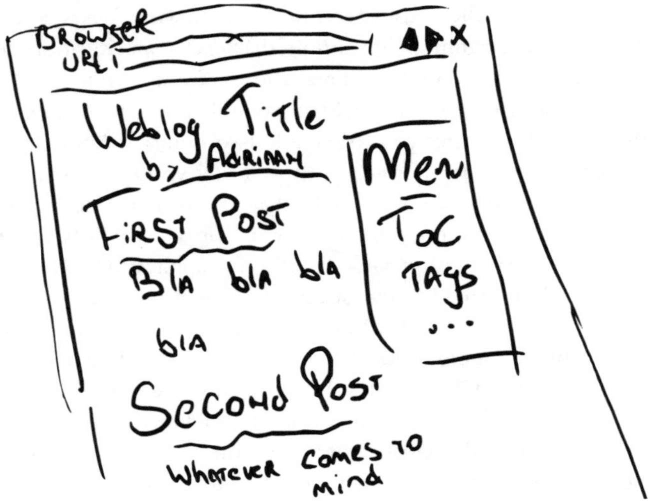

Figure 5.1 Quick sketch of a very basic weblog.

Modeling Data

We must define a number of basic data elements: a *user* who inputs new *posts, external users* who write *comments* to the posts, *tags* with descriptions, a *table of contents* with a *menu*, and the *external feed*.

Now we must consider which of these data elements translate into actual entities in the datastore and how they relate to each other. The post clearly needs its own entity. The main question for the post is how it will store the long text that is inside it. Assuming that the text remains within the 1MB limit, the text should be in a string, which is not indexed.

If you want to introduce a simple searching mechanism and a full text search will not work with the current implementation of the datastore, you could introduce a simplified searching mechanism based on keywords.

> **Full Text Search**
>
> The feature to search on the full text of a document is included on the App Engine roadmap. As soon as the feature is released, the Essential App Engine weblog covers the functionality on www.essentialappengine.com.

The encoding for the text should allow the user to specify keywords, for example, using characters like this: [[keyword]]. In this case, the word "keyword" should be copied to a separate text field that is indexed. The datastore does not allow indexed text fields to be longer than 500 characters, so it follows that the total number of keywords cannot exceed 500 characters. Keywords is a typical feature where searching is a requirement.

The text encoding should support a similar mechanism to extract a small table of contents out of the post. You can think of a notation like {{This is a Subheader}}. There should not be too many within a single post, because tables of content work across multiple posts.

A post should have a single-value property to indicate that it belongs to a series of posts. The question is whether this property is a reference to a series entity or whether it simply uses a string value as an identifying key without using a separate entity. For simplicity, the first version of the software will work with a string identifier containing the series title. The table of contents will be generated in chronological order.

Then there are the tags. As mentioned earlier in this chapter, you may require a description text above a page containing the tag's references and explaining what the tag means. A tag should therefore be a separate entity in order to contain a description text. The next question is whether the tag will refer to the posts or the posts will refer to the tags. This may seem like an easy question. You might reflexively answer that the posts should refer to the tags. Can you be 100 percent sure of your answer? Another question is whether the posts will use key references to tags or simply contain string values. Both are possible. To answer this question, you should know whether the key of a tag contains a string with the actual tag name.

The next question is whether you want to make it easy to add new tags or whether a tag should be preconfigured before you can use it in a post. Assuming you want to add tags on the fly, the string is preferable over the key. Keep in mind that tags are indexed, multivalued properties. This means that there should be no other indexed, multivalued properties in the post entity; only single-valued properties should be used. Read Chapter 4 for an explanation.

Then we have the user. The user is not a conventional entity but a reference to a Google user object. The datastore knows how to handle this.

The comments entity is a bit more complex. If you can store comments in a single string or text property without structure, you may consider adding a nonindexed, multivalued property to the post containing all comments. However, it is more likely that you want to add some structured fields to a comment. In this case, you can only add a separate entity and ask yourself whether the post should refer to the comment using multivalued reference properties or whether the comment should refer to the post. The last option should be most efficient. Some caching doesn't hurt if you want to include the comments under the posts.

Most sites provide a menu with links to other parts of the website to allow visitors to navigate through the site. Weblogs also provide navigation menus. In a typical weblog, a menu in the sidebar should not be an entity in the datastore. Rather, it is extracted from tags, tables of content, and entry dates. Because of the relatively heavy queries behind this functionality, menus should rely on caching most of the time.

Modeling URLs

To support the functionality of a weblog, a number of URLs must be supported. A one-on-one connection does not exist between datastore entities and URLs. Some URLs may be based on a specific field in an entity.

To provide an overview of the inner workings of the weblog, the URLs in Table 5.1 illustrate how the servlets should be set up:

Table 5.1 **Modeling URLs**

URL	Description
http://[appid].appspot.com/	Contains the basic homepage with the five most recent posts
http://[appid].appspot.com/older/5	Contains posts 6–10 that come after the five most recent posts
http://[appid].appspot.com/date/2010/06	Contains all the posts written in June 2010
http://[appid].appspot.com/tag/appengine	Contains all the posts with the tag appengine
http://[appid].appspot.com/author/adriaandejonge	Contains all posts written by the author with the user id adriaandejonge
http://[appid].appspot.com/post/yet-another-article-on-this-subject	Contains a single post with the title "Yet Another Article on This Subject"
http://[appid].appspot.com/post/yet-another-article-on-this-subject/comments	Contains all comments for this post
http://[appid].appspot.com/post/yet-another-article-on-this-subject/comments/new	Contains a form to post new comments and the handler to place them after the form is posted
http://[appid].appspot.com/rss	Contains the RSS feed with the five most recent posts
http://[appid].appspot.com/admin	Contains the homepage for the content administration interface; this URL and underlying URLs are secured
http://[appid].appspot.com/admin/new-post	Contains the form to input new posts and the handler to place them after the form is posted
http://[appid].appspot.com/admin/list-posts	Contains the list view containing all posts in the weblog to allow access to the content administrator
http://[appid].appspot.com/admin/edit-post/yet-another-article-on-this-subject	Contains the editor to modify an existing post

You can imagine adding more URLs for other actions. Every URL space is handled by its own *servlet*. The servlets operate independently of each other, allowing you to extend or simplify the application without repercussions.

Handling Page Flow

With the URLs mentioned in the previous section, you can set up a web application that works without any JavaScript. With the current URL space, every URL contains an atomic transaction, either GET or POST. Instead of aggregating multiple elements on a single page, this mechanism lets the visitor click on URLs to retrieve additional information. For example, the comments for a post are on a separate page.

This is a design choice that improves App Engine scalability with functional consequences on browsers without JavaScript. If those functional consequences are undesirable, you could also let a single URL retrieve both the post and its comments. Although this would work, it would add time for the server to generate the page before it can be sent back to the visitor. Extra time spent on the server harms scalability.

Considering the wide adoption of JavaScript, there is an alternative. With the atomic URLs, you can also consider retrieving additional information on one page using AJAX calls in the background. If JavaScript is turned off, the full content and functionality is available to the user on different pages, because the functionality was already there with links to the atomic URLs. With JavaScript turned on, the pages can be designed to contain additional items without additional mouse clicks. The principle behind this way of adding JavaScript and AJAX is explained in Chapter 8, "Adding Static Interactions Using JavaScript."

Summary

This chapter started with an overview of the requirements for an example weblog application. The requirements are limited but sufficient to require some fundamental design choices. The most difficult step is to decide to stop using the frameworks many Java developers are used to. In the context of the Google App Engine, these frameworks do more harm than good. The next step is to be careful in selecting the libraries to use. Libraries should be kept to an absolute minimum. The same goes for the template engine: this should be as lightweight as possible without harming maintainability and flexibility. The remainder of this chapter discussed how to model data given the functional requirements of the weblog example. An overview was provided of URLs involved in the application, offering a first impression of how the weblog example works.

PART III

User Interface Design Essentials

Chapter 6

Presenting the User Interface with HTML5

This chapter introduces HTML5 and points out why it is the perfect companion to the Google App Engine for creating rich and responsive web applications. It starts with a basic introduction of new HTML5 elements. Next, the HTML5-related JavaScript APIs are discussed. The canvas element for graphical manipulations, rich user interaction with drag and drop, and using new form elements are also discussed. Finally, it explores the possibilities of storing and querying data on the browser side.

Introducing HTML5

Those who were writing HTML during the 1990s remember a time when new features worked only in the newest browsers. You had to explicitly design your website for a limited set of browsers.

In the early 21st century, this problem slowly went away. HTML4 remained unchanged and unchallenged for quite a long time. However, with HTML5 slowly introducing new standardized features to the latest browsers, you will once again have to consider the value of new features against the downside of dropping support for older browsers.

You may think it is a bit early to start using HTML5. At the time of writing, a lot of people are still using Internet Explorer versions 7 and 8, and support for HTML5 in these browsers is somewhat limited.

You may also wonder why there is a full chapter on HTML5 in a Google App Engine book. Strictly speaking, the content of this chapter is not related to the Google App Engine at all. HTML5 is covered here because it is important! And it is particularly well suited to use as a companion to the Google App Engine for several reasons. First of all, most of the added benefit of HTML5 over its predecessors is its focus on rich and interactive web applications. The App Engine is also targeted at web application development.

Second, some of the typical server-side limitations of the App Engine can be overcome by using HTML5 on the client side. For example, the canvas element compensates for the limited ability to manipulate images on the server side. And the Document Object Model (DOM) storage provides a perfect alternative for heavy server-side sessions.

If you want to stay on top of things, now is the time to start adopting HTML5. Better early than late. Just keep in mind that you are working with early technology! You can explore a site like http://html5test.com/ to see what features of HTML5 are currently available in your browser.

This chapter gives you a quick glance at HTML5's possibilities, but a full discussion of HTML5 is beyond the scope of this book.

> **Scoping the Term HTML5**
>
> This book uses the term HTML5 in the broadest possible sense. A lot of what is called HTML5 is actually in separate specifications by the W3C.
>
> If you want to talk about the larger trend of adding new features to browsers, it is hard to avoid the generalized term HTML5 and mention all specifications separately. For that reason, HTML5 is a useful collective noun that is widely used. It is likely that your business customers also talk about HTML5 in general and that they are not interested in formal specifications.
>
> One way to avoid confusion without using too many words is to separate "HTML5 elements" from "HTML5 APIs" or perhaps "HTML5-related APIs" if you like to be more precise.

Using Basic HTML5 Elements

Most of the HTML5-related specifications have little to do with HTML and a lot to do with JavaScript APIs. The writers of the HTML5 specification did update the HTML element library. That is not spectacular in terms of technical possibilities, but it does clean up HTML code in general.

The writers of the specification researched a large number of websites to find out what `class` and `id` attributes people use for their `div` elements. It turned out that there are some common names used across many different websites. Names like `header`, `footer`, `article`, `section`, `nav`, and other names with similar meanings are used everywhere. Code would be cleaner if these names were standardized. With HTML5, they are!

Recent browsers easily work with these new names because they are not strictly tied to the element names in the HTML4 specification. Only Internet Explorer 7 and 8 do not allow styling of new element names without using a JavaScript-based hack to fix it. You can reuse other people's code at http://code.google.com/p/html5shim/ or write your own version limited to the HTML elements you are using.

If you are designing websites that should also work when JavaScript is not available, it may be a bit too soon to start using new HTML5 element names. You should wait until the majority of website visitors moved from Internet Explorer 7 and 8 to version 9.

Listing 6.1 provides a simple HTML layout for a weblog application without using IDs or classes. This example shows just a selection of new HTML5 elements, but there are many more.

Listing 6.1 **A Simple HTML5 Weblog Application**

```
01 <!DOCTYPE html>
02 <html>
03   <meta charset="utf-8">
04   <body>
05     <header>
06       <h1>Blog title</h1>
07       <h2>Written by Adriaan de Jonge</h2>
08     </header>
09     <nav>
10       <a href="/1">First link</a>
11       <a href="/2">Second link</a>
12     </nav>
13     <article>
14       <header>
15         <h1>Post title</h1>
16         <p>Written on <time datetime=2010-10-23 pubdate>
17           the 23rd of October 2010</time></p>
18       </header>
19       <p>Here is the actual content of the article</p>
20       <p> ... and more</p>
21       <footer>
22         Little icons here to publish to Facebook, Twitter, etc.
23       </footer>
24     </article>
25     <article>
26       <header>
27         <h1>Second post</h1>
28         <p>Written on <time datetime=2010-10-24 pubdate>
29           the 24th of October 2010</time></p>
30       </header>
31       <p>Different text</p>
32       <footer>
33         Little icons here to publish to Facebook, Twitter, etc.
34       </footer>
35     </article>
36     <footer>Copyright &copy; 2011 - all rights reserved</footer>
37   </body>
38 </html>
```

On lines 5 and 14, you find a `header` element, each containing an `h1` title. The second `h1` element is scoped within an `article` and therefore can have a different meaning than the first `h1` element.

If you are used to XHTML and not to HTML5, it may seem as if the example contains a lot of sloppy errors. For example, on line 16, the `datetime` attribute has no quotes and the `pubdate` is just floating without a value. In HTML5, you are allowed to leave out quotes when you do not need them. You do need them when there are spaces involved. The `datetime` is unambiguous without quotes. Also, the `pubdate` can stand on its own. You can compare it to the `selected` attribute in an `option` element inside a `select` box. Where XHTML requires you to type `selected="selected"`, HTML5 allows you to abbreviate this.

The `nav` element replaces the usual `div` elements with a `class="nav"` attribute, indicating that the child elements provide a way to navigate through the website. You could nest `ul` and `li` elements inside the `nav` element if you like. This example assumes that the Cascading Style Sheet (CSS) takes care of styling the links to be divided over multiple lines.

Similarly, you can see that an article has its own `footer` element even though there is a `footer` at the end of the document that applies to all.

Chapter 7, "Fine-Tuning the Layout using CSS3," discusses in detail how to apply different styles to `h1` elements on different levels in the tree.

Drawing Images Using the Canvas

Chapter 13, "Manipulating Images with the App Engine Image Service," discusses how to edit images on the Google App Engine. The usual Java APIs for image manipulation are unavailable on the App Engine for performance and security reasons.

App Engine's Images API is somewhat limited. You can resize, rotate 90 degrees, and create composite images, but that is about it.

The HTML5 canvas element comes to the rescue! The canvas provides a relatively rich API to draw, transform, and manipulate images within a browser window. You can also export the resulting image to a PNG or JPEG file. Listing 6.2 shows a small selection of the operations available. Again, there are a lot more possibilities that are beyond the scope of this book.

HTML5 also allows the use of scalable vector graphics (SVG) within your document. An important difference between SVG and the canvas is that SVG allows you to manipulate the XML source of the document. The display automatically reflects the changes. The canvas is more lightweight and is stateless. You need to redraw the image when it should change.

Listing 6.2 **Simple Usage of the HTML5 Canvas Element**

```
<!DOCTYPE html>
<html>
  <meta charset="utf-8">
  <body>
    <header>
      <h1>Try the Canvas</h1>
    </header>
    <article>
      <canvas id="my-canvas" height="200" width="250">
    </article>
  </body>
```

Listing 6.2 **Simple Usage of the HTML5 Canvas Element (Continued)**

```
  <script>
    function drawInCanvas() {
      var canvas = document.getElementById('my-canvas');
      var context = canvas.getContext('2d');
      context.beginPath();
      context.moveTo(10,10);
      context.lineTo(190,190);
      context.stroke();
      context.fillRect(50,10,40,40);
      context.fillStyle = "gray";
      context.rotate(0.1);
      context.fillRect(100,10,40,40);
      context.globalAlpha = 0.5;
      context.fillRect(150,10,40,40);
      context.fillRect(170,10,40,40);
    }
    window.addEventListener('load', drawInCanvas, true);
  </script>
</html>
```

This example draws a line and a rectangle, changes the color of the rectangle from black to gray, and then rotates the view a little. After this rotation, two more rectangles are drawn using an alpha value of 0.5, as shown in Figure 6.1.

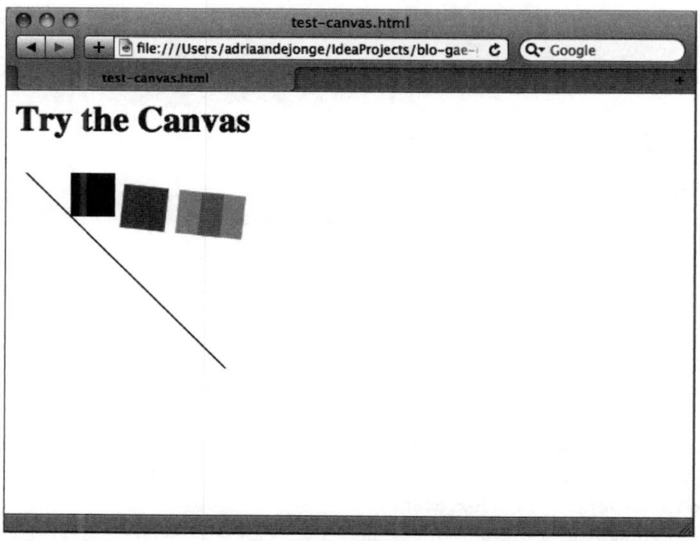

Figure 6.1 The resulting screen after drawing in the canvas.

The canvas element did not originate from the HTML5 specification. It is based on an existing implementation by Apple. Other browser vendors implemented the canvas according to the specification. Starting with version 9, the canvas element works in Internet Explorer.

Dragging and Dropping Items into Pages

As with the canvas element, the support for drag and drop in HTML5 originated from a relatively old implementation by Microsoft in Internet Explorer 5.5. As a result of this origin, some things in the API may seem a little strange.

Drag and drop can be used for more than one purpose. The example code in Listing 6.3 shows you how to drag an element in the page into another element in the same page. This could be useful for applications like shopping baskets, manipulation of data sets, or changing the way a web page looks.

The same API can also be used for communication outside the browser window. Pick a file from your desktop and drag it into the drop area in the example and see what happens.

Listing 6.3 **Marking a `div` as Draggable and Listening for Drop Events**

```
<!DOCTYPE html>
<html>
  <head>
    <meta charset="utf-8">
    <style>
      #drop { height: 100px; border: 4px dashed #c00; }
      #drag { margin: 50px; border: 1px solid #00c; }
    </style>
  </head>
  <body>
    <header>
      <h1>Try Dragging and Dropping</h1>
    </header>
    <article>
      <div id="drag" draggable="true">This element
        is draggable</div>

      <div id="drop"></div>

    </article>
  </body>
  <script>
    var drop = document.getElementById('drop');
    drop.ondrop = function (event) {
      event = event || window.event;
      this.innerHTML += '<p>' +
        event.dataTransfer.getData('Text') + '</p>';
      event.cancelBubble = true;
```

Listing 6.3 **Marking a *div* as Draggable and Listening for Drop Events (Continued)**

```
      return false;
    };

    var appEngineLogo = document.createElement('img');
    appEngineLogo.src = 'http://code.google.com/' +
      'appengine/images/appengine_lowres.png';
    var dragElement = document.getElementById('drag')

    dragElement.ondragstart = function(event) {
      event = event || window.event;
      event.dataTransfer.setDragImage(appEngineLogo, 50, 50);
      event.dataTransfer.setData('Text', dragElement.innerHTML);
    }

    drop.ondragover = function () { return false; };
  </script>
</html>
```

Even though this example is rather simple, it contains a few features worth mentioning. You do not need to take special action to make images within your page draggable. Making text draggable requires the `draggable="true"` attribute. Adding `="true"` is required to make it work in this example. This is why you cannot drag the `h1` element into the drop zone. See Figure 6.2.

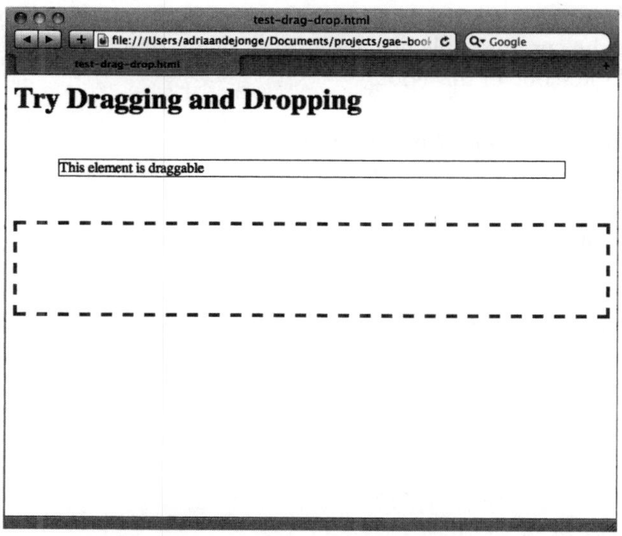

Figure 6.2 The resulting screen with a draggable element and a drop area.

Another feature, not shown in Figure 6.2. is that the drag element changes into an App Engine icon when you start dragging it. Lines 32 through 41 are responsible for this. Also, lines 27 and 40 correspond with each other, passing the text content from the paragraph as content to be added into the drop zone.You can also use this attribute for other purposes.

To make an application that allows dragging and dropping files from the desktop into the browser is beyond the scope of this book. Google uses this API in Gmail for drag-and-drop attachments and in Google Docs to add images. Imagination is the only thing needed to use this API to create richer applications inside your browser.

Improving Form Elements

Some, but not all, of the APIs in HTML5 are based on existing functionality that evolved in one or more browsers independently of existing HTML standards.

HTML5 suggests a richer interface for forms.There are some new kinds of input elements that extend the classic text elements such as dates, range, e-mail, and phone. Despite the lack of support, you can use the newer elements without penalty because older browsers fall back to the text input when they do not recognize a new input element.

Safari already supports a search input box that is shaped similarly to the search box in the upper right of the browser screen. Some mobile devices like BlackBerry already support more advanced date inputs and color choosers. Safari Mobile also supports the date input type, but it is not as user friendly as it could be. Safari Mobile does help the user by changing the onscreen keyboard as appropriate. For example, for typing an e-mail address, the user can press an @ key without switching to special characters.

Listing 6.4 demonstrates a few new input elements so you can try them in your latest browser and see the current implementation status.There are more new features in forms that are beyond the scope of this book.

Listing 6.4 **New HTML5 Input Types in Forms**

```
<!DOCTYPE html>
<html>
  <meta charset="utf-8">
  <body>
    <header>
      <h1>Try the Canvas</h1>
    </header>
    <article>
      <form>
         E-Mail <input type=email id=email><br>
         Search <input type=search><br>
         URL <input type=url><br>
         Date <input type=date><br>
         <input type=submit>

```

Listing 6.4 **New HTML5 Input Types in Forms (Continued)**

```
      </form>
    </article>
  </body>
</html>
```

Another forms standard, by the World Wide Web Consortium, is called XForms. The relation between HTML5 forms and XForms is similar to the relation between the HTML5 canvas element and SVG. HTML5 forms are more lightweight and not bound to an XML model. Where XForms rely on XML technologies, HTML5 forms may use JavaScript to further decorate the interface. Compared to HTML4 forms, the use of JavaScript can be greatly reduced using more powerful and native-looking input types, though.

Detecting a User's Geolocation

The authors of the HTML5 specification kept mobile devices in mind when they wrote it. One of the APIs that makes more sense on a mobile device than on a desktop computer is the Geolocation API.

You can use the Geolocation API to detect your visitor's latitude, longitude, and the precision of this value (but only if the user gives explicit permission to share his or her location with you).

Listing 6.5 shows the basics of the Geolocation API. Make sure you pay attention to the error function, because there's a very real chance that the location will not be available to you.

Listing 6.5 **Asking for the Geolocation of Visitors**

```
<!DOCTYPE html>
<html>
  <meta charset="utf-8">
  <body>
    <header>
      <h1>Try the Geolocation services</h1>
    </header>
    <article>
      <input type=button id=do-get value="Get coordinates">
    </article>
  </body>
  <script>
    function doGet() {
      if (navigator.geolocation) {
        navigator.geolocation.getCurrentPosition(
        function (position) {
          var coords = position.coords;
          alert('coords = ' + coords.latitude +
            ', ' + coords.longitude +
```

(Continues)

Listing 6.5 **Asking for the Geolocation of Visitors (Continued)**

```
20              ' - accuracy = ' + coords.accuracy);
21          },
22          function (error) {
23            alert('error nr ' + error.code);
24          }
25          );
26        }
27      }
28      document.getElementById('do-get')
29        .addEventListener('click', doGet, true);
30    </script>
31  </html>
```

This code may seem a little cluttered. The mechanism is straightforward, though: the `getCurrentPosition` function takes two parameters, which are both functions themselves. The first function is called upon success. The second is called upon error.

An error code could result from everyday events like a user denying permission or a timeout on the location query. If you'd like to display a message to users who do not have support for the Geolocation API, you could implement an `else` block at line 26.

Storing Data on the Client Side

As long as you do not change the settings of the Google App Engine, it is stateless by nature. This means that you cannot temporarily store user data in the session of your web container.

If you change this setting, the App Engine writes sessions to a few special tables in your datastore. This costs both space and performance. If you have the choice, it is preferable to keep your application stateless. See Chapter 3, "Understanding the Anatomy of a Google App Engine Application," for details on this setting.

The classic alternative to keeping web applications stateless is using cookies. Actually, even when you store the user state on the server side, you need a cookie to identify the session if you do not want to modify all URLs or use POSTs for every server call.

If you need to store session data but do not need all data on the server all the time, HTML5 provides a number of alternatives. You can use local storage and session storage to save up to 5MB (10MB on some browsers, but the lower limit is recommended) inside the browser. For more complex operations, there is even database functionality available inside your browser.

Storing Data across Sessions

Storing data across sessions is not limited to sessions. The local storage can store inside your browser data that remains there even after a browser restart or, for that matter, after a full computer restart. This data is accessible only from the domain of the website that wrote the data in the `localStorage`. It is impossible to further scope the data to just part of the website running on that domain, so you may not want to share your App Engine instance with others.

Listing 6.6 provides a simple example of the usage of the local storage. It has three buttons: get, set, and length. If you try the get button without pressing the set button first, you'll find an undefined value. However, if you press the set button and restart your computer, there will be a value the next time you press the get button.

Listing 6.6 **Storing Data Using HTML5 Local Storage**

```
<!DOCTYPE html>
<html>
  <meta charset="utf-8">
  <body>
    <header>
      <h1>Try the localStorage</h1>
    </header>
    <article>
      <input type=button id=do-set value=Set><br>
      <input type=button id=do-get value=Get><br>
      <input type=button id=get-length value=Length>
    </article>
  </body>
  <script>
    function doSet() {
      localStorage.test = 'did set'
      alert('set');
    }
    function doGet() {
      alert('get = ' + localStorage.test);
    }
    function getLength() {
      alert('length = ' + localStorage.length);
    }
    document.getElementById('do-get')
      .addEventListener('click', doGet, true);
    document.getElementById('do-set')
      .addEventListener('click', doSet, true);
    document.getElementById('get-length')
      .addEventListener('click', getLength, true);
  </script>
</html>
```

This API has more methods, such as `removeItem`, `clear`, and options to get a set of keys, but they are beyond the scope of this book.

You may want to avoid storing critical or private data in the local storage. Although browser vendors take great care to avoid leaking data from your website to other websites, other threats remain. For instance, your users may share their computer with others or work on a public computer. You should also consider that a local storage may be wiped any time the user deletes his or her cookies.

Chrome provides a developer tool that allows you to look inside the local storages inside the browser.

Storing Session Data

Listing 6.7 shows you that storing session data works almost the same way as the local storage. Just replace `localStorage` with `sessionStorage` and you're done!

The behavior will change, though. Restarting your browser flushes the content of the storage, so make sure that you only save temporary, disposable data in the session store.

Listing 6.7 **Storing Data Using HTML5 Session Storage**

```
<!DOCTYPE html>
<html>
  <meta charset="utf-8">
  <body>
    <header>
      <h1>Try the sessionStorage</h1>
    </header>
    <article>
      <input type=button id=do-set value=Set><br>
      <input type=button id=do-get value=Get><br>
      <input type=button id=get-length value=Length>
    </article>
  </body>
  <script>
    function doSet() {
      sessionStorage.test = 'did set'
      alert('set');
    }
    function doGet() {
      alert('get = ' + sessionStorage.test);
    }
    function getLength() {
      alert('length = ' + sessionStorage.length);
    }
    document.getElementById('do-get')
      .addEventListener('click', doGet, true);
    document.getElementById('do-set')
      .addEventListener('click', doSet, true);
    document.getElementById('get-length')
      .addEventListener('click', getLength, true);
```

Listing 6.7 **Storing Data Using HTML5 Session Storage (Continued)**

```
  </script>
</html>
```

Dealing with User Permissions

Keep in mind that most browsers do not allow the use of local and session storage if users disallow cookies. These browsers assume that users want the same behavior for these storages as they want for cookies.

If you want to find out more, search the Internet for both "DOM storage" and "web storage." These are different names for the same API. This book uses local and session storage to distinguish between the behavior of the two.

Querying Structured Data Using a Local SQL Database

The web storage APIs are relatively standardized and stable and already work on all recent browsers, including Internet Explorer 8. The SQL database functionality is a bit trickier, though. There are still minor changes in the API, and not all browsers support them. There is even a good chance that the web SQL database specification will never become an official standard. The indexed database API that is currently under development has a better chance of eventually becoming an official recommendation. However, at the time of writing, full implementations of the indexed database API are not available.

Nevertheless, the subject of databases inside browsers is far too interesting to leave out of this book. Without getting into all the details, Listing 6.8 provides a simple code example that creates a SQL database, sets up a table, and fills it with data. Finally, there is a simple SQL query fetching this data.

You can imagine the possibilities of this API. Think of fetching a large search result in JSON format, storing it into the SQL database, and using client-side SQL queries to filter it, responding directly to user input. Faceted search was never this powerful and responsive!

Warning

At the time of writing, Safari is the only browser that runs this example correctly. Keep an eye out for upcoming implementations of the indexed database API to use database functionality inside the database in the future.

Listing 6.8 **Using the Browser's SQL Database**

```
<!DOCTYPE html>
<html>
  <meta charset="utf-8">
  <body>
    <header>
      <h1>Try the local SQL database</h1>
    </header>
    <article>
```

(Continues)

Listing 6.8 **Using the Browser's SQL Database (Continued)**

```
      <input type=button id=do-create value="Create table"><br>
      <input type=button id=do-fill value="Fill table"><br>
      <input type=button id=do-query value="Query database">
    </article>
  </body>
  <script>
    var db;
    if (window.openDatabase) {
        db = openDatabase('mydb', '1.0',
          'My local database', 1024 * 1024);
    }

    function doCreate() {
      db.transaction(function (tx) {
        tx.executeSql('CREATE TABLE ' +
          'IF NOT EXISTS mytable (id, content)');
      });

      alert('created table');
    }
    function doFill() {
      db.transaction(function (tx) {
        tx.executeSql('INSERT INTO mytable (id, content)' +
          'VALUES(?, ?)', [1, 'Test content']);
      });
      alert('filled data');
    }
    function doQuery() {
      db.transaction(function (tx) {
        tx.executeSql('SELECT * FROM mytable WHERE id = ?',
          [1], function (tx, results) {
            for (var i = 0; i < results.rows.length; i++) {
              alert('query result = ' +
              results.rows.item(i).content);
            }
          });
      });

    }
    document.getElementById('do-create')
      .addEventListener('click', doCreate, true);
    document.getElementById('do-fill')
      .addEventListener('click', doFill, true);
    document.getElementById('do-query')
      .addEventListener('click', doQuery, true);
```

Listing 6.8 **Using the Browser's SQL Database (Continued)**

```
54   </script>
55 </html>
```

This code example contains a few other noteworthy things. On line 18, you need to estimate the space required for your database. The example is a bit pessimistic about the size of a single record. You should try to keep your database within the allowable 5MB, though.

On lines 31 and 32, you see the use of prepared statements within JavaScript. This is good practice to avoid SQL injection. Even though you are operating on the client side, or perhaps especially when you are operating on the client side, you should keep security in mind at all times.

On line 38, the `executeSql` function calls a function with the result set as an argument. In this case, it is an inline function. However, this could also be a function defined elsewhere.

Summary

This chapter provided a high-level overview of the new functionalities provided with HTML5. As you begin to use HTML5, be careful to consider older browsers that do not support new functions. Once the majority of your visitors are using Internet Explorer 9 and newer browsers, most of the functions described in this book should work.

HTML5 is a great addition to Google App Engine, providing rich 2D graphics libraries in the form of the canvas and advanced local storage mechanisms using web storage and a browser-side database. HTML5 is equally well suited for such rich web applications as the Google App Engine.

Chapter 7

Fine-Tuning the Layout Using CSS3

This chapter looks at Cascading Style Sheets Level 3 (CSS3) from a software developer's perspective. Instead of explaining how to design a web page, this chapter explains how to keep your HTML and JavaScript clean of layout code. First, the concept of specificity calculation is explained. Next, the most important CSS selectors are introduced and discussed in terms of specificity calculation. The chapter ends with a small selection of new graphical features available in CSS3 to show off its possibilities.

Selecting Elements Using CSS3

Like HTML5, CSS3 is not yet recognized as an official recommendation by the World Wide Web Consortium. This means that the support for CSS3 features will vary between browsers. You can use the features available as long as you do not count on their availability. Consider having a fallback scenario that works if the styles are unavailable.

Web developers with a graphical background tend to focus on the style declarations offered by CSS. They tend to overlook the features in CSS to select elements to which the styles apply. These tendencies lead to large and inefficient CSS files. This book is targeted at technical web developers rather than graphical web developers.

Technical web developers sometimes tend to overlook CSS altogether. To keep a CSS file as small and efficient as possible, a technical view can help the graphical developers. This section focuses on the technical features to select elements inside a document before discussing the actual styling. The underlying message is that you should be involved in the writing of CSS files even if you do not have outstanding graphical skills.

Understanding Specificity Calculation

One of the nice features of the Internet is that you can take a look at the source of CSS files for any site you visit. If you do, you may notice that CSS files for some sites seem to compete with an average phone book in terms of size and readability. And on other sites, the CSS files are small and concise without sacrificing visual attractiveness.

Large CSS files not only hurt maintainability, they also hurt the performance of the browser rendering the page. The question is, How can you keep your CSS files as small as possible?

With a clever setup of your CSS file, you can avoid a lot of duplication. To avoid duplication, you have to understand how you can make a single rule apply to as many HTML elements as possible without concessions to the desired graphical design. Some rules are very specific and apply to only a small number of elements. Other rules may apply to almost any element in the document. You want to declare rules as general as possible, but not more general than that.

Browsers use a simple set of rules to calculate the specificity for a CSS rule:

A = the number of ID selectors

B = the number of class selectors, pseudo-class selectors, and attribute selectors

C = the number type selectors and pseudo-element selectors

A is more specific than B, which in turn is more specific than C. Only style attributes within the HTML are more specific than any CSS rules (and should be avoided at all cost). The universal selector (*) is ignored in specificity calculation.

In the rest of this chapter, the specificity is calculated and presented as:

```
A,B,C = x,y,z
```

> **Considering Performance**
>
> While smaller CSS files save bandwidth and improve maintainability, the choice of your selectors may impact performance of your browser as it evaluates the styles. The evaluation of selectors is from right to left, so the more specific you make the styles and the less depth in selectors, the sooner they match. In real life, the impact is really tiny, though. In this case, easier maintenance of your styles is a better goal than coding for performance.

Using IDs

In many HTML documents, you find code like the following:

```
<div id="main">
```

There can be only one element with the ID `"main"` in the HTML document. This corresponds with the fact that ID selectors are most specific. Consider the use of CSS code like this:

```
#main {
  /* styling here */
}
```

If you use code like this, this rule would have a specificity of:

```
A,B,C = 1,0,0
```

There still is room to create more specific rules, though. In the example HTML, you could have the following instead of the div:

```
<p id="main">
```

With this CSS attached to the HTML document, the #main rules would still apply. To prevent that from happening, you could also provide a more specific rule:

```
div#main {
  /* styling here */
}
```

This rule would have a specificity of:

```
A,B,C = 1,0,1
```

You may sometimes want to be even more specific. An example would be if you wanted to override the styling when the user moves the mouse pointer over the element. In this case, the rule would be:

```
div#main:hover {
  /* styling here */
}
```

The specificity of this rule would be:

```
A,B,C = 1,1,1
```

And if you think that is as specific as you can get, you are mistaken. You could also select a div#main that is inside an element with the ID parent, like this:

```
#parent > div#main {
  /* styling here */
}
```

In this case, the specificity is:

```
A,B,C = 2,0,1
```

You can imagine how to make it more specific from there. However, that is exactly what we're trying to avoid! There is much more to be gained if you can use the least possible number of IDs in your document—preferably none.

If your general CSS file is free of ID attributes, you can easily include an exception in a single page without worrying about name clashes. As the number of exceptions grows, it becomes increasingly risky to add yet another exception.

Chapter 6, "Presenting the User Interface with HTML5," presented a number of new HTML elements that replace the most used IDs and classes in common web pages. The div#main example could easily be replaced with an article element. In that case, the specificity reduces to

```
A,B,C = 0,0,1
```

And you have a lot more ways to override that rule without getting into a hassle.

Selecting Classes

With HTML5's introduction of new element names that replace common classes, the need for classes in a static document is greatly reduced. However, when you are using JavaScript to add interaction to your page, classes are a powerful way to let JavaScript cooperate with your CSS file. This keeps your JavaScript clean of view logic.

You can think of a class called `no-js` like this:

```
<article class="no-js">
```

Following is the CSS style:

```
.no-js {
  display: none;
}
```

This rule has a specificity of

```
A,B,C = 0,1,0
```

You could use a jQuery function in JavaScript to remove this class:

```
$(".no-js").removeClass("no-js");
```

Or, with a bit of extra code, you can remove a class without jQuery.

With this small code example, you can hide screen elements that fail when JavaScript is unavailable. This is the opposite of a `noscript` element. With `noscript` you can show certain content when JavaScript is not available instead of hiding it.

Similarly, you can use the `addClass` method in jQuery to add appropriate styling that occurs during an interaction.

Selecting Pseudo-Classes

Not all interaction is directly JavaScript dependent. A growing number of interactions are detected by the browser without any scripting required. A well-known example is the pseudo-class `:hover`. The following is an example:

```
article {
  border-style: dotted;
  border-width: 1px;
}
article:hover {
  border-style: solid;
}
```

The first rule has specificity

```
A,B,C = 0,0,1
```

The second rule has specificity

```
A,B,C = 0,1,1
```

This means that if the mouse cursor is over an article in this document, the border changes from a dashed border into a solid border. The border width remains unchanged. This is not overruled in the more specific rule, so the less specific rule applies.

CSS3 introduces a large number of new pseudo-classes: `:root`, `:nth-child`, `:checked`, `:invalid`, and `:not()`, to name just a few.

The use of these pseudo-classes allows constructions like:

```
li:nth-child(odd) {
  background-color: white;
}
li:nth-child(even) {
  background-color: gray;
}
```

Both rules have a specificity of

```
A,B,C = 0,1,1
```

In the past, you were required to change the HTML with additional classes to achieve a similar result.

Selecting Attributes

Selecting attributes is particularly useful for applying different styles to input elements in a form. Input elements may look a lot different, depending on the type attribute. From the CSS perspective, they are all the same element, though.

Consider this HTML form element, for example:

```
<input type="text" id="example" value="">
```

This is an input box for text, which looks like a bounded rectangle. It looks a lot different than when the `type` would have been `radio` or `checkbox`. You can select this specific text input element with:

```
input[type="text"] {
  /* styles here */
}
```

The specificity for this rule is:

```
A,B,C = 0,1,1
```

B is 1 because of the attribute selection, C is 1 because of the specific input element.

CSS3 introduces a few variations on this principle. For example, you can select time elements in the year 2011 like this:

```
time[datetime^="2011"] {
  color: blue;
}
```

There are more attribute selectors similar to this one:

^= means "starts with"

$= means "ends with"

*= means "contains"

These attribute selectors allow differences in styling depending on partial content. Of course, this works only for attributes, not for the text inside an element. The specificity remains unchanged.

Selecting Elements

The selection of elements is the least specific way of styling your document. With the introduction of new elements in HTML5, it becomes possible to style your document using much less specific rules.

The most simple element selector works like this:

```
article {
  /* styling here */
}
```

This rule has a specificity of:

```
A,B,C = 0,0,1
```

which is not very specific. Now consider these two rules:

```
body > footer {
  /* styling here */
}

article footer {
  /* styling here */
}
```

Both rules have a specificity of:

```
A,B,C = 0,0,2
```

Their behavior is different, though. The first rule selects a `footer` element only if it is a direct child of the `body` element. The second rule selects any `footer` that is a descendant of an `article` element, direct or indirect.

Especially in these cases, you can clearly see the additional value of the new HTML5 element names. Because these element names are more specific than the general `div` elements by nature, there is less need for additional classes and IDs to point out the element to which you are referring. In many cases, `A` and `B` can remain 0 and only `C` needs a specificity of 1 or 2. This leaves a lot of room to override them if, for example, you need exceptional styling or you need to respond to interactivity in a web application.

Selecting Pseudo-Elements

The first question you should ask is, What is the difference between a pseudo-element and a pseudo-class, and why are they different?

A pseudo-class leaves the element intact and provides an extra property (class) to the element in order to style the full element. In most cases, this helps to render interactivity without requiring JavaScript code.

A pseudo-element applies only to part of the element and not to the full element. Pseudo-elements act as if they are child elements of the real element.

For example, consider the pseudo-element `::first-letter` that applies to a paragraph:

```
<p>This is a paragraph.</p>
```

This is internally considered to be equal to:

```
<p><p::first-letter>T</p::first-letter>his is a paragraph.</p>
```

You can style this line with a larger font for the first letter, like this:

```
p::first-letter {
  font-size: 20px;
}
```

This rule has a specificity of:

```
A,B,C = 0,0,2
```

This means that both the `p` element and the `::first-letter` pseudo-element are counted separately. It is also possible to select only the pseudo-element without specifying a parent element:

```
::first-letter {
  font-size: 20px;
}
```

This has a specificity of

```
A,B,C = 0,0,1
```

Similar to the way you use `::first-letter` to select the first letter in an element, you could use the pseudo-element`::first-line` to select the first line in a paragraph and apply a style to it that is different from the rest of the paragraph.

Using New Graphical Effects in CSS3

So far, this chapter concentrated on the technical side of CSS. Many of the concepts discussed were already possible in CSS2.1. CSS3 mostly adds to the selectors that already exist. These new features combined with HTML5's new element names greatly help reduce the size of your CSS and improve their maintainability.

Quite probably, most people will be more interested in the graphical features of CSS3 than in the selectors. This is a technical book, not a designer's manual. Therefore, this book concentrates on the more technical side of CSS3.

A full discussion of all new graphical possibilities of CSS3 would require a whole separate book. This chapter is limited to a few illustrative examples of what you can do with CSS3.

The CSS file works on an HTML example much like the one in Chapter 6. This example (Listing 7.1) targets the newest versions of the current web browsers and does not work in Internet Explorer versions 7 and 8.

Listing 7.1 **A Simple HTML5-Styled Weblog Application**

```
<! DOCTYPE html>
<html>
  <link rel=stylesheet href="style-article.css">
  <meta charset="utf-8">
  <body>
    <header>
      <h1>Blog title</h1>
      <h2>Written by Adriaan de Jonge</h2>
    </header>
    <nav>
      <a href="/1">First link</a>
      <a href="/2">Second link</a>
    </nav>
    <article>
      <header>
        <h1>Post title</h1>
        <p>Written on <time datetime=2010-10-23 pubdate>
          the 23rd of October 2010</time></p>
      </header>
      <p>Here is the actual content of the article</p>
      <p>…and more</p>
      <footer>
        Little icons here to publish to Facebook, Twitter, etc.
      </footer>
    </article>
    <article>
      <header>
        <h1>Second post</h1>
        <p>Written on <time datetime=2010-10-24 pubdate>
```

Listing 7.1 **A Simple HTML5-Styled Weblog Application (Continued)**

```
            the 24th of October 2010</time></p>
        </header>
        <p>Different text</p>
        <footer>
          Little icons here to publish to Facebook, Twitter, etc.
        </footer>
      </article>
      <footer>Copyright &copy; 2011 - all rights reserved</footer>
  </body>
</html>
```

A simple CSS style sheet for this article is presented in Listing 7.2. Bear in mind that this style sheet is not created by a skilled designer. This is just a simple example to demonstrate some of the graphical capabilities of CSS3.

You should think about the order or your CSS declarations. There is no official standard or authoritative set of rules on how to do this. Some people order the elements alphabetically. Some make distinctions between page layout and text markup. A good practice is to start with the less specific style declarations and then declare more specific exceptions to the general rules.

Listing 7.2 **A CSS Style Sheet for the Weblog Application**

```
body {
  font-family: Verdana, sans-serif;
}
article {
  font-size: 12px;
}
h1 {
  font-size: 50px;
}
h2 {
  font-size: 30px;
  font-style: italic;
}
article {
  border-style: dotted;
  border-width: 1px;
  border-radius: 15px;
  margin: 40px 0px 20px 0px;
  padding: 5px;
}
article:hover {
  border-style: solid;
}
```

(Continues)

Listing 7.2 **A CSS Style Sheet for the Weblog Application (Continued)**

```
24 article h1 {
25   font-size: 25px;
26 }
27 nav a {
28   display: block;
29 }
30 body > footer {
31   margin: 40px 0px 0px 0px;
32   background-color: black;
33   color: white;
34 }
35 article footer {
36   background-color: #DDDDDD;
37 }
38 p::first-letter {
39   font-size: 20px;
40 }
41 time[datetime^="2009"] {
42   color: blue;
43 }
```

This example looks like the screen shown in Figure 7.1.

You'll recognize most of the selector constructs from the first half of this chapter. This illustrates why the global `h1` element and the `article`'s `h1` element have different sizes. This corresponds with their having different meanings.

Rounding Edges

CSS3 offers a wide range of new features, from very simple to amazingly powerful ones. Rounded edges is a simple feature to start with. Many websites have had rounded edges for years, but the tricks these sites used to accomplish this feature were a bit dirty.

Listing 7.2 already contains the code required to create rounded edges on the article borders, as you can see in Figure 7.1. On line 17 of Listing 7.2, you can find `border-radius: 15px;`, which sets the size of the rounded edge.

This feature does not work on all browsers. If the feature is unavailable, the fallback is a border with straight edges. This means graceful degradation by design.

Using 2D Animations

Lines 21, 22, and 23 in Listing 7.2 contain a very basic kind of animation:

```
article:hover {
  border-style: solid;
}
```

Figure 7.1 The resulting screen from Listings 7.1 and 7.2.

If you move the mouse over one of the articles, its border changes from a dashed border into a solid border.

CSS3 enables you to create many other effects. The following example may not be visually appealing to a graphical designer, and the rotation may not follow any logic, but the example illustrates some of CSS3's capabilities.

Add the following lines to the bottom of the stylesheet:

```
article {
  -webkit-transition: -webkit-transform 3s ease-in-out;
  -moz-transition: -moz-transform 3s ease-in-out;
}
article:hover {
        -webkit-transform: rotate(5deg);
        -moz-transform: rotate(5deg);
}
```

If you try this example in the latest versions of Firefox, Chrome, or Safari, you'll see something that looks like Figure 7.2.

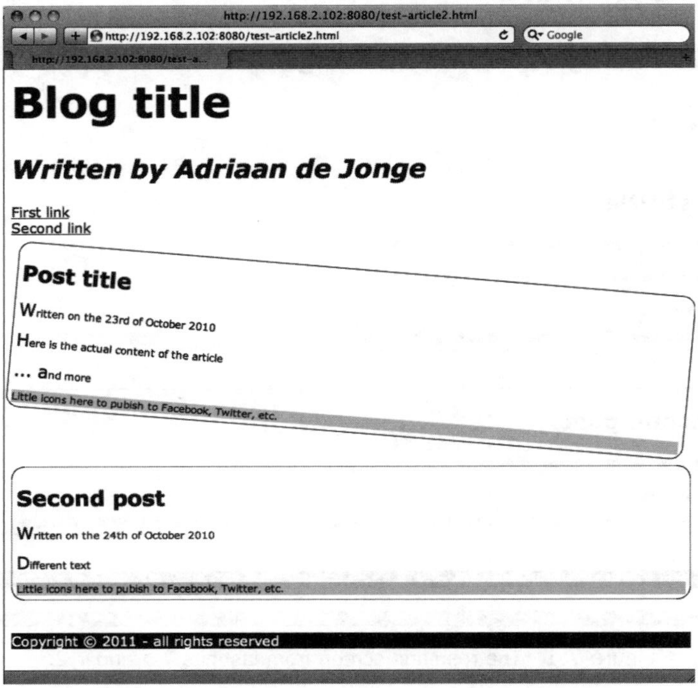

Figure 7.2 Rotating an element when the mouse points to it.

What you notice in the code example is that the style attributes are prefixed with `-webkit-` and `-moz-`. These declarations are more or less duplicates because the transformation attribute has not yet reached the status of W3C Candidate Recommendation at the time of writing. Until it does, behavior and implementation may change and browsers may not render the implementation correctly. The prefix helps to point out where browsers cannot promise to follow the standards.

Using 3D Animations

In addition to 2D animation, Webkit is experimenting with 3D animations. You can find some better-looking (but harder to understand) examples on the Internet. Here is an example based on the HTML from Listing 7.1 and the CSS from Listing 7.2. Add these lines to the CSS instead of the lines you added for 2D animations:

```
article {
  -webkit-transition:-webkit-transform 2s linear;
}
article:hover {
   -webkit-transform: rotateY(40deg) rotateZ(5deg);
}
```

You may be able to tell the difference between the `rotate()` function and the `rotateX()`, `rotateY()`, and `rotateZ()` functions. There are similar `translateX/Y/Z()` functions. Figure 7.3 shows the result of this CSS modification. You can try the code in Safari or Chrome to see the animation.

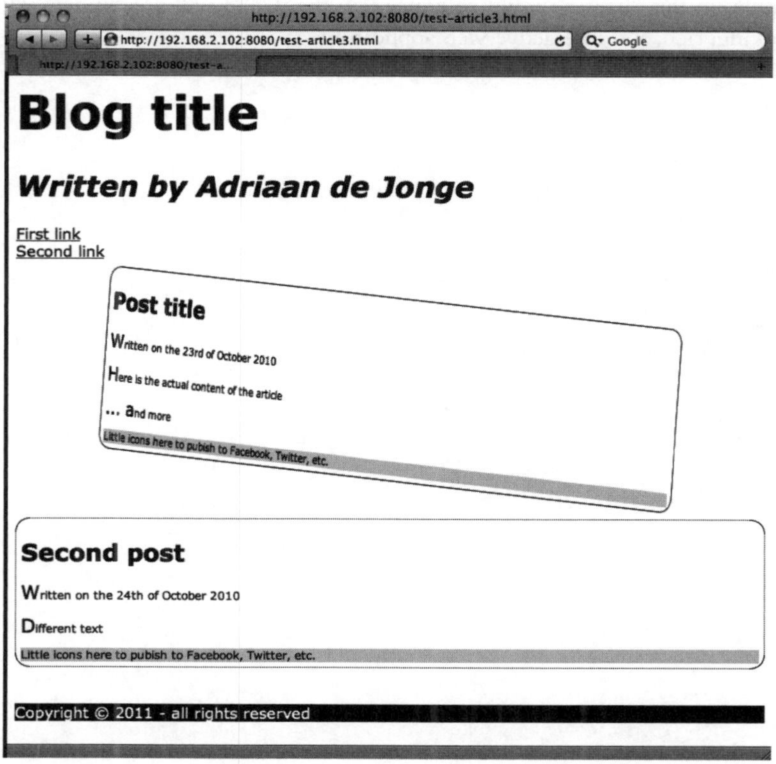

Figure 7.3 3D rotation of an element when the mouse points to it.

CSS3 introduces a seemingly endless number of graphical possibilities to enhance your user experience. Many of these features already work without a single line of JavaScript if you set them up in a clever way. Browser support and standardization will grow over time. Refer to books on CSS3 and to Internet sources for further details.

Summary

This chapter introduced CSS from a technical perspective. An important concept to understand is specificity calculation. To get a small, maintainable CSS file, you need to minimize specificity where possible. This means that elements without classes or IDs are preferable over those that contain classes and IDs. Just a few classes may be helpful to keep JavaScript clean of styling when you want to add interaction. IDs should be avoided and used only in exceptional cases.

The end of the chapter presented a small selection of new graphical features in CSS3. CSS3 offers many other possibilities, which are beyond the scope of this book. However, the examples in this chapter should convince you that CSS3 will greatly help you create good-looking, rich, and interactive web applications.

Chapter 8

Adding Static Interactions Using JavaScript

The last two chapters discussed HTML5 and CSS3. Hopefully, you didn't forget that this is a book about the Google App Engine. One of the most important use cases of the App Engine is creating browser interfaces. This book advocates avoiding frameworks and libraries whenever feasible to optimize performance and minimize resource usage. Many frameworks abstract away from HTML, CSS, and JavaScript. When using frameworks, you may overlook the power of writing code yourself. This part of the book demonstrates the elegance of writing HTML, CSS, and JavaScript and how much you can do with a little code in modern browsers.

Chapter 8 is the last client-side chapter; it discusses how to improve your JavaScript code. To achieve high-performance websites, optimization on the client side is vital. This chapter starts with a simple but flawed example. Throughout the chapter, each flaw is fixed. And even though the performance improvement might not be noticeable in an example this simple, the principles introduced should become clear enough to be applied to larger applications. For the real perfectionist, the chapter includes some suggestions for further improvement.

Setting Up a Simplistic Example

A proper web application may contain several hundred or even thousands of lines of JavaScript code. The performance optimizations suggested in this chapter are more noticeable in larger examples than in small examples. Small examples, however, work better for explaining the principles behind the optimizations in a book. In this chapter, the code from Chapter 7, "Fine-Tuning the Layout Using CSS3," is reused and extended with an extra function: you can minimize a blog post by hiding the content under the title.

Listing 8.1 presents the HTML from Chapter 7 with modifications to minimize the blog posts and get them back on the screen. This example uses an absolute minimum of JavaScript code. The remainder of this chapter explains why it may not be a good idea to insert JavaScript code within the HTML despite the small size of the code.

Listing 8.1 **Minimizing Posts Using Flawed JavaScript Code**

```
<! DOCTYPE html>
<html>
  <link rel=stylesheet href=style-article.css>
  <meta charset="utf-8">
  <body>
    <header>
      <h1>Blog title</h1>
      <h2>Written by Adriaan de Jonge</h2>
    </header>
    <nav>
      <a href="/1">First link</a>
      <a href="/2">Second link</a>
    </nav>
    <article>
      <header>
        <h1 onclick="this.parentNode.parentNode.className =
(this.parentNode.parentNode.className == 'minimized' ? '' :
'minimized')">Post title</h1>
        <p>Written on <time datetime=2010-10-23 pubdate>
          the 23rd of October 2010</time></p>
      </header>
      <p>Here is the actual content of the article</p>
      <p>... and more</p>
      <footer>
        <p>Little icons here to publish to Facebook, Twitter,
        etc.</p>
      </footer>
    </article>
    <article class=minimized>
      <header>
        <h1 onclick="this.parentNode.parentNode.className =
(this.parentNode.parentNode.className == 'minimized' ? '' :
'minimized')">Second post</h1>
        <p>Written on <time datetime=2009-10-24 pubdate>
          the 24th of October 2010</time></p>
      </header>
      <p>Different text</p>
      <footer>
        <p>Little icons here to publish to Facebook, Twitter,
        etc.</p>
      </footer>
    </article>
    <footer>Copyright &copy; 2011 - all rights reserved</footer>
  </body>
</html>
```

On lines 16 through 18 and 31 through 33, you find `onclick` handlers with inline JavaScript code. This approach has two problems: First, it has poor separation of concerns. The JavaScript code is mixed with the HTML, which makes is harder to maintain when you have separate HTML specialists and JavaScript specialists working on the code. It leads to duplication of code that increases as your solutions grow.

The second problem is performance. When the browser is rendering HTML, it pauses every time it encounters a JavaScript fragment in order to interpret it, and then it continues the rendering process. Although you may not notice the overhead of executing just two lines of JavaScript within the HTML, you will notice the difference of executing many lines when building larger web applications.

On line 29, the second post is minimized by default. What happens when JavaScript is turned off? Or when JavaScript stops functioning because of an unexpected error in another part of the page? It means that part of your content becomes inaccessible.

Before continuing with a first improvement step, you need to know something about the appearance of the HTML on screen. Listing 8.2 presents the extended CSS based on the earlier CSS from Chapter 7.

Listing 8.2 **Extending the CSS to Allow Blog Posts to Be Minimized on Screen**

```
body {
    font-family: Verdana, sans-serif;
}
article {
    font-size: 12px;
}
h1 {
    font-size: 50px;
}
h2 {
    font-size: 30px;
    font-style: italic;
}
article {
    border-style: dotted;
    border-width: 1px;
    border-radius: 15px;
    margin: 40px 0px 20px 0px;
    padding: 5px;
}
article:hover {
    border-style: solid;
}
article h1 {
    font-size: 25px;
}
nav a {
```

(Continues)

Listing 8.2 **Extending the CSS to Allow Blog Posts to Be Minimized on Screen (Continued)**

```
28     display: block;
29 }
30 body > footer {
31     margin: 40px 0px 0px 0px;
32     background-color: black;
33     color: white;
34 }
35 p::first-letter {
36     font-size: 20px;
37 }
38 time[datetime^="2009"] {
39     color: blue;
40 }
41 article.minimized p {
42     display: none;
43 }
44 article.minimized h1:after {
45     content: "<<CLICK TO OPEN>>";
46     margin: 0px 0px 0px 10px;
47     color: gray;
48 }
```

The larger part of the CSS file remains unchanged from Chapter 7. The only changes are in the lines added to the bottom of the file. In lines 41, 42, and 43, every paragraph element within an `article` with class `minimized` is hidden. The `article` itself and any other direct child element (like an `h1` or a `footer`) remain visible. The class is called "minimized," after all, not "hidden." It is important, though, that the class is applied to the article and not to the individual paragraphs. You can also create a CSS file that does show all the paragraph elements but decreases the font size of the the whole `article` by several pixels. You can consider that an alternative visual interpretation of the word "minimized." Feel free to modify the CSS to suit your needs!

Figure 8.1 shows the screen output of Listings 8.1 and 8.2 together. The remainder of this chapter provides many enhancements to the technical implementation of the JavaScript, but the screen display will not change (as long as JavaScript is enabled by the end user).

Cleaning Up HTML Using Unobtrusive JavaScript

Mixing HTML and JavaScript, as is done in Listing 8.1, makes it harder for multiple specialists to work together on a piece of code, and inline JavaScript introduces the risk of code duplication. Most important of all, mixing HTML and JavaScript creates a performance penalty during rendering. Every time the browser encounters a piece of JavaScript, it pauses the rendering process to interpret the JavaScript code. The penalty grows as the size of the JavaScript code increases.

Figure 8.1 The resulting screen from Listings 8.1 and 8.2.

As you write your code, you should consider not only total loading time but also *perceived loading time*. Perceived loading time is the time the website visitor is waiting to see something meaningful appear on the screen. One way to improve this perception is to load JavaScript at the bottom of the page instead at the top so the browser can render all visual elements from HTML and CSS before interpreting and executing the JavaScript code.

Listing 8.3 shows a cleaned-up version of Listing 8.1. The HTML no longer contains any `onclick` attributes, and at the bottom of the page, a new JavaScript is loaded.

Listing 8.3 Removing Inline JavaScript and Referring to External JavaScript

```
<! DOCTYPE html>
<html>
  <link rel=stylesheet href="style-article.css">
  <meta charset="utf-8">
  <body>
    <header>
      <h1>Blog title</h1>
      <h2>Written by Adriaan de Jonge</h2>
    </header>
    <nav>
```

(Continues)

Listing 8.3 **Removing Inline JavaScript and Referring to External JavaScript (Continued)**

```
11        <a href="/1">First link</a>
12        <a href="/2">Second link</a>
13      </nav>
14      <article>
15        <header>
16          <h1>Post title</h1>
17          <p>Written on <time datetime=2010-10-23 pubdate>
18            the 23rd of October 2010</time></p>
19        </header>
20        <p>Here is the actual content of the article</p>
21        <p>... and more</p>
22        <footer>
23          <p>Little icons here to publish to Facebook, Twitter,
24          etc.</p>
25        </footer>
26      </article>
27      <article class=minimized>
28        <header>
29          <h1>Second post</h1>
30          <p>Written on <time datetime=2009-10-24 pubdate>
31            the 24th of October 2010</time></p>
32        </header>
33        <p>Different text</p>
34        <footer>
35          <p>Little icons here to publish to Facebook, Twitter,
36          etc.</p>
37        </footer>
38      </article>
39      <footer>Copyright &copy; 2011 - all rights reserved</footer>
40    </body>
41    <script src=script-article.js></script>
42 </html>
```

The `script` introduced on line 41 replaces the `onclick` attributes that were removed from lines 16 and 31, although from the code presented so far, there is no guarantee that it does. Instead, it might contain a script that adds Twitter feeds to the footers of the articles—who knows?

Listing 8.4 provides a bit more certainty on the behavior of the `script-article.js` script that is loaded at line 41. It provides a simple and unobtrusive way to add event handlers after the HTML is rendered.

Warning

This script uses no frameworks like jQuery and is set up to work in the newest browsers, like Safari 5, Firefox 4, Chrome 5, and Internet Explorer (IE) 9. To simplify code examples, there is no support for IE 6, 7, and 8. The general principles introduced in this chapter are more important than the coding details for browsers that do not comply with standards. Please keep these details in mind when you are working on production code though!

To fix this:

- In IE 8, use `window.event` instead of the event function parameter.
- In IE 8, use `event.srcElement` instead of `event.target`.
- In older browsers, replace `document.querySelectorAll` with the jQuery framework.
- In older browsers, avoid the `Object.create` introduced in the last code example, and do a Google search for the Revealing Module pattern.

Listing 8.4 **Implementing `onclick` Handlers in an Unobtrusive Fashion**

```
01 var searchAncestorByName = function(node, name) {
02   if(node.tagName == name.toUpperCase()) {
03     return node;
04   } else if(node.parentNode != undefined) {
05     return searchAncestorByName(node.parentNode, name);
06   }
07 }
08
09 var hasClicked = function(e) {
10   var ancestor = searchAncestorByName(e.target, "article");
11   if(ancestor.className == "minimized") ancestor.className = "";
12   else ancestor.className = "minimized";
13 }
14
15 var initEvents = function() {
16   var selected = document.querySelectorAll('article h1');
17
18   for(var i = 0; i < selected.length; i++) {
19     selected.item(i).addEventListener('click', hasClicked, false);
20   }
21 }
22
23 document.addEventListener('DOMContentLoaded', initEvents, false);
```

It seems an enormous increase from only two lines of JavaScript in Listing 8.1 to 23 lines of JavaScript code in Listing 8.4. And it is! Keep in mind the principles introduced here are meant to be applied to larger web applications, and this is a very small code example. The overhead is relatively large compared to the actual code. This ratio changes in the real world.

Let's walk through the code. On lines 1, 9, and 15, a (global) variable declaration assigns a function definition to the variable. Global variables should be avoided whenever possible. We'll get back to that later.

More important for now is the assignment of a function to a variable. This is something you cannot do in the Java 6 language. If you haven't looked at the JavaScript language in the past few years, its powerful features might surprise you. In this case, you can use JavaScript as a *functional language*. First you assign a function to a variable like this:

```
var myFunction = function() { /* … */ }
```

Then you can call this function with the following statement:

```
myFunction();
```

You can also pass the function as an argument to another function, just as you can pass any variable as an argument to a function:

```
anotherFunction(myFunction);
```

Passing a variable referring to a function as an argument to a function is exactly what line 23 does. It passes the `initEvents` function declared on line 15 as an argument to the `addEventListener` method to register it as an event listener. Once the `DOMContentLoaded` event is fired on the document, the `initEvent` function is called.

The `initEvent` function itself registers additional events only after the document rendering is complete. To be more specific, it searches the document for all `h1` elements contained in an `article` element and adds the `hasClicked` function as the handler to `click` events.

Finally, the `hasClicked` function replaces the code in Listing 8.1 within the `onclick` attributes. The ugly `this.parentNode.parentNode` construction is replaced with a recursive function called `searchAncestorByName`. The remainder of the function does exactly what you saw earlier: it adds and removes the `minimized` class.

Reducing JavaScript Dependence by Progressively Enhancing the HTML

The next flaw to be fixed is the JavaScript dependence of the examples so far. Try disabling JavaScript in your browser and reloading the code from Listings 8.1 and 8.3. You will not be able to read the content in the second blog post.

A more elegant way to write web applications is to start writing them with JavaScript disabled and do the best possible job you can to invent a usable web application without JavaScript. In most cases, this leads to more page switches, more page reloading, and heavier reliance on the server side.

In our simple code example, it means displaying all blog posts and not minimizing any by default. Minimization by default can be added using JavaScript during the initialization phase. The only minor disadvantage is that the visitor may notice the posts being disabled during the loading of the page.

The changes to the HTML are minor. Listing 8.5 shows only a fragment of the original HTML from Listing 8.3 to indicate the change.

Listing 8.5 **Removing Undesirable Classes by Default**

```
27 [...]
28     <article>
29       <header>
30         <h1>Second post</h1>
31         <p>Written on <time datetime=2009-10-24 pubdate>
32           the 24th of October 2010</time></p>
33       </header>
34       <p>Different text</p>
35       <footer>
36         <p>Little icons here to publish to Facebook, Twitter,
37         etc.</p>
38       </footer>
39     </article>
40 [...]
```

The class attribute is removed on line 28. When JavaScript is turned off, the result on the screen looks like Figure 8.2.

Figure 8.2 The resulting screen from Listing 8.5 when JavaScript is turned off.

You can move the minimization of articles 2 (and further, if any) to JavaScript, as shown in Listing 8.6. During event initialization, there is already a loop through all articles. This loop can be reused to minimize any article except the first.

Listing 8.6 **Minimizing Articles on Page Load Using JavaScript**

```
01 var searchAncestorByName = function(node, name) {
02   if(node.tagName == name.toUpperCase()) {
03     return node;
04   } else if(node.parentNode != undefined) {
05     return searchAncestorByName(node.parentNode, name);
06   }
07 }
08
09 var hasClicked = function(e) {
10   var ancestor = searchAncestorByName(e.target, "article");
11   if(ancestor.className == "minimized") ancestor.className = "";
12   else ancestor.className = "minimized";
13 }
14
15 var initialHide = function(sourceElement) {
16   var ancestor = searchAncestorByName(sourceElement, "article");
17   ancestor.className = "minimized";
18 }
19
20 var initEvents = function() {
21   var selected = document.querySelectorAll('article h1');
22
23   for (var i = 0; i < selected.length; i++) {
24     selected.item(i).addEventListener('click', hasClicked, false);
25     if(i > 0) initialHide(selected.item(i));
26   }
27 }
28
29 document.addEventListener('DOMContentLoaded', initEvents, false);
```

Line 25 checks whether the first article is being processed, in which case, minimization is ignored. In any other case, the `initialHide` function is called to minimize the `article`.

The `initialHide` function on lines 15 through 18 first obtains the `article` element from the `h1` element being processed. After all, the code was reused from the event initialization and the events were bound to the `h1` elements.

When the `article` elements are found, reusing existing code from the `onclick` processing, the actual minimization is trivial, as you can see on line 17.

Optimizing Performance Using Event Delegation

In larger and richer web applications, the number of elements that should respond to events may grow. Looping through all elements and binding events during initialization also costs performance at some point. Again, in this small code example, the performance penalty of looping through two elements is trivial. However, the code example is sufficient to explain the principle of event delegation that allows you to avoid the event binding loop.

When your web application is very dynamic and screen elements are added and removed on the fly, you have another challenge. Let's say you want to add a third `article` to the code example after the page was loaded. The event initialization loop runs only once at page load time. Using the approach so far, you would need to introduce code to bind an `onclick` event to the newly introduced article somewhere.

Assuming that your page elements and their behavior is relatively predictable and generic, you can optimize your code using the principle of event delegation. To put it simply, event delegation means that instead of binding event handlers to the HTML elements targeted by the end user, you bind the event handler to a parent element that contains one or more of the target HTML elements.

The reason this works is called *event bubbling*. When an event is not sufficiently handled by the target element, the event is passed to its parent element, and this goes on recursively until either the document root or an event handler actively cancels the bubbling process.

Using this approach, you can monitor events on several thousands of HTML elements (or more) using only a single event handler. And dynamically adding or removing HTML elements from their container does not affect the event handler.

Listing 8.7 illustrates the principle by binding the `onclick` handlers to the body element instead of to the `h1` elements. For other applications, a body element might be too generic. You can also select more specific elements that contain multiple children for which you want to handle events.

Listing 8.7 **Reducing the Number of `click` Event Listeners to a Single Instance Attached to the `body` Element**

```
var searchAncestorByName = function(node, name) {
  if(node.tagName == name.toUpperCase()) {
    return node;
  } else if(node.parentNode != undefined) {
    return searchAncestorByName(node.parentNode, name);
  }
}

var hasClicked = function(e) {
  if(e.target.nodeName == "H1") {
    var ancestor = searchAncestorByName(e.target, "article");
    if(ancestor.className == "minimized") ancestor.className = "";
    else ancestor.className = "minimized";
```

(Continues)

Listing 8.7 **Reducing the Number of `click` Event Listeners to a Single Instance Attached to the `body` Element (Continued)**

```
14   }
15 }
16
17 var initialHide = function(sourceElement) {
18   sourceElement.className = "minimized";
19 }
20
21 var initEvents = function() {
22   var bodyEl = document.getElementsByTagName('body');
23   if(bodyEl.length > 0) bodyEl.item(0).addEventListener('click',
24       hasClicked, false);
25
26   var selected = document.querySelectorAll('article');
27
28   for (var i = 1; i < selected.length; i++) {
29     initialHide(selected.item(i));
30   }
31 }
32
33 document.addEventListener('DOMContentLoaded', initEvents, false);
```

On lines 23, 24, and 25, only the body element is selected, and the `onclick` listener is added. This is not very different from adding `onclick` handlers to multiple HTML elements in a loop.

On lines 29 through 32, there is still a loop through the articles, but it is simpler. Instead of selecting `h1` elements within an `article`, the `articles` themselves are selected. The advantage is that the `initialHide` function can be reduced to a single line of code. It is no longer necessary to go from the `h1` to its `article` ancestor. In fact, the `initialHide` function is trivial enough for you to place it in the loop itself if you want to.

The actual event handling is now on lines 9 through 15. Please be careful here: binding the `onclick` handler to the body element means that *every* `onclick` on *any* element is captured by the `hasClicked` function. Within the event handling function, you need to select exactly which `onclick` events you are listening for.

Frameworks like jQuery may help a little here. The code in Listing 8.7 simply checks whether the `event.target` is an `h1` element. However, this means that `h1` elements that are not contained within an `article` element are also caught. Because `searchAncestorByName` does not find an `article` ancestor, the other `h1` elements are ignored. It would be even better to make that a little more explicit than it is in the current code.

Avoiding Global Variables

The final flaw in the code examples presented so far is the unnecessary use of global variables. JavaScript specialists introduced clever ways to avoid global variables. You can find these on the Internet if you search for namespaces, modules, or the Revealing Module pattern. Most of these patterns require a bit more explanation than is possible in the context of this chapter. Some of them require frameworks like the Yahoo! User Interface (YUI) library or jQuery; others can stand alone. Most of them also work in older browsers.

The code examples in this chapter are optimized for the newer browsers for simplicity. This allows for a very simple solution to minimize the number of global variables used: the use of new features introduced in ECMAScript 5 (also known as JavaScript 1.8.5).

Listing 8.8 shows how you can hide all functions within a single global variable using the newly introduced `Object.create` method. This method takes a property map as a parameter, which is used as the prototype for the newly created object. You can add more properties in a second argument to the `Object.create` method.

Listing 8.8 Reducing the Number of Global Variables to a Single Container Object

```
"use strict";

var myModule = Object.create({
  searchAncestorByName : function(node, name) {
    if(node.tagName == name.toUpperCase()) {
      return node;
    } else if(node.parentNode != undefined) {
      return myModule.searchAncestorByName(node.parentNode, name);
    }
  },
  hasClicked : function(e) {
    if(e.target.nodeName == "H1")
    {
      var ancestor = myModule.searchAncestorByName(e.target,
          "article");
      if(ancestor.className == "minimized") ancestor.className = "";
      else ancestor.className = "minimized";
    }
  },
  initialHide : function(sourceElement) {
    sourceElement.className = "minimized";
  },
  initEvents : function() {
    var bodyEl = document.getElementsByTagName('body');
    bodyEl.item(0).addEventListener('click', myModule.hasClicked,
        false);

    var selected = document.querySelectorAll('article');

    for (var i = 1; i < selected.length; i++) {
      myModule.initialHide(selected.item(i));
```

(Continues)

Listing 8.8 **Reducing the Number of Global Variables to a Single Container Object (Continued)**

```
32       }
33     }
34 });
35
36 document.addEventListener('DOMContentLoaded', myModule.initEvents,
37       false);
```

On line 3 and further, you find the creation of a single global variable, which is the container of all other variables (in this case functions).

Apart from this global declaration, two things that change in the code example are worth mentioning. The function definitions are no longer assignments to global variables, but declarations of properties in a map, and the calls to the functions need to be prefixed with the global variable to be accessible.

The last minor change you find in Listing 8.8 is on line 1: `"use strict"`. This declaration tells ECMAScript 5–aware JavaScript interpreters to enforce stricter rules in the code. This helps you avoid common pitfalls and security risks. Be careful though! Violations lead to hard errors. The current browser implementations might not catch all errors that future browsers will.

> **Reading More on JavaScript**
>
> You are strongly encouraged to read additional literature on JavaScript elaborating on the basic topics introduced in this chapter. Backwards compatibility with non–standards-compliant browsers and additional, more powerful ways to build modules are essential for larger web applications.
>
> You may want to consider a framework like jQuery to assist you with that. If you can limit yourself to the newest browsers, then a pure, frameworkless approach may be preferable. To explain the principles in this chapter, working without frameworks is the cleanest approach.

Summary

This chapter introduced a few fundamental techniques to improve your JavaScript code in terms of both performance and maintainability. Unobtrusive JavaScript allows a clean separation between HTML and JavaScript. Progressive enhancement improves your support for users who disable JavaScript or for devices in which JavaScript is unavailable. Event delegation improves performance when events from large numbers of elements need to be caught. Finally, ECMAScript 5 introduces new methods that help you avoid global variables.

Chapter 9

Adding Dynamic Interactions Using AJAX

This chapter discusses how to add interactions to a page or web application that depends on server interaction. The chapter starts with classic AJAX (Asynchronous JavaScript and XML) calls in which the client initiates an asynchronous connection to the server and the server responds as quickly as possible. After that, the Channel API is introduced. Using the Channel API, a connection between the browser and the Google App Engine is kept open for a longer time, allowing the server to notify clients quickly when events occur. Both the client side and the server side of the Channel API are discussed.

Using Classic AJAX without Frameworks

Chapter 8, "Adding Static Interactions Using JavaScript," explained how to write high-performing JavaScript code without using frameworks. Every developer reading this book has likely worked with AJAX before, but perhaps not without using frameworks.

The purpose of minimizing the use of frameworks is to increase the performance of our web applications. The purpose of frameworks is to simplify life, save code, and avoid common errors.

It is useful to reconsider frameworks occasionally to see if they are still required. If you need to support older versions of Internet Explorer, AJAX frameworks are really useful. In those browsers, AJAX calls work in a different way than in other browsers. For example, you need to create an ActiveX component to invoke calls to the server. In addition, you must consider small but essential differences, such as accessing the event object and the event target.

For simplicity, this book requires Internet Explorer version 9 or any recent version of Chrome, Safari, or Firefox for the code examples to work. In these browsers, JavaScript frameworks like jQuery still help to create code that is easier to maintain. It is not strictly necessary to use jQuery, though. The burden of not using jQuery seems acceptable, but it depends on your exact implementation choices. This chapter reviews XML, JavaScript Object Notation (JSON), and plain HTML.

Communicating with the Server Using XML

Originally, the X in the AJAX acronym stood for XML. When you need to connect to the server asynchronously, you create an object called `XMLHttpRequest`. Listing 9.1 shortens the HTML from earlier chapters to serve as a placeholder for AJAX examples. In all the following examples, you should click on the article header called Dynamic text box to trigger the interactions. Although the user should click on the article headers, the event handler is attached to the document's body element following the event delegation principle described in Chapter 8.

Listing 9.1 **Setting Up the HTML for the AJAX Examples**

```
01 <!DOCTYPE html>
02 <html>
03   <link rel=stylesheet href=style-article.css>
04   <meta charset="utf-8">
05   <body>
06     <header>
07       <h1>Blog title</h1>
08       <h2>Written by Adriaan de Jonge</h2>
09     </header>
10     <nav>
11       <a href="/1">First link</a>
12       <a href="/2">Second link</a>
13     </nav>
14     <article>
15       <header>
16         <h1>Dynamic text box</h1
17       </header>
18       <p id=replace>Replace this text</p>
19     </article>
20     <footer>Copyright &copy; 2011 - all rights reserved</footer>
21   </body>
22   <script src=script-article.js></script>
23 </html>
```

Apart from the minor reduction in the size of the HTML file, there are no fundamental changes. Still, the only link to a JavaScript file is at the bottom on line 22, to make sure the rest of the page is rendered as fast as possible. If JavaScript is turned off, the basic page can still be read. The JavaScript–AJAX interaction adds only features that, if left out, will not cause page rendering to fail.

In the HTML file, you cannot see whether or not the JavaScript file is going to perform AJAX calls. The only part of the HTML that may hint toward interactions is the `id=replace` attribute on line 18. Adding an `id` attribute with that name does not make sense in the context of CSS styling. The purpose of this identifier is to simplify the element selection in JavaScript.

Listing 9.2 provides the content of the script-article.js file. This script selects the paragraph from line 18 in the HTML file and replaces the text with some values returned from the server.

Listing 9.2 **Interacting with the Server Using XML**

```
"use strict";

var myModule = Object.create({
ajaxHandler : function(e) {
 if(this.readyState == 4 && this.status == 200) {
   var name = this.responseXML.getElementsByTagName('name');
   var description =
     this.responseXML.getElementsByTagName('description');
   var lastChange =
     this.responseXML.getElementsByTagName('lastChange');
   var newText = name.item(0).firstChild.nodeValue + ' '
     + description.item(0).firstChild.nodeValue + ' '
     + lastChange.item(0).firstChild.nodeValue + ' ';
   var selected = document.querySelectorAll('p#replace');
   selected.item(0).firstChild.nodeValue = newText;
 } else if (this.readyState == 4 && this.status != 200) {
   // error handling
 } else {
   // status handling
 }
},
hasClicked : function(e) {
  if(e.target.nodeName == "H1") {
    var xhr = new XMLHttpRequest();
    xhr.onreadystatechange = myModule.ajaxHandler;
    xhr.open("GET", "values.xml");
    xhr.send();
  }
},
initEvents : function() {
  var bodyEl = document.getElementsByTagName('body');
  if(bodyEl.length > 0) bodyEl.item(0).addEventListener('click',
myModule.hasClicked, false);
}});

document.addEventListener('DOMContentLoaded', myModule.initEvents,
false);
```

The code is set up similarly to the final example in Chapter 8. A module is created to prevent name collisions. The code starts adding a `click` event listener after the page has loaded.

The event listener, on lines 22 through 29, invokes an AJAX call, a `GET` request to the file values.xml. In this example, the call is static, but it could just as easily be a dynamic server call.

Lines 4 through 22 implement the `ajaxHandler` function that is invoked when the result is returned from the server. The code in this function queries both the HTML document and the XML returned from the server. The HTML is queried for placeholders. The XML is queried for its content.

Error handling and status handling are skipped in this example because they are not strictly necessary. In larger web applications, the request status can be monitored using the `readyState` attribute found on lines 5 and 16. This attribute can contain five values:

- 0: The object is created but not yet opened.
- 1: The request is opened, but send has not been called.
- 2: Send has been called, but no data is available yet.
- 3: Data is received, but no `responseText` is available.
- 4: All data has been received.

The response status can be found in the status attribute:

- 100–199: informational
- 200–299: success
- 300–399: multiple choices
- 400–499: client error
- 500–599: server error

See IETF RFC 2616 for more details. This is the specification of the HTTP protocol and can be found at www.ietf.org/rfc/rfc2616.txt.

The server output in XML format is provided in Listing 9.3.

Listing 9.3 **The XML Output in values.xml**

```
<values xmlns="">
  <name>Adriaan</name>
  <description>Author</description>
  <lastChange>2011-04-03</lastChange>
</values>
```

The content is not extremely useful, just a couple of values with which to test the server interaction. The XML is as simple as it can be. No namespaces are used, but the default namespace is explicitly defined to be empty, just in case.

Communicating with the Server Using JSON

Creating AJAX calls that communicate in XML is becoming less popular, and JSON notation is becoming more popular these days. JSON is simple to read and write, contains little overhead, and is naturally suited for use in JavaScript. In fact, JSON notation is borrowed from the JavaScript language itself. Any valid JSON is valid JavaScript.

Interpreting JSON by interpreting the string value is a convenient way to parse the data extremely fast. It may not be the safest way to read the data, though. For mission-critical applications, you should consider frameworks that help interpret JSON data.

Listing 9.4 provides an example of how you can read JSON data with relative ease. Apart from the change of XML to JSON, Listing 9.4 provides the same functionality as Listing 9.2.

Listing 9.4 **Replacing XML Reading with JSON Evaluation**

```
01 "use strict";
02
03 var myModule = Object.create({
04 ajaxHandler : function(e) {
05  if(this.readyState == 4 && this.status == 200) {
06    var values = eval('('+this.responseText+')');
07    var newText = values.name
08        + ' ' + values.description
09        + ' ' + values.lastChanged;
10    var selected = document.querySelectorAll('p#replace');
11    selected.item(0).firstChild.nodeValue = newText;
12  } else if (this.readyState == 4 && this.status != 200) {
13    // error handling
14  } else {
15    // status handling
16  }
17 },
18 hasClicked : function(e) {
19   if(e.target.nodeName == "H1") {
20     var xhr = new XMLHttpRequest();
21     xhr.onreadystatechange = myModule.ajaxHandler;
22     xhr.open("GET", "values.json");
23     xhr.send();
24   }
25 },
26 initEvents : function() {
27   var bodyEl = document.getElementsByTagName('body');
28   if(bodyEl.length > 0) bodyEl.item(0).addEventListener('click',
29       myModule.hasClicked, false);
30 }});
31
32 document.addEventListener('DOMContentLoaded', myModule.initEvents,
33     false);
```

First, there is a very minor but essential change on line 22. The AJAX call connects to a different URL: values.json instead of values.xml.

Second, the `ajaxHandler` on lines 5 through 16 is greatly simplified. The code still needs to select an HTML element as a placeholder for the values received from the server. The interpretation of the JSON code is reduced to a single line of code: the `eval` statement on line 6.

You might say that `eval` is evil: it is not limited to interpreting JSON values; it also executes any JavaScript code inside the file. This could be a reason to switch to a JSON interpretation library. Another option is to first check the JSON string using a regular expression before feeding it to `eval`.

Listing 9.5 shows how the XML from Listing 9.3 could be translated to JSON.

Listing 9.5 **Replacing XML with JSON Values**

```
{
  "name": "Adriaan",
  "description": "Author",
  "lastChanged": "2011-04-03"
}
```

Even though the `"name"` key is enclosed in quotes, after evaluation it can be accessed as a normal object property, as shown on line 7 of Listing 9.4. Please note that JSON is not limited to such a simple structure. It can also contain nested maps and lists to create large content trees.

Communicating with the Server Using HTML

Both XML and JSON are useful in web applications, where values are processed by application code before being presented to the visitor. For websites presenting a lot of content in a relatively straightforward way, XML and JSON may lead to a lot of superfluous code on the client, though.

Sometimes an AJAX call is used only to prevent a click to a new page and load some content quickly or more smoothly. If so, you should consider retrieving HTML directly from the server. In most cases, the server is already capable of delivering HTML and the HTML template is already there, so it also simplifies life on the server side.

In Listing 9.6, HTML instead of XML or JSON is retrieved from the server. This code example does a little bit more than Listings 9.2 and 9.4: it replaces the full article instead of just a single line.

Listing 9.6 **Fetching HTML from the Server and Displaying the Result in the Page**

```
"use strict";

var myModule = Object.create({
ajaxHandler : function (e) {
 if(this.readyState == 4 && this.status == 200) {
```

Listing 9.6 **Fetching HTML from the Server and Displaying the Result in the Page (Continued)**

```
06
07     var selected = document.querySelectorAll('article');
08     selected.item(0).innerHTML = this.responseText;
09
10   } else if (this.readyState == 4 && this.status != 200) {
11     // error handling
12   } else {
13     // status handling
14   }
15 },
16 hasClicked : function(e) {
17   if(e.target.nodeName == "H1") {
18     var xhr = new XMLHttpRequest();
19     xhr.onreadystatechange = myModule.ajaxHandler;
20     xhr.open("GET", "values.html");
21     xhr.send();
22   }
23 },
24 initEvents : function() {
25   var bodyEl = document.getElementsByTagName('body');
26   if(bodyEl.length > 0) bodyEl.item(0).addEventListener('click',
27       myModule.hasClicked, false);
28 }});
29
30 document.addEventListener('DOMContentLoaded', myModule.initEvents,
31     false);
```

This code replaces the full article in just two lines of code: lines 7 and 8. Agreed, having an extra line to check whether the article element is correctly found would have helped prevent errors, but this code proves the power of exchanging simple HTML fragments.

Listing 9.7 provides a simple example of the HTML fragment.

Listing 9.7 **An Example HTML Fragment**

```
<header>
<h1>New content</h1>
</header>
<p>Hello world!</p>
<footer>bye world...</footer>
```

This HTML mostly speaks for itself. It should be noted that the HTML fragment does not contain an `article` element. If the fragment were contained inside an `article`, the code in Listing 9.6 would lead to two nested `articles`.

Using Google App Engine's Channel API

AJAX code examples, to this point in the chapter, have used a simple and direct request-response model. Although asynchronous, the server needs to respond within 30 seconds. This makes it impossible for the server to reach the client when the client is not asking. Furthermore, developers are encouraged to make the server respond as quickly as possible. A purposely delayed response using the normal App Engine code would not be advisable.

For highly interactive web applications, *long polls* are increasingly popular. When using a long poll, an AJAX request connects to the server and waits as long as required for a response—far beyond the 30-second limit. This way, when the server has a notification for the client, the client receives it instantaneously, with no lag from an update polling interval.

Google added such a mechanism to the App Engine: the Channel API. It works a bit differently from the other APIs. Google provides a client-side JavaScript library to help interact with the server channels.

The Channel API can be used to notify browsers of updates on the server. This is especially useful if your site has a high update frequency and it is important for your visitors to see changes right away. Also, websites that are highly interactive may benefit from the Channel API.

Opening a Channel from the Server

To set up a channel, you need three things:

- a way to identify the channel on the server
- a way to identify the channel on the client
- the channel itself

From the server perspective, the client that needs to receive a notification may not always be the client requesting the current URL. Consider a chat application, for example: the message needs to be delivered to another client, not to the poster.

From the client perspective, only one channel is opened per page. The client may have more than one tab or browser window connecting to the same server, though. An identifier is needed beyond the session identifier—if there even is a session. Moreover, channeling is something different from keeping state. Strictly speaking, a channel is stateless. It just takes longer than usual to retrieve the server response.

Listing 9.8 provides the server-side Java code to set up a new channel and return an identifier to the client.

Listing 9.8 **Setting Up a New Channel from the Server**

```
package com.appspot.channel;

import com.google.appengine.api.channel.ChannelService;
import com.google.appengine.api.channel.ChannelServiceFactory;
import org.antlr.stringtemplate.StringTemplate;
```

Listing 9.8 Setting Up a New Channel from the Server (Continued)

```
06 import org.antlr.stringtemplate.StringTemplateGroup;
07
08 import javax.servlet.ServletException;
09 import javax.servlet.http.Cookie;
10 import javax.servlet.http.HttpServlet;
11 import javax.servlet.http.HttpServletRequest;
12 import javax.servlet.http.HttpServletResponse;
13 import java.io.IOException;
14
15 public class OpenChannelServlet extends HttpServlet {
16   @Override
17   protected void doGet(HttpServletRequest request,
18       HttpServletResponse response)
19       throws ServletException, IOException {
20
21     ChannelService channelService =
22         ChannelServiceFactory.getChannelService();
23     // PLEASE NOTE: this value should be different
24     //         for EACH user in most cases:
25     String token = channelService.createChannel("1");
26
27     StringTemplateGroup group = new StringTemplateGroup("xhtml",
28         "WEB-INF/templates/channel");
29     StringTemplate hello = group.getInstanceOf("index");
30     hello.setAttribute("token", token);
31     response.getWriter().write(hello.toString());
32
33   }
34 }
```

The server-side identifier for this channel is on line 25. For simplicity, the value is `1`. Note that as soon as a second user comes online, this value may become problematic: both users share the same channel now. Very few cases require this functionality. A better approach is to replace this value with a value that is specific to the current user, like a user ID.

Also on line 25, the Channel API returns a token that should be sent to the client. Lines 27 through 31 insert this value into the HTML template that is returned to the visitor. This template is discussed later in this chapter.

Listing 9.9 shows the code that sends a message to a channel.

Listing 9.9 Sending Messages to a Channel

```
package com.appspot.channel;

import com.google.appengine.api.channel.ChannelMessage;
```

(Continues)

Listing 9.9 **Sending Messages to a Channel (Continued)**

```
import com.google.appengine.api.channel.ChannelService;
import com.google.appengine.api.channel.ChannelServiceFactory;
import org.antlr.stringtemplate.StringTemplate;
import org.antlr.stringtemplate.StringTemplateGroup;

import javax.servlet.ServletException;
import javax.servlet.http.HttpServlet;
import javax.servlet.http.HttpServletRequest;
import javax.servlet.http.HttpServletResponse;
import java.io.IOException;

public class SendMessageServlet extends HttpServlet {
  @Override
  protected void doPost(HttpServletRequest request,
      HttpServletResponse response) throws ServletException,
      IOException {

    ChannelService channelService =
        ChannelServiceFactory.getChannelService();

    // PLEASE NOTE (again) that this value should be different
    //          for each user in most cases:
    channelService.sendMessage(new ChannelMessage("1",
        "hello world!"));

  }
}
```

Again, the channel is identified by the value `1`. Sending a message to the channel is straightforward. Using this servlet, sharing a channel with multiple clients leads to all clients being notified with the message. In the few cases that you need such behavior, that seems quite useful. It is better to avoid it, though. The behavior of a shared channel can be unpredictable.

Handling Messages on the Client

The client-side code to handle messages from the Channel API is a bit larger than the original HTML in Listing 9.1 that is used for the classic AJAX example. Listing 9.10 shows that using the Channel API makes it harder to avoid JavaScript within the HTML. It would have been possible by inserting the client token inside the HTML and retrieving it using JavaScript. It would also have been possible by retrieving an external JavaScript generated by the server on the fly. Neither option feels natural, though. So instead, some basic code is added inside the HTML, still at the bottom of the page.

Listing 9.10 **Returning the Token to the Visitor**

```
<!DOCTYPE html>
<html>
  <link rel=stylesheet href=style-article.css>
  <meta charset="utf-8">
  <body>
    <header>
      <h1>Blog title</h1>
      <h2>Written by Adriaan de Jonge</h2>
    </header>
    <nav>
      <a href="/1">First link</a>
      <a href="/2">Second link</a>
    </nav>
    <article>
      <header>
        <h1>Dynamic text box</h1>
      </header>
      <p>Opened: <span id="opened">none yet</span></p>
      <p>Message: <span id="message">none yet</span></p>
      <p>Error: <span id="error">none yet</span></p>
      <p>Close: <span id="close">none yet</span></p>
    </article>
    <footer>Copyright &copy; 2011 - all rights reserved</footer>

    <script type="text/javascript" src="/_ah/channel/jsapi">
    </script>

    <script type="text/javascript" src="/script-article.js">
    </script>

    <script>
    var myModule = Object.create({
    sendMessage : function() {
      var xhr = new XMLHttpRequest();
      xhr.open('POST', '/send-message', true);
      xhr.send();
    },
    initChannel : function() {
      var channel = new goog.appengine.Channel('$token$');
      var socket = channel.open();
      socket.onopen = channelHandler.onOpened;
      socket.onmessage = channelHandler.onMessage;
      socket.onerror = channelHandler.onError;
      socket.onclose = channelHandler.onClose;
      var selected = document.querySelectorAll('article h1');
```

(Continues)

Listing 9.10 **Returning the Token to the Visitor (Continued)**

```
46         selected.item(0).addEventListener('click',
47             myModule.sendMessage, false);
48       }});
49       document.addEventListener('DOMContentLoaded',
50           myModule.initChannel, false);
51       </script>
52
53     </body>
54 </html>
```

Lines 38 through 48 initialize the channel from the client side. Note that the `$token$` is replaced by the server-side StringTemplate library with the actual token received on the server. This token looks a bit like this: `channel-4rw5e-1`.

The functions called by the API refer to JavaScript functions that are implemented in an external file. Lines 41 through 44 correspond with the functions in Listing 9.11, the demonstration implementation for this chapter.

Listing 9.11 **Demonstrating the Channel API**

```
"use strict";
var channelHandler = Object.create({
onOpened : function() {
  var el = document.getElementById('opened');
  el.firstChild.nodeValue = 'opened';
},
onMessage : function(message) {
  var el = document.getElementById('message');
  el.firstChild.nodeValue = message.data;
},
onError : function() {
  var el = document.getElementById('error');
  el.firstChild.nodeValue = 'error';
},
onClose : function() {
  var el = document.getElementById('close');
  el.firstChild.nodeValue = 'close';
}
});
```

This code selects span elements from the HTML template and inserts the responses from the server. If it is a message, the message itself is displayed. If it is an opening, closing, or error event, the event name is added.

If you open the example, the opened event is fired. If you click on the article header, a Hello World message is added. If you shut down the server instance, an error occurs. The channel is closed after 2 hours.

Keep in mind that the Channel API allows only a single channel connection with the server per page. This means you must invent a sharing mechanism if you want to pass messages for more than one concern.

Summary

This chapter revisited classic AJAX interactions without frameworks. Using modern browsers, frameworks may still be helpful, but they are not strictly necessary. The developer has the choice to work with XML, JSON, or plain HTML. The use of XML may be more complicated than necessary. JSON is a practical alternative for web applications as long as security concerns are kept in mind. For content-driven websites, it could be beneficial to replace XML/JSON with plain and simple HTML. This makes both client and server easier to maintain.

Next, Google's Channel API was introduced. The Channel API allows long polling on the Google App Engine. It takes relatively few lines of code to implement the server side. The amount of code on the client side is kept to a minimum because of the client-side JavaScript library provided by Google. Although the use of libraries should be minimized, the use of some libraries cannot (and should not) be avoided.

PART IV

Using Common App Engine APIs

Chapter 10

Storing Data in the Datastore and Blobstore

This chapter demonstrates how to write code to communicate with the Google App Engine datastore and the Blobstore. It builds on the theory presented in Chapter 4, "Data Modeling for the App Engine Datastore." It starts with storing, querying, and retrieving data synchronously. Next, the changes in the code to process data asynchronously are presented. Two simple examples demonstrate how to work with multitenancy and transactions. Finally, storing, querying, and retrieving blobs from the Blobstore are demonstrated.

Processing Data Synchronously

Google provides three APIs to work with the datastore: Java Data Objects (JDO), Java Persistence API (JPA), and the low-level API. In addition, the open source community provides APIs like Objectify, SimpleDS, and Twig Persist.

This book works with the low-level API. Working with the low-level API, you force yourself to think about the exact data structures in the datastore. You prevent yourself from focusing on the object model rather than on the structure in the datastore. It saves startup time because there are fewer classes to load.

Also, it is questionable whether you actually need all the high-level APIs. As the code in this chapter demonstrates, using the StringTemplate library, it is relatively simple to use datastore entities directly in your templates without setting up data transfer objects.

If you feel you need to map data into Java objects, you should start investigating Objectify, SimpleDS, and Twig Persist. The advantage of those libraries is that they specifically target the App Engine datastore. JDO and JPA were originally designed mainly for object-relational mapping. There is a higher risk of setting up a data model that does not perform well on the App Engine with the datastore. See Chapter 4 for more background on this.

Using the low-level API, you have full control over the way datastore requests are processed. For example, the API distinguishes between synchronous and asynchronous requests. After you invoke a synchronous call, the code blocks until the response from the datastore is returned. Asynchronous requests allow you to perform other work parallel to waiting for the response from the datastore.

Storing Data Synchronously

To store data, first you need to retrieve data. Listing 10.1 implements a `GET` method to show a form for data input and a `POST` method to store the values provided in the form. Note that you need to restrict access to this servlet to administrators. This example contains no checks on script injections!

Listing 10.1 **Fetching Data from a Form and Storing in Datastore**

```
package com.appspot.datastore;

import com.google.appengine.api.datastore.DatastoreService;
import com.google.appengine.api.datastore.DatastoreServiceFactory;
import com.google.appengine.api.datastore.Entity;
import com.google.appengine.api.users.User;
import com.google.appengine.api.users.UserService;
import com.google.appengine.api.users.UserServiceFactory;
import org.antlr.stringtemplate.StringTemplate;
import org.antlr.stringtemplate.StringTemplateGroup;

import javax.servlet.ServletException;
import javax.servlet.http.HttpServlet;
import javax.servlet.http.HttpServletRequest;
import javax.servlet.http.HttpServletResponse;
import java.io.IOException;
import java.util.Date;

public class StoreDataServlet extends HttpServlet {

  protected void doGet(HttpServletRequest request,
                       HttpServletResponse response)
      throws ServletException, IOException {



    StringTemplateGroup group = new StringTemplateGroup("xhtml",
        "WEB-INF/templates/xhtml");
    StringTemplate html = group.getInstanceOf("store-blog-post");
    response.getWriter().write(html.toString());
  }

  protected void doPost(HttpServletRequest request,
                        HttpServletResponse response)
```

Listing 10.1 **Fetching Data from a Form and Storing in Datastore (Continued)**

```
35         throws ServletException, IOException {
36
37       DatastoreService datastoreService = DatastoreServiceFactory
38           .getDatastoreService();
39
40       String title = request.getParameter("title");
41       Entity blogPost = new Entity("BlogPost", normalize(title));
42       blogPost.setProperty("title", title);
43
44       String author = request.getParameter("author");
45       blogPost.setProperty("author", author);
46       String content = request.getParameter("content");
47       blogPost.setProperty("content", content);
48       blogPost.setProperty("date", new Date());
49
50       // if any: (be careful with Task Queue)
51       UserService userService = UserServiceFactory.getUserService();
52       User user = userService.getCurrentUser();
53       blogPost.setProperty("user", user);
54
55       datastoreService.put(blogPost);
56
57       StringTemplateGroup group = new StringTemplateGroup("xhtml",
58           "WEB-INF/templates/xhtml");
59       StringTemplate html = group.getInstanceOf("done-blog-post");
60       html.setAttribute("title", title);
61       html.setAttribute("author", author);
62       html.setAttribute("content", content);
63       response.getWriter().write(html.toString());
64
65     }
66
67     private String normalize(String str) {
68       String trimmedLower = str.toLowerCase().trim();
69       return trimmedLower.replaceAll("\\W+", "-");
70     }
71 }
```

Lines 21 through 31 present the input form provided in Listing 10.2. Lines 37 and 38 initialize the connection to the datastore. Lines 40, 41, and 42 translate the title field from the form into a value that can easily be used to model a URL to retrieve the data again. Lines 41 through 53 enter the values into the entity. Finally, line 55 stores the data. The rest of the code example is used to present values in HTML to the browser.

Line 50 warns you to be careful with the Task Queue API because in the Task Queue, line 52 does not return the user who requested this task. Instead, the system returns the technical user invoking this task. In the Task Queue, this is the admin user. A reference to the user who requested this task should have been set up when handling the user interaction and posting details to the Task Queue for later execution.

Keep in mind that Listing 10.1 does not explicitly catch exceptions and does not provide different handlers for different situations. Production code could benefit from additional exception handling.

Listing 10.2 **Setting Up the Form to Fetch Data**

```
01 <html>
02 <body>
03 <form action="" method="post">
04 <p>
05 <label for="title">Title</label>
06 <input type="text" name="title">
07 </p>
08 <p>
09 <label for="author">Author</label>
10 <input type="text" name="author">
11 </p>
12 <p>
13 <label for="content">Content</label>
14 <textarea type="text" name="content" rows=40 cols=80></textarea>
15 </p>
16 <p>
17 <input type="submit" value="Send">
18 </p>
19 </form>
20 </body>
21 </html>
```

Because the `action` attribute on line 3 is empty, the simple form posts to the current URL, the servlet that provided this HTML to the browser using a `GET` request.

After storing the data in the datastore, the user receives a confirmation screen set up on lines 57 through 64 showing the values entered in the form. A simple example of an HTML template presenting these values is provided in Listing 10.3.

Listing 10.3 **Presenting the Stored Data**

```
<html>
<body>
<h1>A Blog Post has been saved</h1>

<p>
Title: $title$
</p>
```

Listing 10.3 **Presenting the Stored Data (Continued)**

```
<p>
Author: $author$
</p>
<p>
Content: $content$
</p>
</body>
</html>
```

This HTML example is too simplistic for real-world usage. It can easily be replaced by a more elaborate HTML snippet, as used in Chapters 6 through 9, which present the front end.

On your development server, you can go to http://localhost:8888/_ah/admin and check that the data is added as expected. On a production machine, you can check the *datastore viewer* on http://appengine.google.com/.

Querying Data Synchronously

The datastore does not provide a query language like SQL or XQuery. Although some high-level frameworks may emulate a query language, under the hood all you need to do is set up a query object and provide filters and sort orders. Listing 10.4 demonstrates a query on `BlogPost` entities that are older than 5 seconds. It sorts by date.

Listing 10.4 **Querying Data from the Datastore**

```
package com.appspot.datastore;

import com.google.appengine.api.datastore.*;
import org.antlr.stringtemplate.StringTemplate;
import org.antlr.stringtemplate.StringTemplateGroup;

import javax.servlet.ServletException;
import javax.servlet.http.HttpServlet;
import javax.servlet.http.HttpServletRequest;
import javax.servlet.http.HttpServletResponse;
import java.io.IOException;
import java.util.Date;
import java.util.List;

public class QueryDataServlet extends HttpServlet {

  protected void doGet(HttpServletRequest request,
                       HttpServletResponse response)
      throws ServletException, IOException {

```

(Continues)

Listing 10.4 **Querying Data from the Datastore (Continued)**

```
21      DatastoreService datastoreService = DatastoreServiceFactory
22          .getDatastoreService();
23
24      Query query = new Query("BlogPost");
25      query.addFilter("date", Query.FilterOperator.LESS_THAN,
26          new Date(System.currentTimeMillis() - 5000));
27      query.addSort("date", Query.SortDirection.DESCENDING);
28      PreparedQuery preparedQuery = datastoreService.prepare(query);
29
30      List list = preparedQuery.asList(
31          FetchOptions.Builder.withLimit(10));
32
33      StringTemplateGroup group = new StringTemplateGroup("xhtml",
34          "WEB-INF/templates/xhtml");
35      StringTemplate html = group.getInstanceOf("query-blog-post");
36      html.setAttribute("items", list);
37      response.getWriter().write(html.toString());
38    }
39 }
```

The actual query is set up in lines 24 through 28. Although there is a bit more code than in a SQL statement, there is no risk of code injection and there is an absolute minimum of code required to process the result set.

Lines 30 and 31 use a limit to restrict the number of results. You might also use an offset with similar code to implement a paging algorithm. In some scenarios, where the queries are specific to a single user, you might be interested in *cursors*. A cursor is a base64-encoded string indicating the current position in a result set. A cursor may be stored in the datastore or in memcache or may be passed to the client. Cursors do not work in all situations. For example, there are problems with inequality filters, multivalued properties, and changing index configurations. Because of the drawbacks of cursors, they are not further discussed in this book.

Lines 33 through 39 refer to the HTML template presented in Listing 10.5 displaying the list of posts.

Listing 10.5 **Presenting the Links to the Posts in HTML**

```
<html>
<body>
<p>Query Blog Post</p>
<ul>
$items:{<li>View post: <a href="/retrieve-data/$it.key.name$">
                        $it.properties.title$</a></li>}$
</ul>
</body>
</html>
```

This HTML template relies on a StringTemplate construction to present multiple items. Lines 5 and 6 contain a construction that looks like a closure. The `it` variable is introduced implicitly for each item in the items list. The `it.key.name` and `it.properties.title` are actually calls to the entity class API.

Retrieving Data Synchronously

The HTML in Listing 10.5 provided links to blog posts with the post ID in the URL. These URLs are configured in web.xml to refer to a servlet that reads and presents single posts. This servlet is presented in Listing 10.6.

Listing 10.6 **Reading a Single Post from the Datastore**

```
package com.appspot.datastore;

import com.google.appengine.api.datastore.*;
import org.antlr.stringtemplate.StringTemplate;
import org.antlr.stringtemplate.StringTemplateGroup;

import javax.servlet.ServletException;
import javax.servlet.http.HttpServlet;
import javax.servlet.http.HttpServletRequest;
import javax.servlet.http.HttpServletResponse;
import java.io.IOException;

public class RetrieveDataServlet extends HttpServlet {

  protected void doGet(HttpServletRequest request,
                       HttpServletResponse response)
      throws ServletException, IOException {

    String id = request.getRequestURI()
        .replaceAll("/retrieve-data/", "");
    DatastoreService datastoreService =
        DatastoreServiceFactory.getDatastoreService();

    Entity blogPost = null;
    try {
      blogPost = datastoreService.get(
          KeyFactory.createKey("BlogPost", id));
    } catch (EntityNotFoundException e) {
      // This should not happen: let the 500 page handle it
      throw new ServletException(e);
    }


    StringTemplateGroup group = new StringTemplateGroup("xhtml",
        "WEB-INF/templates/xhtml");
```

(Continues)

Listing 10.6 **Reading a Single Post from the Datastore (Continued)**

```
36       StringTemplate html = group.getInstanceOf("retrieve-blog-post");
37       html.setAttributes(blogPost.getProperties());
38
39       response.getWriter().write(html.toString());
40     }
41 }
```

In lines 19 and 20, the `BlogPost` ID is extracted from the URL by removing the rest of the URL. The code example might be a bit more hardcoded than you'd want in a production version. A more dynamic regular expression or a configurable value would be preferable in real life. The important thing is that the ID is inside the URL path and not passed as a URL parameter. This helps for search engine optimization and caching in proxy servers.

Lines 24 through 31 fetch the post, and lines 34 through 39 present the values. Apart from the obvious exception handling construction, this code is relatively straightforward. Listing 10.7 provides simple HTML to present values.

Listing 10.7 **Presenting a Single Post in HTML**

```
<html>
<body>
<h1>$title$</h1>
<h2>$author$</h2>
<p>
 $content$
</p>
</body>
</html>
```

Again, you may want more sophisticated HTML for production use. This snippet simply presents the general concept.

Processing Data Asynchronously

The low-level datastore API also provides a variant allowing you to process calls to the datastore asynchronously. The construction is similar to the construction in Chapter 15, "Retrieving External Data Using URL Fetch." The API returns a `Future` class that returns the end result using generics.

This allows you to perform tasks in parallel while the datastore is processing the request. As a result, the total processing time for the query is smaller than using the synchronous API, which waits for the datastore to respond before making the next request. The next request should not depend on the results returned by the datastore though.

Storing Data Asynchronously

In Listing 10.8, the example from Listing 10.1 is modified to use the asynchronous API. The resulting HTML template is processed while the datastore processes the inserted data.

Listing 10.8 **Building the HTML Template while Storing Values in the Datastore**

```
package com.appspot.datastore;

import com.google.appengine.api.datastore.*;
import com.google.appengine.api.users.User;
import com.google.appengine.api.users.UserService;
import com.google.appengine.api.users.UserServiceFactory;
import org.antlr.stringtemplate.StringTemplate;
import org.antlr.stringtemplate.StringTemplateGroup;

import javax.servlet.ServletException;
import javax.servlet.http.HttpServlet;
import javax.servlet.http.HttpServletRequest;
import javax.servlet.http.HttpServletResponse;
import java.io.IOException;
import java.util.Date;
import java.util.concurrent.ExecutionException;
import java.util.concurrent.Future;

public class StoreDataAsyncServlet extends HttpServlet {

  protected void doGet(HttpServletRequest request,
                       HttpServletResponse response)
      throws ServletException, IOException {



    StringTemplateGroup group = new StringTemplateGroup("xhtml",
        "WEB-INF/templates/xhtml");
    StringTemplate html = group.getInstanceOf("store-blog-post");
    response.getWriter().write(html.toString());
  }

  protected void doPost(HttpServletRequest request,
                        HttpServletResponse response)
      throws ServletException, IOException {

    AsyncDatastoreService datastoreService =
        DatastoreServiceFactory.getAsyncDatastoreService();

    String title = request.getParameter("title");
    Entity blogPost = new Entity("BlogPost", normalize(title));
```

(Continues)

Listing 10.8 **Building the HTML Template while Storing Values in the Datastore (Continued)**

```
42      blogPost.setProperty("title", title);
43
44      String author = request.getParameter("author");
45      blogPost.setProperty("author", author);
46      String content = request.getParameter("content");
47      blogPost.setProperty("content", content);
48      blogPost.setProperty("date", new Date());
49
50      // if any: (be careful with Tasks Queue)
51      UserService userService = UserServiceFactory.getUserService();
52      User user = userService.getCurrentUser();
53      blogPost.setProperty("user", user);
54
55      Future<Key> key = datastoreService.put(blogPost);
56
57      // do something else, for example process the result template
58      StringTemplateGroup group = new StringTemplateGroup("xhtml",
59          "WEB-INF/templates/xhtml");
60      StringTemplate html = group.getInstanceOf("done-blog-post");
61      html.setAttribute("title", title);
62      html.setAttribute("author", author);
63      html.setAttribute("content", content);
64
65      try {
66        // block until the result is available
67        key.get();
68        // and do nothing with the resulting key
69      } catch (InterruptedException e) {
70        throw new ServletException(e);
71      } catch (ExecutionException e) {
72        throw new ServletException(e);
73      }
74
75      response.getWriter().write(html.toString());
76    }
77
78    private String normalize(String str) {
79      String trimmedLower = str.toLowerCase().trim();
80      return trimmedLower.replaceAll("\\W+", "-");
81    }
82  }
```

Lines 37 and 38 contain the key to the API variant: you create an `AsyncDatastoreService` instead of a `DatastoreService`. In line 55, you find the first change in using this API: it returns a `Future` and continues processing lines 57 through 63 immediately. On line 67, the code blocks execution until the background thread is finished. Or it returns directly if the datastore answered before the template processing that occurred in the meantime was done. Apart from the exception handling, the rest of the code remains unchanged. Overall, processing tasks in parallel when possible should make the request more efficient. The possible gain depends on the amount of work that can be processed in parallel.

Querying Data Asynchronously

At first sight, the code for querying data asynchronously seems a bit different from the code in the previous example for storing data. As you can see in Listing 10.9, the API does not explicitly return `Futures`. As long as you use an `Iterator` or `Iterable` instead of a `List`, however, the results are processed asynchronously.

Listing 10.9 **Processing a Query in Parallel with Other Code**

```
package com.appspot.datastore;

import com.google.appengine.api.datastore.*;
import org.antlr.stringtemplate.StringTemplate;
import org.antlr.stringtemplate.StringTemplateGroup;

import javax.servlet.ServletException;
import javax.servlet.http.HttpServlet;
import javax.servlet.http.HttpServletRequest;
import javax.servlet.http.HttpServletResponse;
import java.io.IOException;
import java.util.Date;
import java.util.Iterator;
import java.util.List;

public class QueryDataAsyncServlet extends HttpServlet {

  protected void doGet(HttpServletRequest request,
                       HttpServletResponse response)
      throws ServletException, IOException {

    AsyncDatastoreService datastoreService = DatastoreServiceFactory
        .getAsyncDatastoreService();

    Query query = new Query("BlogPost");
    query.addFilter("date", Query.FilterOperator.LESS_THAN,
        new Date(System.currentTimeMillis() - 5000));
    query.addSort("date", Query.SortDirection.DESCENDING);
    PreparedQuery preparedQuery = datastoreService.prepare(query);

    Iterator iterator = preparedQuery.asIterator();
```

(Continues)

Listing 10.9 **Processing a Query in Parallel with Other Code (Continued)**

```
32
33     StringTemplateGroup group = new StringTemplateGroup("xhtml",
34         "WEB-INF/templates/xhtml");
35     StringTemplate html = group.getInstanceOf("query-blog-post");
36     html.setAttribute("items", iterator);
37     response.getWriter().write(html.toString());
38   }
39 }
```

Lines 22 and 23 are similar to Listing 10.8. On line 31, note the change from a `List` to an `Iterator`. The code continues execution directly. Lines 33 through 36 are processed in parallel with the query. Line 37 starts a process that requires the iterator to have the data available. During this process, reading from the iterator blocks until the datastore returns the query results.

Retrieving Data Asynchronously

Data retrieval uses `Futures` like Listing 10.8 does, as demonstrated in Listing 10.10.

Listing 10.10 **Reading a Single Post Asynchronously**

```
package com.appspot.datastore;

import com.google.appengine.api.datastore.AsyncDatastoreService;
import com.google.appengine.api.datastore.DatastoreServiceFactory;
import com.google.appengine.api.datastore.Entity;
import com.google.appengine.api.datastore.KeyFactory;
import org.antlr.stringtemplate.StringTemplate;
import org.antlr.stringtemplate.StringTemplateGroup;

import javax.servlet.ServletException;
import javax.servlet.http.HttpServlet;
import javax.servlet.http.HttpServletRequest;
import javax.servlet.http.HttpServletResponse;
import java.io.IOException;
import java.util.concurrent.ExecutionException;
import java.util.concurrent.Future;

public class RetrieveDataAsyncServlet extends HttpServlet {

  protected void doGet(HttpServletRequest request,
                       HttpServletResponse response)
      throws ServletException, IOException {

    String id = request.getRequestURI()
```

Listing 10.10 **Reading a Single Post Asynchronously (Continued)**

```
25         .replaceAll("/retrieve-data/", "");
26     AsyncDatastoreService datastoreService =
27         DatastoreServiceFactory.getAsyncDatastoreService();
28
29     // start asynchronous call
30     Future<Entity> blogPostFuture =
31         datastoreService.get(KeyFactory.createKey("BlogPost", id));
32
33     // do something else
34
35     Entity blogPost = null;
36     try {
37       // and block until result is available
38       blogPost = blogPostFuture.get();
39     } catch (InterruptedException e) {
40       throw new ServletException(e);
41     } catch (ExecutionException e) {
42       throw new ServletException(e);
43     }
44
45
46     StringTemplateGroup group = new StringTemplateGroup("xhtml",
47         "WEB-INF/templates/xhtml");
48     StringTemplate html = group.getInstanceOf("retrieve-blog-post");
49     html.setAttributes(blogPost.getProperties());
50
51     response.getWriter().write(html.toString());
52   }
53 }
```

Lines 26 and 27 are similar to Listings 10.8 and 10.10. Lines 30 and 31 retrieve a `Future` you can refer to later. On line 33 is a placeholder for for a task that could be executed while waiting for the datastore to return the result. On lines 35 through 43, the `Future` is asked for the result. In this case, you are more interested in the end result than you were in Listing 10.8. In Listing 10.8, it was mostly waiting and checking that nothing went wrong. In Listing 10.10, you actually want the end result to present it to the visitor.

Setting Up Transactions

Chapter 4 discusses the theory behind transactions. Entities need to be grouped together in order to be processed together in a single transaction. This also means that grouped data is stored on the same machine, which may hurt scalability. Both entity grouping and transactions should be used sparingly, only when you really need to use them. The general rule of thumb is to put only a single user's worth of data in the same entity group.

Listing 10.11 demonstrates how to store a blog post and a child element in a single transaction.

Listing 10.11 Storing Data in a Transaction

```
package com.appspot.datastore;

import com.google.appengine.api.datastore.*;
import com.google.appengine.api.users.User;
import com.google.appengine.api.users.UserService;
import com.google.appengine.api.users.UserServiceFactory;
import org.antlr.stringtemplate.StringTemplate;
import org.antlr.stringtemplate.StringTemplateGroup;

import javax.servlet.ServletException;
import javax.servlet.http.HttpServlet;
import javax.servlet.http.HttpServletRequest;
import javax.servlet.http.HttpServletResponse;
import java.io.IOException;
import java.util.Date;
import java.util.concurrent.ExecutionException;
import java.util.concurrent.Future;

public class StoreDataTransactionServlet extends HttpServlet {

  protected void doGet(HttpServletRequest request,
                       HttpServletResponse response)
      throws ServletException, IOException {



    StringTemplateGroup group = new StringTemplateGroup("xhtml",
        "WEB-INF/templates/xhtml");
    StringTemplate html = group.getInstanceOf("store-blog-post");
    response.getWriter().write(html.toString());
  }

  protected void doPost(HttpServletRequest request,
                        HttpServletResponse response)
      throws ServletException, IOException {

    AsyncDatastoreService datastoreService =
        DatastoreServiceFactory.getAsyncDatastoreService();

    Future<Transaction> tx = datastoreService.beginTransaction();

    String title = request.getParameter("title");
```

Listing 10.11 **Storing Data in a Transaction (Continued)**

```
    Key parentKey =
        KeyFactory.createKey("BlogPost", normalize(title));
    Entity blogPost = new Entity(parentKey);
    blogPost.setProperty("title", title);

    String author = request.getParameter("author");
    blogPost.setProperty("author", author);
    String content = request.getParameter("content");
    blogPost.setProperty("content", content);
    blogPost.setProperty("date", new Date());

    // if any: (be careful with Tasks Queue)
    UserService userService = UserServiceFactory.getUserService();
    User user = userService.getCurrentUser();
    blogPost.setProperty("user", user);

    // asynchronous put, ignore output
    datastoreService.put(blogPost);

    // create a child within the same transaction
    Entity child = new Entity("Child", "child-key", parentKey);
    child.setProperty("test", "value");
    datastoreService.put(child);

    // do something else, for example print the result

    StringTemplateGroup group = new StringTemplateGroup("xhtml",
        "WEB-INF/templates/xhtml");
    StringTemplate html = group.getInstanceOf("done-blog-post");
    html.setAttribute("title", title);
    html.setAttribute("author", author);
    html.setAttribute("content", content);
    response.getWriter().write(html.toString());

    try {
      // synchronous commit (can also be async)
      tx.get().commit();
    } catch (InterruptedException e) {
      throw new ServletException(e);
    } catch (ExecutionException e) {
      throw new ServletException(e);
    }

  }

  private String normalize(String str) {
```

(Continues)

Listing 10.11 **Storing Data in a Transaction (Continued)**

```
89     String trimmedLower = str.toLowerCase().trim();
90     return trimmedLower.replaceAll("\\W+", "-");
91   }
92 }
```

The most important differences between Listing 10.11 and Listing 10.8 are on lines 40 and 77 through 85: this is where the transaction begins and commits. In addition, lines 62 through 65 introduce the concept of an entity group by setting the `BlogPost` as the parent for the child entity.

Using Multitenancy to Introduce Namespaces

App Engine instances may run on multiple domains for several users. There is only one conceptual datastore behind the App Engine, though. You want to limit the risk of users accessing each other's data. This is discussed in more detail in Chapter 16, "Securing a Web Application Using Google Accounts, OpenID, and OAuth."

Multitenancy also affects your datastore entities. The simplest (although not the safest) way to introduce a namespace is presented in Listing 10.12. A safer way to introduce multitenancy is to use a *servlet filter* configured for all servlets.

Listing 10.12 **Setting a Namespace for Multitenancy**

```
package com.appspot.datastore;

import com.google.appengine.api.NamespaceManager;
import com.google.appengine.api.datastore.*;
import com.google.appengine.api.users.User;
import com.google.appengine.api.users.UserService;
import com.google.appengine.api.users.UserServiceFactory;
import org.antlr.stringtemplate.StringTemplate;
import org.antlr.stringtemplate.StringTemplateGroup;

import javax.servlet.ServletException;
import javax.servlet.http.HttpServlet;
import javax.servlet.http.HttpServletRequest;
import javax.servlet.http.HttpServletResponse;
import java.io.IOException;
import java.util.Date;
import java.util.concurrent.ExecutionException;
import java.util.concurrent.Future;

public class StoreDataMultitenancyServlet extends HttpServlet {

  protected void doGet(HttpServletRequest request,
```

Listing 10.12 **Setting a Namespace for Multitenancy (Continued)**

```
                          HttpServletResponse response)
      throws ServletException, IOException {


    StringTemplateGroup group = new StringTemplateGroup("xhtml",
        "WEB-INF/templates/xhtml");
    StringTemplate html = group.getInstanceOf("store-blog-post");
    response.getWriter().write(html.toString());
  }

  protected void doPost(HttpServletRequest request,
                          HttpServletResponse response)
      throws ServletException, IOException {

    NamespaceManager.set("development");

    AsyncDatastoreService datastoreService = DatastoreServiceFactory
        .getAsyncDatastoreService();
    Future<Transaction> tx = datastoreService.beginTransaction();

    String title = request.getParameter("title");
    Key parentKey =
        KeyFactory.createKey("BlogPost", normalize(title));
    Entity blogPost = new Entity(parentKey);
    blogPost.setProperty("title", title);

    String author = request.getParameter("author");
    blogPost.setProperty("author", author);
    String content = request.getParameter("content");
    blogPost.setProperty("content", content);
    blogPost.setProperty("date", new Date());

    // if any: (be careful with Tasks Queue)
    UserService userService = UserServiceFactory.getUserService();
    User user = userService.getCurrentUser();
    blogPost.setProperty("user", user);

    // asynchronous put, ignore output
    datastoreService.put(blogPost);

    // create a child within the same transaction
    Entity child = new Entity("Child", "child-key", parentKey);
    child.setProperty("test", "value");
    datastoreService.put(child);

```

(Continues)

Listing 10.12 **Setting a Namespace for Multitenancy (Continued)**

```
68      // do something else, for example print the result
69
70      StringTemplateGroup group = new StringTemplateGroup("xhtml",
71          "WEB-INF/templates/xhtml");
72      StringTemplate html = group.getInstanceOf("done-blog-post");
73      html.setAttribute("title", title);
74      html.setAttribute("author", author);
75      html.setAttribute("content", content);
76      response.getWriter().write(html.toString());
77
78      try {
79        // synchronous commit (can also be async)
80        tx.get().commit();
81      } catch (InterruptedException e) {
82        throw new ServletException(e);
83      } catch (ExecutionException e) {
84        throw new ServletException(e);
85      }
86
87    }
88
89    private String normalize(String str) {
90      String trimmedLower = str.toLowerCase().trim();
91      return trimmedLower.replaceAll("\\W+", "-");
92    }
93 }
```

The important difference between Listing 10.11 and Listing 10.12 is on line 37. The `NamespaceManager` is called to set the new namespace. In this example, it is used to create separate spaces for development, test, and production. After storing data in a namespace, refer to the Admin console to see what happens with your data.

Storing and Retrieving Large Files

Although the datastore allows you to store binaries and larger texts, there is a limit to the size of the data you can store. Currently, the limit is 1MB per datastore item. Google provides the Blobstore to overcome these limits.

Storing Large Files in the Blobstore

Storing a file in the Blobstore is easy if you allow Google to help you a little. The only drawback is that you have a bit less control over the interaction. You can let the user send the file to a location handled by Google. To do so, you need to get a URL from the Blobstore service. After the file uploads, you can retrieve the key ID for the stored blob.

Then the servlet is supposed to redirect the visitor to a location to proceed the interaction. Listing 10.13 demonstrates both of these steps.

Enabling Billing for the Blobstore

Although the Blobstore has free quota, you need to have billing enabled in order to be able to use the API.

Listing 10.13 **Storing Blobs**

```
package com.appspot.datastore;

import com.google.appengine.api.blobstore.BlobKey;
import com.google.appengine.api.blobstore.BlobstoreService;
import com.google.appengine.api.blobstore.BlobstoreServiceFactory;
import org.antlr.stringtemplate.StringTemplate;
import org.antlr.stringtemplate.StringTemplateGroup;

import javax.servlet.ServletException;
import javax.servlet.http.HttpServlet;
import javax.servlet.http.HttpServletRequest;
import javax.servlet.http.HttpServletResponse;
import java.io.IOException;
import java.util.Map;

public class StoreBlobServlet extends HttpServlet {

  protected void doGet(HttpServletRequest request,
                       HttpServletResponse response)
      throws ServletException, IOException {

    BlobstoreService blobstoreService =
        BlobstoreServiceFactory.getBlobstoreService();
    String url = blobstoreService.createUploadUrl("/store-blob");

    StringTemplateGroup group = new StringTemplateGroup("xhtml",
        "WEB-INF/templates/xhtml");
    StringTemplate template = group.getInstanceOf("upload-file");
    template.setAttribute("url", url);
    response.getWriter().write(template.toString());
  }

  protected void doPost(HttpServletRequest request,
                        HttpServletResponse response)
      throws ServletException, IOException {

    BlobstoreService blobstoreService =
        BlobstoreServiceFactory.getBlobstoreService();
```

(Continues)

Listing 10.13 **Storing Blobs (Continued)**

```
39
40     Map<String, BlobKey> uploadedFiles =
41         blobstoreService.getUploadedBlobs(request);
42     BlobKey blobKey = uploadedFiles.get("myfile");
43
44     // do something with blobKey - in this example: IGNORE!
45
46     response.sendRedirect("/query-files");
47   }
48 }
```

Lines 22, 23, and 24 retrieve the URL to post the file to. Lines 26 through 30 set up the HTML template containing the form that posts the file to the URL received from the `BlobstoreService` as a multipart MIME (Multipurpose Internet Mail Extensions) request. That HTML template is presented in Listing 10.14.

Lines 37 through 42 ask the `BlobstoreService` to handle the mutlipart MIME request and store the file. In Chapter 13, "Manipulating Images with the App Engine Image Service," the code for handling multipart MIME requests without Google's help is presented. The `BlobstoreService` saves a lot of code.

Remember the key `"myfile"` in line 42. You'll find the same key in the HTML in Listing 10.14. On line 44, you typically store a reference to the returned `blobKey` in a related record in the datastore.

After storing the blob, the App Engine expects a redirect to the URL where the user interaction should continue. You may pass the `blobKey` as a parameter if your system needs it later. In this example, the visitor is simply redirected to the query page. Listing 10.14 provides the HTML form for uploading a file to the Blobstore.

Listing 10.14 **Presenting an HTML Form to Upload a File**

```
<html>
<body>
<h1>File upload</h1>
<form action="$url$" enctype="multipart/form-data" method="post">
<p>
Please specify a file, or a set of files:<br>
<input type="file" name="myfile" size="40">
</p>
<p>
<input type="submit" value="Send">
</p>
</form>
</body>
</html>
```

On line 4 is a placeholder for the URL to post the file to. The form contains only a file upload control and no other input fields for simplicity. Setting up your file upload dialog this way may affect the interaction design of your web application.

Querying for the Content of Blobstore

Strictly speaking, you cannot query the Blobstore for its content. You can, however, query the datastore for the content of the Blobstore, which is contained in the `__BlobInfo__` entity kind. Listing 10.15 provides an example query.

Listing 10.15 **Querying Metadata for Available Blobs**

```
package com.appspot.datastore;

import com.google.appengine.api.datastore.*;
import org.antlr.stringtemplate.StringTemplate;
import org.antlr.stringtemplate.StringTemplateGroup;

import javax.servlet.ServletException;
import javax.servlet.http.HttpServlet;
import javax.servlet.http.HttpServletRequest;
import javax.servlet.http.HttpServletResponse;
import java.io.IOException;
import java.util.List;

public class QueryFilesServlet extends HttpServlet {

  protected void doGet(HttpServletRequest request,
                       HttpServletResponse response)
      throws ServletException, IOException {

    DatastoreService datastoreService = DatastoreServiceFactory
        .getDatastoreService();

    Query query = new Query("__BlobInfo__");
    PreparedQuery preparedQuery = datastoreService.prepare(query);

    List list = preparedQuery.asList(
        FetchOptions.Builder.withLimit(10));

    StringTemplateGroup group = new StringTemplateGroup("xhtml",
        "WEB-INF/templates/xhtml");
    StringTemplate html = group.getInstanceOf("query-files");
    html.setAttribute("items", list);
    response.getWriter().write(html.toString());
  }
}
```

Lines 23 through 27 set up the query just as Listing 10.4 does. Lines 29 through 33 pass the result to a simple HTML template that displays the fields returned by the query to the visitor.

The easiest way to discover the fields available in the `__BlobInfo__` entities is to visit http://localhost:8080/_ah/admin/datastore or a similar address if your development server runs on a different port.

Listing 10.16 provides a simple, unordered list with links to the servlet that retrieves the blobs and returns them to the visitor.

Listing 10.16 **Presenting a List of Available Blobs in HTML**

```
01 <html>
02 <body>
03 <p>Query Blog Post</p>
04 <ul>
05 $items:{<li>View file: <a href="/retrieve-blob/$it.key.name$">
06                          $it.properties.filename$</a></li>}$
07 </ul>
08 </body>
09 </html>
```

On line 5, the key of the Blobstore is used similarly to the way Listing 10.5 uses it with the blog posts. The key is different from the file name presented. You could consider using the file name as a key, but this is not unique by default. Using the file name ensures that the user downloading the file gets a pretty file name in his or her download folder. It involves a few extra steps while uploading and downloading, though.

Retrieving Files from the Blobstore

Retrieving files from the Blobstore is surprisingly simple, especially when you know what kind of data is sent over the line. Large files can be sent in chunks, requiring continuation requests from the browser fetching the next chunk. The Blobstore API handles all complexity under the hood. Listing 10.17 implements a servlet that connects to the Blobstore service and asks it to serve a specified file.

Listing 10.17 **Retrieving the Blob**

```
package com.appspot.datastore;

import com.google.appengine.api.blobstore.BlobKey;
import com.google.appengine.api.blobstore.BlobstoreService;
import com.google.appengine.api.blobstore.BlobstoreServiceFactory;

import javax.servlet.ServletException;
import javax.servlet.http.HttpServlet;
import javax.servlet.http.HttpServletRequest;
```

Listing 10.17 **Retrieving the Blob (Continued)**

```
10 import javax.servlet.http.HttpServletResponse;
11 import java.io.IOException;
12
13 public class RetrieveBlobServlet extends HttpServlet {
14
15   protected void doGet(HttpServletRequest request,
16                        HttpServletResponse response)
17       throws ServletException, IOException {
18
19     String id = request.getRequestURI()
20         .replaceAll("/retrieve-blob/", "");
21
22     BlobstoreService blobstoreService =
23         BlobstoreServiceFactory.getBlobstoreService();
24
25     blobstoreService.serve(new BlobKey(id), response);
26   }
27 }
```

Lines 19 through 23 are similar to the previous examples. Most interesting is line 25, where the key of the blob and the HTTP response object are passed to the Blobstore API to take over the rest of the work.

Uploading Bulk Data Using the Remote API

When you are setting up your application for the first time, you may want to preload the datastore with larger quantities of data. You could design servlets and scheduled tasks for this, but the limited time allowed to process a request quickly makes things difficult.

Google helps out with a special API for this purpose, the Remote API. This API works interchangeably between Python and Java, and you can reuse clients written for Python App Engine applications.

Setting up the Remote API on the server is as simple as configuring a servlet that is already provided by Google. Listing 10.18 provides the code to add to the web.xml file.

Listing 10.18 **Configuring the Remote API on the Server**

```
<servlet>
  <servlet-name>RemoteApiServlet</servlet-name>
  <servlet-class>com.google.apphosting.utils
  .remoteapi.RemoteApiServlet</servlet-class>
</servlet>
<servlet-mapping>
  <servlet-name>RemoteApiServlet</servlet-name>
  <url-pattern>/remote-api</url-pattern>
</servlet-mapping>
```

Communicating with the Remote API from the client requires writing a standalone Java file that sets up a connection and then starts creating entity objects, just as in Listing 10.1 on storing objects synchronously.

To connect to the Remote API, you need to add the appengine-remote-api.jar file from the App Engine SDK to your class path and write code similar to that presented in Listing 10.19.

Listing 10.19 **Communicating with the Remote API from the Client**

```
package client;

import com.google.appengine.api.datastore.DatastoreService;
import com.google.appengine.api.datastore.DatastoreServiceFactory;
import com.google.appengine.api.datastore.Entity;
import com.google.appengine.tools.remoteapi.RemoteApiInstaller;
import com.google.appengine.tools.remoteapi.RemoteApiOptions;

import java.io.IOException;

public class RemoteApiClient {
    public static void main(String[] args) {
        try {

            String username = "test";
            String password = "test";

            RemoteApiOptions options = new RemoteApiOptions()
                    .server("localhost", 8085)
                    .remoteApiPath("/my-remote-api")
                    .credentials(username, password);
            RemoteApiInstaller installer = new RemoteApiInstaller();
            installer.install(options);

            DatastoreService datastoreService =
                DatastoreServiceFactory.getDatastoreService();

            for(int i = 0; i < 10; i++) {
                Entity entity = new Entity("AutoCount");
                entity.setProperty("ColA", "a" + i);
                entity.setProperty("ColB", "b" + i);
                entity.setProperty("ColC", "c" + i);
                entity.setProperty("ColD", "d" + i);
                entity.setProperty("ColE", "e" + i);
                entity.setProperty("ColF", "f" + i);
                datastoreService.put(entity);
            }

```

Listing 10.19 **Communicating with the Remote API from the Client (Continued)**

```
39             installer.uninstall();;
40
41         } catch (IOException e) {
42             e.printStackTrace();
43         }
44     }
45 }
```

Lines 15 and 16 hardcode the user account. When connecting to the production server instead of the local development server, you should consider replacing this with code that reads user input for security reasons.

Lines 18 through 23 set up a connection to the server—in this example, the development server, which is listening on port 8085 on the path /my-remote-api. If you prefer to use the default configuration, you can remove the port number and the `remoteApiPath`. The default configuration is port 8080, and the URL path is /remote_api (notice the dash [-] becomes an underscore [_]).

Lines 25 through 37 are written exactly as they would have been on the server side, only there is no limit to the processing time of the requests. In this example, 10 rows are filled with 10 columns just to demonstrate that the API works correctly.

Summary

This chapter started with a brief discussion of libraries available to communicate with the Google App Engine datastore. The examples in this book focus on the low-level API because it is sufficient for the demonstration and it gives the most control over the performance. The low-level API should be considered as your first choice. Readers who require mapping to objects are encouraged to look at APIs such as Objectify, SimpleDS, and Twig Persist. JDO and JPA have a higher risk of bad performance.

The rest of the chapter provided code examples for both synchronous and asynchronous storing, querying, and retrieving. There was a brief introduction on storing data within a transaction, with a reference to the theory presented in Chapter 4. This chapter also provided a first encounter with multitenancy, a topic explored more elaborately in Chapter 16.

Next, the Blobstore was introduced. The Blobstore can be used for larger files, particularly for files larger than 1MB that do not fit into the datastore. The chapter provided code examples for storing, retrieving, and querying the datastore for the content of the Blobstore.

The last part of this chapter demonstrated how to upload bulk data to the datastore. This is most useful for initial data setup or larger maintenance actions. For periodic updates, scheduled tasks are preferable.

Chapter 11

Sending and Receiving E-Mail

This chapter demonstrates how to send and receive e-mail on the Google App Engine. First, it shows how to send a full-featured e-mail with HTML markup and an attachment. Then it shows how an application on the App Engine can receive e-mail and store it. Google offers two APIs to send e-mail: the JavaMail API and a low-level API. While presenting examples, this chapter draws a comparison between both APIs.

An App Engine application can use e-mail for many purposes:

- Notify users when changes are made.
- Store details that are hard to remember in the user's mailbox.
- Deliver electronic products.
- Authenticate website visitors for low trust levels.
- Reach website visitors after they leave the site.

In this chapter, e-mail is used to send a confirmation to a visitor who left a comment on a web log.

Sending Confirmation E-Mails with HTML and Attachments

Let's start with sending an e-mail using Google's low-level mail API for the App Engine. The example shown in Listing 11.1 is a `Servlet` that sends a confirmation e-mail to the recipient specified in the URL parameter. This servlet can be triggered after a visitor leaves a comment.

Confirmation e-mails to visitors should contain both plain text and XHTML formatting. In addition, they should contain the visitor's comment as an attachment. The text of the e-mail contains additional URL parameters, like the post that was modified with a comment and its URL. The security issues that arise from using URL parameters are discussed in the next section.

Listing 11.1 **Sending a Confirmation Using the Low-Level API**

```
package com.appspot.mail;

import java.io.IOException;

import javax.servlet.ServletException;
import javax.servlet.http.HttpServlet;
import javax.servlet.http.HttpServletRequest;
import javax.servlet.http.HttpServletResponse;

import org.antlr.stringtemplate.StringTemplate;
import org.antlr.stringtemplate.StringTemplateGroup;

import com.google.appengine.api.mail.MailService;
import com.google.appengine.api.mail.MailServiceFactory;
import com.google.appengine.api.mail.MailService.Message;

/**
 * Low-level alternative to SendConfirmationJMServlet.
 */
public class SendConfirmationLLServlet extends HttpServlet {

  private static final String SENDER =
    "No Reply <info@blo-gae.appspotmail.com>";
  private static final StringTemplateGroup templates =
    new StringTemplateGroup("mail", "WEB-INF/templates/mail");

  private static final long serialVersionUID = 818089810592369246L;

  protected void doPost(HttpServletRequest request,
          HttpServletResponse response)
      throws ServletException, IOException {

    String recipient = request.getParameter("recipient");
    String thread = request.getParameter("thread");
    String url = request.getParameter("url");
    String message = request.getParameter("message");

    String subject = createSubject(thread);
    String body = createBody(url, thread);
    String htmlBody = createHtmlBody(url, thread);
    String attachment = createAttachment(message);

    sendMail(recipient, subject, body, htmlBody, attachment);
  }

  private void sendMail(String recipient, String subject,
```

Listing 11.1 **Sending a Confirmation Using the Low-Level API (Continued)**

```
      String body, String htmlBody, String attachment)
      throws IOException {
    MailService mailService = MailServiceFactory.getMailService();
    Message mail = new Message(SENDER, recipient, subject, body);
    mail.setHtmlBody(htmlBody);
    mail.setAttachments(new MailService.Attachment("message.txt",
        attachment.getBytes()));
    mailService.send(mail);
  }

  private String createBody(String url, String thread) {
    StringTemplate body =
      templates.getInstanceOf("confirmation-body");
    body.setAttribute("url", filter(url));
    body.setAttribute("thread", filter(thread));
    return body.toString();
  }

  private String createHtmlBody(String url, String thread) {
    StringTemplate body =
      templates.getInstanceOf("confirmation-html-body");
    body.setAttribute("url", filter(url));
    body.setAttribute("thread", filter(thread));
    return body.toString();
  }

  private String createSubject(String thread) {
    StringTemplate subject =
      templates.getInstanceOf("confirmation-subject");
    subject.setAttribute("thread", filter(thread));
    return subject.toString();
  }

  private String createAttachment(String message) {
    StringTemplate subject =
      templates.getInstanceOf("confirmation-attachment");
    subject.setAttribute("message", filter(message));
    return subject.toString();
  }

  private String filter(String text) {
    if (text == null)
      return "";
    return text.replaceAll("<?>?", "");
  }
}
```

This example uses Google's low-level mail API, designed for the App Engine. Although titles like "low-level" may seem scary, this shows you need only five or six lines of code to send the e-mail—and that includes both HTML markup and attachments!

Of course, the code preparing the input is left out of this line count. That part does not change when you replace the low-level API with JavaMail.

Parameterizing the Mail Body

On lines 38 through 41 of Listing 11.1, the example starts reading request parameters. These parameters turn out to be extra useful when this `Servlet` is invoked using the Task Queue API presented in Chapter 12, "Running Background Work with the Task Queue API and Cron." These parameters create flexibility on the input side.

The output of this `Servlet` also needs to be flexible. To achieve this, the mail body is not hardcoded but externalized to a template file using the same StringTemplate API that is used in other chapters. Listing 11.2 contains a small template to parameterize the mail body. This template is loaded by the `createHtmlBody()` method on line 65 of Listing 11.1.

Listing 11.2 **The Contents of confirmation-html-body.st**

```
<html>
  <body>
    <h1>Confirmation</h1>
   <p>You have posted a comment on <em>$thread$</em>.</p>
   <p><a href="$url$">Review your comment</a></p>
  </body>
</html>
```

The confirmation-subject.st and confirmation-body.st template files used to parameterize the mail body and subject line are similar but smaller.

Securing the Servlet

It is a security risk to write a `Servlet` that sends e-mails, especially when you introduce parameters for flexibility. Access to this `Servlet` should be limited to machines or people with administrator privileges. The Google App Engine allows you to restrict access with relative ease by modifying web.xml and adding a `security-constraint`, as shown in Listing 11.3.

Listing 11.3 **Adding *`security-constraints`* to web.xml**

```
<security-constraint>
     <web-resource-collection>
     <web-resource-name>send-mail-url</web-resource-name>
         <url-pattern>/mail/*</url-pattern>
     </web-resource-collection>
     <auth-constraint>
```

Listing 11.3 **Adding *`security-constraints`* to web.xml (Continued)**

```
            <role-name>admin</role-name>
        </auth-constraint>
    </security-constraint>
```

These access restrictions do not prevent insertion of malicious code by website visitors writing the comments and thread titles, though. Many e-mail clients interpret HTML code sent in e-mails. Some HTML code might contain harmful JavaScript code. To prevent this, template parameters are filtered using the `filter()` method on line 87 of Listing 11.1. The filtering in this example is straightforward and very restrictive. It filters out all < and > characters to make HTML impossible. Depending on your use case, you could implement a more sophisticated filter that allows a small subset of HTML.

Adding attachments to the e-mail requires thinking about what files can be attached. For the purpose of confirmations, the attachments are limited to text files. In other use cases, you should be careful not to e-mail any file uploaded by a website visitor for security reasons. You cannot be sure that the attachment is virus free. Google restricts the types of files that can be attached to an e-mail. This list of allowed types is slowly growing and can be found on Google's website: http://code.google.com/appengine/docs/java/mail/overview.html#Attachments.

Logging Sent Mails on the Development Server

When you send e-mails from your development server, you also want to know what was sent using the e-mail API. Currently, it is not possible to configure an SMTP server in the development environment. Instead, you can set the Log level to `INFO` and see logging information on sent mails. To achieve this, change the logging.properties file in /WEB-INF and add the following line above the other configuration line:

```
.level = INFO
```

Using the JavaMail API as an Alternative

The example in Listing 11.1 uses Google's low-level API to send the notifications. Although it might hurt cold startup time a bit, you could also use the JavaMail API to send e-mail. It requires just a small change to the implementation of the `sendMail()` method, as demonstrated in Listing 11.4.

Listing 11.4 **Sending a Confirmation with the JavaMail API**

```
private void sendMail(String recipient, String subject,
        String body, String htmlBody, String attachment)
        throws UnsupportedEncodingException, ServletException {
    try {
        InternetAddress senderAddress = new InternetAddress(
                SENDER_MAIL, SENDER_NAME);
```

(Continues)

Listing 11.4 **Sending a Confirmation with the JavaMail API (Continued)**

```
        InternetAddress recipientAddress = new InternetAddress(
                recipient);

        Multipart multipart = new MimeMultipart();

        MimeBodyPart plainPart = new MimeBodyPart();
        plainPart.setContent(body, "text/plain");
        multipart.addBodyPart(plainPart);

        MimeBodyPart htmlPart = new MimeBodyPart();
        htmlPart.setContent(htmlBody, "text/html");
        multipart.addBodyPart(htmlPart);

        MimeBodyPart attPart = new MimeBodyPart();
        attPart.setContent(attachment, "text/plain");
        attPart.setFileName("message.txt");
        multipart.addBodyPart(attPart);

        Properties props = new Properties();
        Session session = Session.getDefaultInstance(props, null);
        Message mail = new MimeMessage(session);

        mail.setFrom(senderAddress);
        mail.addRecipient(Message.RecipientType.TO,
          recipientAddress);
        mail.setSubject(subject);
        mail.setContent(multipart);
        Transport.send(mail);

      } catch (AddressException e) {
        throw new ServletException(e);
      } catch (MessagingException e) {
        throw new ServletException(e);
      }
    }
```

This example uses the JavaMail API to create a MIME message and send it. Google's JavaMail implementation works similarly to other implementations of JavaMail. The main difference is that the App Engine does not require configuration of an SMTP server.

If you have existing code that works with the JavaMail API, it is easy to migrate existing code. If you ever want to move away from the App Engine in the future, there is less lock-in to deal with.

What you see in Listing 11.4 is that every MIME part is added separately. If you know the resulting text that is sent over the SMTP protocol, you'll recognize the resemblance with the API.

Instead of attaching a text file, you can also attach binary files. One way to do this is to replace line 21, attPart.setContent(attachment, "text/plain");, with attPart.attachFile(new File("/my/file"));.

Comparing the Low-Level API to JavaMail

For the confirmation example, the low-level API is simpler than the JavaMail API. There is a minor risk, however, that Google will decide to change the API later. On the upside, this API is a bit more efficient in terms of performance. This is further explained in the section "Considering Performance and Quota."

The low-level API calls are more concise than the JavaMail API calls. The low-level API abstracts away from the multipart MIME nature of the messages that are sent to the recipient. But if you start adding static files as binary attachments, it may be easier to use JavaMail instead of the low-level API. The JavaMail API does not require you to read the file into a byte array.

Other than that, there are many good reasons to consider the low-level API if you are not afraid to risk a little rework on the code if the API happens to change.

Receiving E-Mail

The App Engine has a clever mechanism to receive mail. Instead of setting up slow connections to POP3 or IMAP servers, the App Engine infrastructure sends the e-mail directly to the web application using an HTTP POST request.

Configuring the Servlet to Receive Mail

Unlike sending mail, you have to change configurations before you can receive e-mail. First, you have to configure the receiving Servlet under the URL where Google expects it. You can do this in your web.xml in two ways: you can declare a single Servlet to handle all e-mail, regardless of the target address, or you can declare a specific Servlet to handle a specific e-mail address. Listing 11.5 shows how you can receive every e-mail on any address that points to the App Engine instance.

Listing 11.5 **Configuring web.xml to Listen for Every E-Mail Address**

```
<servlet>
  <servlet-name>ReceiveMailServlet</servlet-name>
  <servlet-class>com.appspot.mail.ReceiveMailServlet</servlet-class>
</servlet>
<servlet-mapping>
  <servlet-name>ReceiveMailServlet</servlet-name>
  <url-pattern>/_ah/mail/*</url-pattern>
</servlet-mapping>
```

E-mail addresses pointing to the App Engine are composed as <anything>@<instance-name>.appspotmail.com. With this information, you can also configure a specific

`Servlet` to listen for a specific e-mail address by modifying web.xml the way Listing 11.6 does.

Listing 11.6 Configuring web.xml to Listen for a Specific E-Mail Address

```
<servlet>
  <servlet-name>ReceiveMailServlet>/servlet-name>
  <servlet-class>com.appspot.mail.ReceiveMailServlet</servlet-class>
</servlet>
<servlet-mapping>
  <servlet-name>ReceiveMailServlet</servlet-name>
  <url-pattern>/_ah/mail/info@blo-gae.appspotmail.com</url-pattern>
</servlet-mapping>
```

But that is not all the configuration needed to receive e-mail. The next step is to secure these URLs to prevent malicious requests being sent from sources other than the App Engine system. You need to add a `security-constraint` to your web.xml, as in Listing 11.7.

Listing 11.7 Configuring web.xml to Secure the `Servlet`

```
<security-constraint>
  <web-resource-collection>
    <url-pattern>/_ah/mail/*</url-pattern>
  </web-resource-collection>
  <auth-constraint>
    <role-name>admin</role-name>
  </auth-constraint>
</security-constraint>
```

Now you're almost there. The `Servlet` is set up and secured, but the Google App Engine does not let any e-mails through. You can change the appengine-web.xml file in your /WEB-INF folder with the lines presented in Listing 11.8.

Listing 11.8 Configuring Inbound E-Mail in appengine-web.xml

```
<inbound-services>
  <service>mail</service>
</inbound-services>
```

Implementing the Servlet to Store Received Mail

If you want a `Servlet` that automatically responds to e-mails by adding a line above the received e-mail, you can use the code in Listing 11.9. The code uses the JavaMail API to parse the raw mail sent in the HTTP `POST` request and stores the message using the low-level datastore API, as explained in Chapter 10, "Storing Data in the Datastore and Blobstore."

Listing 11.9 **Receiving E-Mail Using JavaMail and Storing in the Datastore**

```
package com.appspot.mail;

import com.google.appengine.api.datastore.DatastoreService;
import com.google.appengine.api.datastore.DatastoreServiceFactory;
import com.google.appengine.api.datastore.Entity;

import javax.mail.Address;
import javax.mail.BodyPart;
import javax.mail.MessagingException;
import javax.mail.Session;
import javax.mail.internet.AddressException;
import javax.mail.internet.MimeMessage;
import javax.mail.internet.MimeMultipart;
import javax.servlet.ServletException;
import javax.servlet.http.HttpServlet;
import javax.servlet.http.HttpServletRequest;
import javax.servlet.http.HttpServletResponse;
import java.io.IOException;
import java.util.Date;
import java.util.Properties;

public class ReceiveJMMailServlet extends HttpServlet {

  protected void doPost(HttpServletRequest request,
                        HttpServletResponse response)
      throws ServletException, IOException {

    Properties props = new Properties();
    Session session = Session.getDefaultInstance(props, null);

    try {
      MimeMessage receivedMessage = new MimeMessage(session, request
          .getInputStream());

      DatastoreService datastoreService = DatastoreServiceFactory
          .getDatastoreService();

      Entity mail = new Entity("ReceivedJMMail");

      mail.setProperty("subject", receivedMessage.getSubject());
      mail.setProperty("content", readMessage(receivedMessage));
      mail.setProperty("sender", readSender(receivedMessage));
      mail.setProperty("date", new Date());

      datastoreService.put(mail);

```

(Continues)

Listing 11.9 **Receiving E-Mail Using JavaMail and Storing in the Datastore (Continued)**

```
47     } catch (MessagingException e) {
48       throw new ServletException(e);
49     }
50   }
51
52   private Object readMessage(MimeMessage receivedMessage)
53       throws MessagingException, IOException, ServletException {
54
55     Object multipartObject = receivedMessage.getContent();
56
57     if (multipartObject instanceof MimeMultipart) {
58       MimeMultipart multipart = (MimeMultipart) multipartObject;
59       BodyPart bodypart = multipart.getBodyPart(0);
60       return bodypart.getContent();
61     }
62     return null;
63   }
64
65   private String readSender(MimeMessage receivedMessage)
66       throws ServletException, MessagingException {
67     try {
68       Address[] addresses = receivedMessage.getFrom();
69
70       if (addresses.length > 0) {
71         return addresses[0].toString();
72       }
73       return "";
74     } catch (AddressException e) {
75       throw new ServletException(e);
76     }
77   }
78 }
```

Listing 11.9 shows that an e-mail is received as `POST` data and can be read as an `InputStream`. It also shows that it is relatively simple to read an `InputStream` using the JavaMail API to parse the message on line 32 and simplify processing. The parsed message is stored in the App Engine datastore using the low-level API, as explained in Chapter 10.

If you want to test this code on your local development environment, you have to improvise a little. The only way to test e-mail is by a fake form in the administrative interface for the development environment. See Figure 11.1 for an example of this environment.

You can access this e-mail form on this address, where you should replace 8888 with the port number you configured for your development server: http://localhost:8888/_ah/admin/inboundmail.

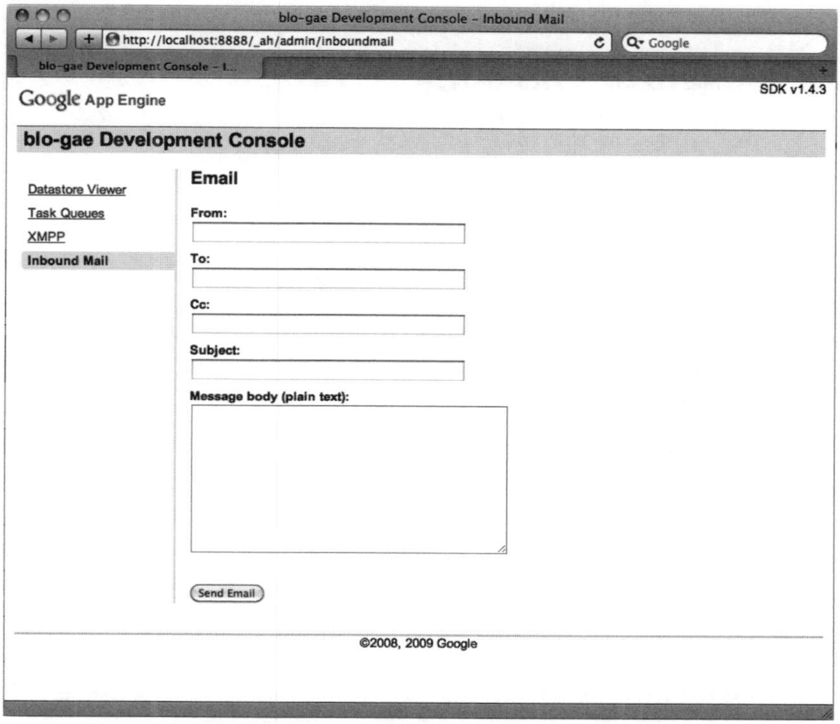

Figure 11.1 The e-mail form in the development environment.

Reading E-Mail without the JavaMail API

After looking at the first example to read e-mails, you might wonder whether you need the JavaMail API to read the messages when they arrive as plain text in an `InputStream`.

The answer depends on the application. For very simple processing, you may consider reading the `InputStream` manually. For example, the code in Listing 11.10 stores the received e-mail as plain text without parsing it.

Listing 11.10 **Receiving E-Mail without JavaMail and Storing in the Datastore**

```
package com.appspot.mail;

import com.google.appengine.api.datastore.DatastoreService;
import com.google.appengine.api.datastore.DatastoreServiceFactory;
import com.google.appengine.api.datastore.Entity;

import java.io.BufferedReader;
import java.io.IOException;
import java.util.Date;

```

(Continues)

Listing 11.10 **Receiving E-Mail without JavaMail and Storing in the Datastore (Continued)**

```
import javax.servlet.ServletException;
import javax.servlet.http.HttpServlet;
import javax.servlet.http.HttpServletRequest;
import javax.servlet.http.HttpServletResponse;

/**
 * Low-level alternative to ReceiveJMMailServlet.
 */
public class ReceiveLLMailServlet extends HttpServlet {

  protected void doPost(HttpServletRequest request,
          HttpServletResponse response)
      throws ServletException, IOException {

    String rawMail = readMailFromRequest(request);
    DatastoreService datastoreService = DatastoreServiceFactory
          .getDatastoreService();

      Entity mail = new Entity("ReceivedLLMail");

      mail.setProperty("rawmail", rawMail);
      mail.setProperty("date", new Date());

      datastoreService.put(mail);
  }

  private String readMailFromRequest(HttpServletRequest request)
      throws IOException {
    BufferedReader reader = request.getReader();
    StringBuilder stringBuilder = new StringBuilder(1000);
    char[] buffer = new char[1024];
    int length = 0;
    while ((length = reader.read(buffer)) > 0) {
      String readData = String.valueOf(buffer, 0, length);
      stringBuilder.append(readData);
    }
    reader.close();
    String result = stringBuilder.toString();
    return result;
  }
}
```

This example is not very useful, though. As soon as you want to read actual fields from the `InputStream`, you end up with very complex regular expressions, and you might as well have used the JavaMail API.

Failures

The error handling in the example code may seem crude. Throwing a `ServletException` results in large stack traces in browser screens on some application servers. The Google App Engine does not display stack traces. A `ServletException` results in a brief error message, which is not elegant but does not reveal internal system like a stack trace.

More important is that a `ServletException` leads to a 500 error status code sent to the App Engine instead of a 200 OK message. In most cases, the servlets presented in this chapter are invoked only by machines, not directly by visitors. The App Engine interprets the 500 code as an error. After receiving a 500 error code, the App Engine retries the same request later. For the mail API, this automatically leads to new attempts to send the mail.

Considering Performance and Quota

The way the App Engine handles e-mail, potential performance issues are not directly visible to website visitors. Receiving e-mail is a process without user interaction. Sending e-mail can be configured to run in the background using the Task Queue API introduced in Chapter 12.

Nevertheless, it is good practice to be economical with resources even if there is no direct user interaction. One good reason for this is to save money when your application is over quota.

The App Engine offers two APIs to send e-mail: the JavaMail API and a low-level API. Google recommends using the JavaMail API because the low-level API may be subject to change. The low-level API documentation is published for API authors. At the time of writing, there are no alternative mail APIs based on the low-level API.

This can mean two things:

- The JavaMail API is sufficiently fast and well-functioning.
- The low-level API is simple enough to use directly, whereas JavaMail is too heavy.

This chapter compares both APIs. The differences in code were presented in the previous sections. This section investigates the differences in response times.

How Long Does It Take to Send an E-Mail?

Assuming an already initialized App Engine instance, after class loading, sending an e-mail takes roughly 50ms regardless of the API. After the instance has started and classes have loaded, the overhead of the JavaMail API over the low-level API is not significant.

This means that sending two e-mails takes roughly 100ms, and sending five e-mails takes roughly 250ms, although the intervals are not perfectly linear. It may take even longer.

> **Caution**
>
> Don't send five e-mails at once on a production version of an unpaid App Engine instance. You'll run through your quota faster than you can imagine!

On a paid instance of the App Engine, sending 100 separate change notification e-mails quickly adds an undesirable waiting period to the request. If your messages are not personalized, you could consider adding 100 addresses to the To-field of a single mail. However, that creates privacy issues and makes it easy for senders of spam to collect e-mail addresses of a target audience. You can add them to the BCC-field of a single mail, but then the risk of deletion by spam filters increases.

To avoid this, you want to introduce task queuing when sending e-mails. On an unpaid instance, you need task scheduling to control the use of quotas. On a paid instance, you need task scheduling for performance. Task scheduling is discussed in the next chapter.

What Is the Overhead on a Cold Instance?

If the performance of fully initialized instances is already an issue, how does this change on cold startup? There are two stages in cold startups:

- 100 percent cold: The Mail API calls are the first request on the instance.
- 50 percent cold: The App Engine instance has already been initialized by another request, but the Mail API classes have not been loaded yet.

A simple way to measure the net execution time of the Mail API calls is to call the `System.currentTimeMillis()` method twice and compare the difference. Although there are more sophisticated tools available, this way of measuring provides a good indication of the execution time of a small code snippet.

If you take this approach, you'll see the following execution times on a 50 percent cold instance:

- Mail API: 500ms average
- Low-level API: 250ms average

The execution times on a 100 percent cold instance are comparable but a bit less reliable.

This means that if you are sending e-mail, particularly when not using the task scheduler, you may benefit from using the low-level API. But what functionality do you need, and does the API help you sufficiently?

As long as you don't send static files as binary attachments, the low-level API is almost always simpler than the JavaMail API.

How Does the Mail Receiver Perform?

The way Google implemented the receiving of e-mail is a good example of performance by design. Before the App Engine, it was not uncommon for a server to periodically connect to a POP3 or an IMAP server and read new e-mails. An App Engine instance is not allowed to create Socket connections to POP3 or IMAP servers. Instead, the App Engine receives e-mails as HTTP `POST` requests.

This has functional implications, though. The web server has to provide and handle its own mail storage. The HTTP `POST` is a fire and forget protocol. Also, the web server can only receive and read e-mail that is specifically addressed to this server. A shared mail repository is not possible using the default e-mail standards.

When receiving e-mail, the added value of the JavaMail API easily outweighs the disadvantage of a small amount of extra class loading. Most uses of receiving e-mail need the MIME message rather than a large unstructured text to be parsed.

Summary

This chapter shows how to use e-mail on the Google App Engine to send confirmation messages with XHTML content and attachments. In addition, this chapter compared the JavaMail API and the low-level Mail API in terms of both performance and code efficiency.

The low-level API turns out to be slightly more efficient on cold startup. On warm requests, the overhead of the JavaMail API over the low-level API is not significant.

Next the actual code calling both APIs was compared. For sending e-mail, the low-level API is easier for almost every application except sending static binary files. When receiving e-mail, the JavaMail API helps parse the raw data from an `InputStream`. Then you can read the mail using standard JavaMail API calls. The raw API requires a lot of text processing and holds only for extremely simple applications. The performance overhead of JavaMail is hardly noticed. In addition, receiving e-mail is a background process that is not directly noticed by the website visitor.

In many ways, the mechanism for receiving e-mail behaves similarly to the Task Queue presented in Chapter 12. You'll find out that the simplistic examples for sending e-mail can easily be modified to implement a task in the queue.

Chapter 12

Running Background Work with the Task Queue API and Cron

This chapter introduces the task scheduling mechanisms built into the App Engine. There are two ways to schedule tasks used for different purposes. Cron (the task scheduler) should be used to plan repetitive tasks at fixed times for structural work. The Task Queue can be used to execute tasks without making the end user wait for them. This chapter starts with the Task Queue API before introducing cron tasks. At the end of the chapter, both ways of scheduling come together for the App Engine–specific HTTP headers passed to task servlets.

Task Queuing

The task queuing mechanism is a key part of the Google App Engine for at least three reasons. First, and most important, it improves performance. Tasks with lower priority can be executed without the website visitor having to wait for them to end. Multiple subtasks can be split over multiple requests so they can be executed in parallel.

Second, if you run into the 30-second time limit of a user request, you should definitely consider moving the work to the Task Queue. In fact, you should consider queuing tasks as soon as your request takes more than a second. Especially when larger datastore operations are involved, task queues provide a noticeable improvement in responsiveness to the visitor.

A third reason task queues are important is that they facilitate a lightweight programming model. Every queued task leads to a new HTTP `POST` request. This means you can write a separate servlet for every task. If you do this well, you end up with small atomic servlets, each customized to perform a single responsibility. Small atomic servlets that respond within hundreds of milliseconds rather than multiple seconds improve the scalability of your web application.

Queuing Send Mails

Chapter 11, "Sending and Receiving E-Mail," presented a servlet that sends an e-mail, partly based on input read from request parameters. For the complete code, you can review Listing 11.1. Listing 12.1 contains only the excerpt with the necessary details to start up a task.

Listing 12.1 **Reading Task Details from Request Parameters**

```
package com.appspot.mail;

import java.io.IOException;

import javax.servlet.ServletException;
import javax.servlet.http.HttpServlet;
import javax.servlet.http.HttpServletRequest;
import javax.servlet.http.HttpServletResponse;

// [...]

public class SendConfirmationLLServlet extends HttpServlet {

  // [...]

  private static final long serialVersionUID = 8168089810592369246L;

  protected void doPost(HttpServletRequest request,
          HttpServletResponse response)
      throws ServletException, IOException {

    String recipient = request.getParameter("recipient");
    String thread = request.getParameter("thread");
    String url = request.getParameter("url");
    String message = request.getParameter("message");

    // [...] (perform rest of task)
  }
  // [...]
}
```

How does the task receive these parameters? A task can be scheduled from any servlet that calls the Task Queue API, including from servlets that were themselves invoked by the Task Queue API.

Listing 12.2 shows code that invokes the task in Listing 12.1 with a few simple, hardcoded parameters.

Listing 12.2 **Launching a Task with Hardcoded Parameters**

```
package com.appspot.tasks;

import java.io.IOException;

import javax.servlet.ServletException;
import javax.servlet.http.HttpServlet;
import javax.servlet.http.HttpServletRequest;
import javax.servlet.http.HttpServletResponse;

import com.google.appengine.api.taskqueue.Queue;
import com.google.appengine.api.taskqueue.QueueFactory;
import com.google.appengine.api.taskqueue.TaskOptions;

public class QueueMailTaskServlet extends HttpServlet {

  private static final long serialVersionUID =
    9026042431554327176L;

  protected void doGet(HttpServletRequest request,
          HttpServletResponse response)
      throws ServletException, IOException {

    TaskOptions task = TaskOptions.Builder
        .withUrl("/mail/low-level")
        .param("recipient", "adriaandejonge+1@gmail.com")
        .param("thread", "Question about JavaMail API")
        .param("url", "http://my-url/post/news-about-javamail")
        .param("message", "What is faster, JavaMail or the\n" +
                "low-level Google API?\n" +
                "\n" +
                "Kind regards,\n" +
                "\n" +
                "Me.");
    Queue queue = QueueFactory.getDefaultQueue();
    queue.add(task);
  }
}
```

As you can see, there is no direct reference to the class, code, or servlet performing the requested task. There is only the path of the URL, which is connected to the servlet using web.xml. There could also be a completely different handler behind this address: a Java Server Page (JSP), a heavyweight Model-View-Control (MVC) framework, or even JRuby code.

Configuring Task Queues

Listing 12.1 uses the default task queue. For this to work, you need not configure anything except default security measures. In Chapter 11, the URLs starting with /mail/ were already secured in web.xml. Listing 12.3 provides a quick reminder how to do this for URLs starting with /tasks/. For the Task Queue API, it does not matter in which URL space the tasks live. But for your security, it does matter!

Listing 12.3 **Securing a URL Space Meant for Tasks**

```
<security-constraint>
    <web-resource-collection>
        <web-resource-name>tasks-url</web-resource-name>
        <url-pattern>/tasks/*</url-pattern>
    </web-resource-collection>
    <auth-constraint>
        <role-name>admin</role-name>
    </auth-constraint>
 </security-constraint>
```

Without any additional configuration, the code should already work because the code uses the default queue. And the default queue requires no further configuration. The default queue handles a maximum of five tasks per second. You can adjust this rate by providing a queue.xml file in the WEB-INF directory. Listing 12.4 shows an example reducing the maximum to 1000 tasks per day.

Listing 12.4 **Modifying the Default Queue in queue.xml**

```
<queue-entries>
  <queue>
    <name>default</name>
    <rate>1000/d</rate>
    <bucket-size>10</bucket-size>
  </queue>
</queue-entries>
```

In Listing 12.4, you also find an entry called `bucket-size`, which helps to control resource usage on the system. For example, if tasks in this queue perform many write actions on the datastore, limiting resource usage can help avoid concurrency issues. You can consider the bucket size to be a rough equivalent of "maximum number of tasks running simultaneously."

Managing Quota

This chapter references a code example from Chapter 11 to send e-mail. Sending e-mail on the App Engine is bound by quota. Especially on unpaid instances, you easily run into maximum numbers of 8 e-mails per minute and 100 e-mails per day at the time of writing.

If you limit your queue to 8 e-mails a minute, you can still exceed 100 e-mails per day. Theoretically, the queue allows 11,520 calls to the send-mail API, resulting in an `OverQuotaException`. The other way around, if you limit the queue to 100 e-mails per day, you may still exceed the rate of 8 e-mails per minute if they are sent all at once.

Although reducing the bucket size may help a little, it gives no guarantee. If you want to be absolutely safe, you could invent your own mechanism using two queues: one with a maximum of 100 e-mails a day that does nothing but read task parameters and post them to the actual mail queue with a maximum of 8 tasks each minute. A configuration like this is shown in Listing 12.5. You could implement the first mail queue by combining code from Listing 12.1 and 12.2. The second mail queue should not be much different from Listing 12.2.

Listing 12.5 **Modifying Mail Queues in queue.xml**

```
<queue-entries>
  <queue>
    <name>mail-queue</name>
    <rate>100/d</rate>
  </queue>
  <queue>
    <name>second-mail-queue</name>
    <rate>8/m</rate>
  </queue>
</queue-entries>
```

However, if you exceed these quota on a regular basis, this may not be a structural solution. In such cases, you should either consider sending fewer e-mails or moving to a paid instance of the App Engine.

Specifying Additional Options

The URL in Listing 12.2 is built using a *Fluent API*. With the Fluent API, every method returns a handle to the object and guarantees it'll never return null. This way you can make many method calls with a single concise statement.

By default, this API calls the `POST` method of the servlet. You can change this by explicitly specifying a parameter telling the App Engine to invoke the `GET` method, as shown in Listing 12.6.

Listing 12.6 **Calling Tasks Using the *GET* Method**

```
TaskOptions task = TaskOptions.Builder
  .url("/mail/low-level")
    .param("recipient", "adriaandejonge+1@gmail.com")
    // […]
    .method(TaskOptions.Method.GET);
Queue queue = QueueFactory.getDefaultQueue();
queue.add(task);
```

Under some circumstances, you may want to delay the execution of an action for a specified time. You can do so by specifying the `countdownMillis` property as Listing 12.7 does. The example specifies an equation to make the interval of 2 minutes more explicit. It could also have said 120,000 instead. In both cases, these are magic numbers, and they should be in a constant or in a property from a configuration file.

Listing 12.7 **Delaying the Task by 2 Minutes**

```
TaskOptions task = TaskOptions.Builder
  .url("/mail/low-level")
    .param("recipient", "adriaandejonge+1@gmail.com")
    // […]
    .countdownMillis(2 * 60 * 1000);
Queue queue = QueueFactory.getDefaultQueue();
queue.add(task);
```

Instead of specifying a delay, you can set a fixed date and time for a task to perform. Like the delay time, the fixed date and time are set using a `long`. The main difference is that the delay time is specified in milliseconds from *now*. The time and date are specified in milliseconds since January 1, 1970, just as `System.currentTimeMillis()` and all Java dates do.

The advantage is that regular Java helper classes can be used to compute these numbers. Listing 12.8 shows how to use `GregorianCalendar` to set a specific date. You can also specify the time on that day. Note that at the time of writing, this example does not work. Tasks should be scheduled less than 30 days ahead in time.

Listing 12.8 **Scheduling the Task for a Specific Date and Time**

```
TaskOptions task = TaskOptions.Builder
  .url("/mail/low-level")
    .param("recipient", "adriaandejonge+1@gmail.com")
    // […]
    .etaMillis(new GregorianCalendar(2011,
         Calendar.NOVEMBER, 20).getTimeInMillis());
Queue queue = QueueFactory.getDefaultQueue();
queue.add(task);
```

Using the Task Queue API, you can specify more details than can be discussed in this book. Refer to the online manual at http://code.google.com/appengine/docs/java/taskqueue/ to review them. There is one option that deserves attention here, though: the payload method.

Instead of URL parameters, you can provide a payload in the form of a large string or as a byte array. This functionality can be particularly useful for passing small files, such as XML files or small pictures, to a task to process. The files should be smaller than 10KB. Listing 12.9 shows how to pass a string as payload to a task.

Listing 12.9 **Specifying a String as Payload to a Task**

```
TaskOptions task = TaskOptions.Builder2
  .url("/mail/low-level")
    .payload("This String could grow up to 10KB.");
Queue queue = QueueFactory.getDefaultQueue();
queue.add(task);
```

In the servlet receiving this payload, you need to modify your code a little to process the input. Instead of reading parameters, you should read the `InputStream` or reader from the request object. If the payload is a string, readers work best. If it is a byte array, then an `InputStream` is more appropriate. Listing 12.10 shows how to read the string specified in Listing 12.9.

Listing 12.10 **Reading a String Payload in a Task Servlet**

```
package com.appspot.tasks;

import java.io.IOException;
import java.io.Reader;

import javax.servlet.ServletException;
import javax.servlet.http.HttpServlet;
import javax.servlet.http.HttpServletRequest;
import javax.servlet.http.HttpServletResponse;

public class PayloadServlet extends HttpServlet {

  private static final long serialVersionUID =
    -7897709050363917514L;

  protected void doGet(HttpServletRequest request,
          HttpServletResponse response)
          throws ServletException, IOException {

    Reader reader = request.getReader();
    StringBuilder stringBuilder = new StringBuilder();
    int length;
    char[] buffer = new char[1024];

    while ((length = reader.read(buffer)) >= 0) {
      stringBuilder.append(buffer, 0, length);
    }

    String result = stringBuilder.toString();

    // do something with result

  }
}
```

Instead of a string, you can provide a byte array as payload. To do so, you must set the content type. Listing 12.11 provides an example PNG image as payload to demonstrate this functionality.

Listing 12.11 Specifying a Byte Array as Payload to a Task

```
TaskOptions task = TaskOptions.Builder
  .url("/mail/low-level")
    .payload(imageByteArray, "image/png");
Queue queue = QueueFactory.getDefaultQueue();
queue.add(task);
```

Reading a byte array from an `InputStream` has many similarities to reading a `String` from a `Reader`, but there are also subtle differences. The buffer becomes a byte array instead of a character array, and the `StringBuffer` becomes a `ByteArrayOutputStream`. Listing 12.12 provides the modified code.

Listing 12.12 Reading a Byte Array Payload in a Task Servlet

```
package com.appspot.tasks;

import java.io.ByteArrayOutputStream;
import java.io.IOException;
import java.io.InputStream;

import javax.servlet.ServletException;
import javax.servlet.http.HttpServlet;
import javax.servlet.http.HttpServletRequest;
import javax.servlet.http.HttpServletResponse;

public class PayloadServlet extends HttpServlet {

  private static final long serialVersionUID =
    -7897709050363917514L;

  protected void doGet(HttpServletRequest request,
          HttpServletResponse response)
          throws ServletException, IOException {

   InputStream inputStream = request.getInputStream();
   ByteArrayOutputStream byteArrayStream =
     new ByteArrayOutputStream();
   int length;
   byte[] buffer = new byte[1024];

   while((length = inputStream.read(buffer)) >= 0) {
```

Listing 12.12 **Reading a Byte Array Payload in a Task Servlet (Continued)**

```
            byteArrayStream.write(buffer, 0, length);
        }

        byte[] result = byteArrayStream.toByteArray();

         // do something with result

    }
}
```

With the Task Queue API, you can provide a name for a task in order to have it execute once and only once. And you can schedule a task within a *transaction* and make sure the task is executed only if the transaction succeeds.

Taking Advantage of Task Queues

Normal HTTP requests invoked by the end user are subject to a time limit of 30 seconds. Tasks invoked by cron or the Task Queue have a time limit of 10 minutes. If tasks run longer than the time limit, the App Engine interrupts the running task with a `DeadlineExceededException`.

For requests by the end user, it should be evident that 30 seconds is way too long to respond. Task queues help out here because parts of the task can be externalized out of sight of the website visitor.

Even though response time to the visitor is not a direct issue for task processing, there are still many good reasons to speed up the task as much as possible. Google App Engine scales best with short-running tasks.

If you want to execute multiple tasks, it is recommended to execute them in separate tasks and add them all to the queue. The total execution time can be optimized by the App Engine. Using task queues, multiple tasks can run simultaneously, which, at the time of writing, is impossible within a single task because of the security limitations disallowing you to start your own threads.

To scale well when many tasks are executed, the App Engine infrastructure may even decide to launch a new instance of your application in order to process the queued tasks more quickly.

Where necessary, tasks themselves can add new tasks to the task queue. This is especially useful when a task depends on the successful execution of other tasks.

If a task leads to a failure, it should return a 500 HTTP status code in the response. The App Engine interprets HTTP response codes and acts accordingly. Failed tasks are rescheduled on an exponentially increasing interval up to 1 hour. Tasks are retried until they succeed with an HTTP status code 200. The HTTP header contains a counter of the number of tries. HTTP headers are further discussed later in the chapter. A repetitively failing task can be stopped only if the servlet reads the retry count and sets a maximum.

Scheduling Tasks Using Cron

A web application should not be limited to respond only to visitor requests. Many web applications require regular maintenance tasks running independently of visitor requests. For example, data from external sources must be periodically refreshed, and old data from the datastore must be thrown away.

On regular computers, the operating system provides mechanisms to run tasks periodically. Windows has the *task scheduler* in the Control Panel's administrative tools section. UNIX machines have the *crontab* configuration file used by the cron daemon to execute tasks in the background.

Because the App Engine does not allow access to the operating system, it provides a different mechanism, also called *cron*. To configure cron, you need to provide a file called cron.xml.

Configuring Tasks Using cron.xml

In comparison to the Task Queue API, the capabilities of cron tasks are somewhat limited because cron tasks are specified in a simple static XML file instead of invoked by a rich and dynamic API.

Basically, the XML file just specifies the path of the servlet to be called. This servlet receives a `GET` request. The more sophisticated part of the cron.xml task specification format is where you set the dates and times to execute. Listing 12.13 gives an example cron.xml.

Listing 12.13 **Configuring Multiple Tasks at Different Intervals**

```
<?xml version="1.0" encoding="UTF-8"?>
<cronentries>
  <cron>
    <url>/cron/spam-mail</url>
    <description>Send a spam mail…</description>
    <schedule>every 2 minutes</schedule>
  </cron>
  <cron>
    <url>/cron/read-rss</url>
    <description>Read RSS feed…</description>
    <schedule>every day 22:00</schedule>
    <timezone>Africa/Johannesburg</timezone>
  </cron>
</cronentries>
```

The schedule specification needs some explanation before you can use it to its full extent. The values for `schedule` (and for `timezone`) seem like English language, but cron does not allow just any English expression.

Rather than providing a formal grammar, Listing 12.14 displays a number of examples explaining how to write your own specifications. If you do prefer the formal grammar, you can find it on Google's website at http://code.google.com/appengine/docs/java/config/cron.html.

Listing 12.14 Specifying Cron Start Times

```
every 2 minutes
every 2 hours
every 2 hours synchronized
every 2 minutes from 9:00 to 17:00
every day 22:00
every monday of november 22:00
first monday of november
first,second monday of november
every 2,9,16,23 of month 22:00
```

Most of these examples should be self-explanatory, but the post-fix `synchronized` is unclear at first sight. The addition of `synchronized` after `2 hours` means that the task starts exactly every 2 hours. Without this addition, tasks are run 2 hours after the completion of the last task. This means if the task takes roughly 20 seconds to complete, tasks are run every 2 hours and 20 seconds on average.

The second entry that needs further explanation is `timezone`. There are many ways to specify a time zone. Some systems use abbreviations like CET, PST, and MST. Other systems express time zones as UTC, UTC+01, and UTC-08. The problem is that these time zones do not take into account daylight savings time (or summer time, as it is called in many countries).

The App Engine uses a combination of continent and city and does take into account daylight savings time. This results in values like the following:

```
Europe/Andorra
Asia/Dubai
Asia/Kabul
America/Antigua
America/Anguilla
Europe/Tirane
Asia/Yerevan
America/Curacao
[…]
```

If you are using an Apple computer, you can find the list of time zones on your own computer. Open a terminal and type the following command:

```
systemsetup -listtimezones
```

On Ubuntu Linux, you can find all the time zones on your file system in the following directory.

```
/usr/share/zoneinfo
```

Windows users can search on Google for timezones.txt for the complete list.

Taking Advantage of Cron

Cron can help to improve performance when it is used for regular preprocessing. For example, instead of reading an RSS (Really Simple Syndication) feed live within a web visitor's request, a cron task can read the RSS feed periodically and store the contents in the datastore.

Another way to use cron to improve performance is by preloading caches. Although the content of the cache cannot be guaranteed to be available later on, preloading certainly helps to reduce load time. The caching mechanism is discussed in Chapter 14, "Optimizing Performance Using the Memory Cache."

Some clever developers may try to use cron tasks to keep App Engine instances warm. First of all, Google tells you not to do this. So don't. Second, just running tasks does not keep the instances warm. Although you might invent clever mechanisms to work around that, in the long run you are trying to take away symptoms instead of fixing actual performance problems. The App Engine infrastructure works best if you put all your effort into serving pages as efficiently as possible.

Reading HTTP Headers

Regardless whether tasks are scheduled using the Task Queue API or using cron, servlets receive some HTTP headers that are App Engine specific. They are mixed with some more general HTTP headers.

Listing 12.15 provides simple example code for retrieving HTTP headers for App Engine tasks. Because cron jobs work with `GET` requests and Task Queue jobs work with `POST` requests by default, the example servlet implements both methods, each optimized for its respective purpose.

Listing 12.15 **Reading App Engine–Specific HTTP Headers**

```
package com.appspot.tasks;

import java.io.IOException;

import javax.servlet.ServletException;
import javax.servlet.http.HttpServlet;
import javax.servlet.http.HttpServletRequest;
import javax.servlet.http.HttpServletResponse;

public class TaskHeaderServlet extends HttpServlet {

  private static final long serialVersionUID =
```

Listing 12.15 **Reading App Engine–Specific HTTP Headers (Continued)**

```
     -1137258632691070463L;

   /**
    * Called by default when scheduled by CRON
    */
   protected void doGet(HttpServletRequest request,
           HttpServletResponse response) throws ServletException,
           IOException {


     String userAgent = request.getHeader("User-Agent");
     String host = request.getHeader("Host");

     boolean isCronTask = "true".equals(
             request.getHeader("X-AppEngine-Cron"));
     String queueName = request.getHeader("X-AppEngine-QueueName");
     assert !isCronTask || "__cron".equals(queueName);

     String taskName = request.getHeader("X-AppEngine-TaskName");
     String taskRetryStr =
       request.getHeader("X-AppEngine-TaskRetryCount");
     int taskRetryCount = taskRetryStr == null ? -1 :
       Integer.parseInt(taskRetryStr);

     if(taskRetryCount > 25) return; // and give up

     // Perform task knowing all above fields

   }

   /**
    * Called by default when scheduled by Task Queue API
    */
   protected void doPost(HttpServletRequest request,
           HttpServletResponse response) throws ServletException,
           IOException {

     String contentType = request.getHeader("Content-Type");
     String userAgent = request.getHeader("User-Agent");
     String referer = request.getHeader("Referer");
     String host = request.getHeader("Host");
     String contentLengthStr = request.getHeader("Content-Length");
     int contentLength = contentLengthStr == null ? -1 :
       Integer.parseInt(contentLengthStr);

     String queueName = request.getHeader("X-AppEngine-QueueName");
```

(Continues)

Listing 12.15 **Reading App Engine–Specific HTTP Headers (Continued)**

```
59      String taskName = request.getHeader("X-AppEngine-TaskName");
60      String taskRetryStr =
61        request.getHeader("X-AppEngine-TaskRetryCount");
62      int taskRetryCount = taskRetryStr == null ? -1 :
63        Integer.parseInt(taskRetryStr);
64
65      if(taskRetryCount > 25) return; // and give up
66
67      // Perform task knowing all above fields
68    }
69
70  }
```

The HTTP header `X-AppEngine-TaskRetryCount` may be the most important of all. If you don't read this parameter and act accordingly, an unmonitored task may continue to be retried and fail forever as long as the HTTP status code finally returned is 500.

Line 29 contains an assert that you could leave out of your code. Its main purpose is to make sure there are two ways to confirm your task was launched by cron and not by a nondefault call to the Task Queue API explicitly asking for a `GET` request.

Other HTTP headers can be used for application-specific purposes. You may have reasons to make slight modifications to the behavior of a task depending on the task queue that launched it.

Using Pull API, REST API, and Backends for Heavy Background Work

In May 2011, Google extended the App Engine Task Queue API with additional mechanisms specialized for lifting heavy workloads to make the App Engine more attractive to use in larger companies.

The Task Queue API discussed in this chapter so far is now called the Push API. When you queue a task, the App Engine handles the execution using the code you provided.

In comparison, the Pull API allows you to post tasks to a task queue, but the tasks posted there are not automatically executed if you do not implement a mechanism handling the workload.

Google provides a REST API that allows you to fetch the tasks in the queue so you can execute them and delete them from the queue. You can perform the tasks on a machine outside the App Engine. It could be a specialized machine running within your company.

The task could also be handled by an App Engine instance configured to run as a *backend*. Backends are dedicated paid instances allowing you to run tasks beyond the 10-minute time limit and use more CPU and memory than regular instances to handle background work.

The Pull API, REST API, and backends are beyond the scope of this book. As the APIs evolve and lose their experimental status, there will be posts on the Essential App Engine weblog covering their functionality.

Summary

This chapter covered the App Engine's capabilities for running background work while the website visitor continues his or her activities without having to wait for a direct response. The App Engine, via the Task Queue API, allows invoking background tasks as a result of a visitor's action. It also allows regular scheduling of background work regardless of user interaction with cron.

The Task Queue API is a key part of the App Engine for multiple reasons. It improves end user performance by processing lower priority tasks after the user is served. It also improves the scalability of the infrastructure because work can be split over small atomic servlets that can be executed independently. The Task Queue API provides a rich tool set for parameterizing tasks to be delayed.

Cron allows regular scheduling of tasks independent of the activity of website visitors. Regular scheduling of tasks can be used to improve performance by preprocessing content, performing slow activities, or preloading the cache.

Regardless of the mechanism that queues tasks, the servlets performing the task receive App Engine–specific HTTP headers that can be used to influence the actions.

Chapter 13

Manipulating Images with the App Engine Image Service

Google App Engine does not allow using `java.awt.Image` and related classes. Instead, it offers its own service for image manipulation. This chapter starts with a brief discussion of when to use the Image API and when not to. Then it provides code examples for frequently used features of the API. Finally, this chapter explores other uses of the API by showing how to place, for example, copyright notices over images.

Minimizing the Use of the Image API

The App Engine provides an Image API allowing you to perform a small number of rudimentary manipulations on images server side. Although it is good to have such an API at your disposal, it should be used sparingly. In many cases, there are alternatives that perform better, offer more features, or produce higher-quality results.

For example, HTML5 offers a canvas function with which you can draw and manipulate richer images without using server resources. The downside is that it requires modern browsers, so the possibilities depend on your user group and their adoption of the latest software.

Sometimes, manipulation on the client side creates a large overhead of network traffic. Think of a page filled with thumbnails, for example. Downscaling in the browser means that all large images should be transferred before they can be minimized.

Reading and Writing Images

The App Engine Image API can read and write raw byte arrays containing serialized PNG, GIF, or JPEG files. It can detect the format from the byte stream. Most image formats contain a byte combination at the start of the file that reveals their format.

Reading from User Input

If a website visitor uploads a file, an HTTP header also provides a field containing the file format. This is not reliable, though. The file might as well contain an executable file with malicious code in it. Although this would not directly cause problems on the App Engine itself, by redistributing a malicious file, you could inadvertently help a hacker do harm on other machines.

In addition to resizing, cutting, and otherwise changing images, manipulating images uploaded by anonymous end users has the positive side effect of making sure you are not spreading malicious code to your visitors. Reading an unrecognized file format results in an `IllegalArgumentException`. Reading files that are too large results in a `RequestTooLargeException`. The current file size limit is 32MB. For the most recent values, check Google's website: http://code.google.com/appengine/docs/java/images/overview.html.

The code in Listing 13.1 implements two HTTP request types: `GET` and `POST`. The `GET` method displays a simple form that allows you to upload a file. The `POST` method reads the file and instantiates an image object. You'll notice that with this code, the exceptions mentioned earlier won't be thrown. This is because the image is just a data container. The byte arrays are treated as actual images only when you start applying transformations.

Listing 13.1 **Reading Image Data from User Input**

```
package com.appspot.images;

import java.io.ByteArrayOutputStream;
import java.io.IOException;
import java.io.InputStream;
import java.util.HashMap;
import java.util.Map;

import javax.servlet.ServletException;
import javax.servlet.http.HttpServlet;
import javax.servlet.http.HttpServletRequest;
import javax.servlet.http.HttpServletResponse;

import org.antlr.stringtemplate.StringTemplate;
import org.antlr.stringtemplate.StringTemplateGroup;
import org.apache.commons.fileupload.FileItemIterator;
import org.apache.commons.fileupload.FileItemStream;
import org.apache.commons.fileupload.FileUploadException;
import org.apache.commons.fileupload.servlet.ServletFileUpload;
import org.apache.commons.fileupload.util.Streams;

import com.google.appengine.api.images.Image;
import com.google.appengine.api.images.ImagesServiceFactory;

public class ReceiveImageServlet extends HttpServlet {

  private static final long serialVersionUID = 2380641632803777837L;
```

Listing 13.1 **Reading Image Data from User Input (Continued)**

```

    protected void doGet(HttpServletRequest request,
            HttpServletResponse response) throws ServletException,
            IOException {
    StringTemplateGroup group = new StringTemplateGroup("xhtml",
            "WEB-INF/templates/xhtml");
    StringTemplate template = group.getInstanceOf("upload-file");
    response.getWriter().write(template.toString());
  }

  protected void doPost(HttpServletRequest request,
          HttpServletResponse response) throws ServletException,
          IOException {

    if (ServletFileUpload.isMultipartContent(request)) {
      Map<String, String> formValues =
          new HashMap<String, String>();
      byte[] imageBytes = null;
      try {
        ServletFileUpload upload = new ServletFileUpload();
        FileItemIterator iterator = upload.getItemIterator(request);
        while (iterator.hasNext()) {
          FileItemStream item = iterator.next();

          if (item.isFormField()) {
            formValues.put(item.getFieldName(), Streams.asString(
                    item.openStream()));
          } else {
            InputStream inputStream = item.openStream();
            imageBytes = inputStreamToBytes(inputStream);
          }
        }
      } catch (FileUploadException e) {
        throw new ServletException(e);
      }

      Image image = ImagesServiceFactory.makeImage(imageBytes);
      // do something with image
    }
  }

  public byte[] inputStreamToBytes(InputStream inputStream)
          throws IOException {

    ByteArrayOutputStream byteArrayOutputStream =
        new ByteArrayOutputStream(1024);
```

(Continues)

Listing 13.1 **Reading Image Data from User Input (Continued)**

```
74     byte[] buffer = new byte[1024];
75     int length;
76
77     while ((length = inputStream.read(buffer)) >= 0) {
78       byteArrayOutputStream.write(buffer, 0, length);
79     }
80
81     inputStream.close();
82     return byteArrayOutputStream.toByteArray();
83   }
84 }
```

Note that for this code example to work, you must include the Apache Commons Fileupload library on your classpath. With the current servlet specification, it seems impractical to try to read multipart form requests without this library. When the Servlet 3.0 specification is implemented by major application servers and by Google, this library should be superfluous. That might take a while, though.

Commons Fileupload generally has two ways to retrieve multipart requests. The classic version writes temporary files on the file system. A more sophisticated alternative works with streaming data. This example uses the streaming variant. Storing temporary files on an App Engine instance is not an option.

The code consists of two parts: lines 46 through 62 are used to read the submitted files and put other form values in a `HashMap`. After line 62, the byte array is retrieved and the `HashMap` can be used as a substitute for the usual `request.getParameter()` method calls.

Writing to the Datastore

One of the most common things you can do after retrieving the multipart form data is to store it to the Google App Engine datastore. Storing data in a simple data structure is relatively easy, but there are pitfalls.

Consider the example in Listing 13.2. The complete code is roughly the same as Listing 13.1 except for a few important lines. The listing contains some abbreviations to save space. Line 14 in Listing 13.2 corresponds with line 64 in Listing 13.1.

Listing 13.2 **Writing an Image to the Datastore**

```
01 //[…see listing 13.1…]
02 protected void doPost(HttpServletRequest request,
03         HttpServletResponse response) throws ServletException,
04         IOException {
05
06   if (ServletFileUpload.isMultipartContent(request)) {
07     Map<String, String> formValues =
```

Listing 13.2 **Writing an Image to the Datastore (Continued)**

```
            new HashMap<String, String>();
        byte[] imageBytes = null;
        try {
            //[…see listing 13.1…]
        }

        DatastoreService datastoreService = DatastoreServiceFactory
                .getDatastoreService();
        Entity imageEntity = new Entity("ImageEntity");
        if (imageBytes != null) {
          imageEntity.setProperty("data", new Blob(imageBytes));
        }
        imageEntity.setProperty("caption", formValues.get("caption"));
        datastoreService.put(imageEntity);
    }
  }
  //[…see listing 13.1…]
```

One noticeable difference is that Listing 13.2 does not attempt to read the byte array into an image object. The image object is not necessary because images are stored as byte arrays.

The big downside of directly storing uninterpreted byte arrays is that you might store something that is not an image. You might be storing an executable containing a virus, a ZIP with illegal software, unwanted movies, or worse.

Loading the byte array into an image object will not help here. Only performing an actual transformation reveals files that are not images. Although it costs in terms of performance and quota, there might be a good case for a routine transformation even if it is only a security check. Generating thumbnails has positive side effects!

> **Warning**
>
> Keep in mind that the maximum size of a datastore item is currently 1MB. You may prefer the Blobstore over the datastore, as explained in Chapter 10, "Storing Data in the Datastore and Blobstore."

Reading from the Datastore

Listing 13.3 presents the code to retrieve an image from the datastore and send it to the website visitor.

Listing 13.3 **Reading an Image from the Datastore**

```
package com.appspot.images;

import java.io.IOException;

```

(Continues)

Listing 13.3 **Reading an Image from the Datastore (Continued)**

```
05 import javax.servlet.ServletException;
06 import javax.servlet.http.HttpServlet;
07 import javax.servlet.http.HttpServletRequest;
08 import javax.servlet.http.HttpServletResponse;
09
10 import com.google.appengine.api.datastore.Blob;
11 import com.google.appengine.api.datastore.DatastoreService;
12 import com.google.appengine.api.datastore.DatastoreServiceFactory;
13 import com.google.appengine.api.datastore.Entity;
14 import com.google.appengine.api.datastore.EntityNotFoundException;
15 import com.google.appengine.api.datastore.KeyFactory;
16
17 public class RetrieveDatastoreImageServlet extends HttpServlet {
18
19   private static final long serialVersionUID =
20       -6510323320594401293L;
21
22   protected void doGet(HttpServletRequest request,
23           HttpServletResponse response) throws ServletException,
24           IOException {
25     String keyStr = request.getParameter("key");
26     if(keyStr == null) return;
27     long key = Long.parseLong(keyStr);
28
29     response.setContentType("image/png");
30     DatastoreService datastoreService = DatastoreServiceFactory
31     .getDatastoreService();
32     try {
33       Entity entity = datastoreService.get(
34          KeyFactory.createKey("ImageEntity", key));
35       Blob data = (Blob) entity.getProperty("data");
36       response.getOutputStream().write(data.getBytes());
37     } catch (EntityNotFoundException e) {
38          throw new ServletException(e);
39     }
40   }
41 }
```

Just as in Listing 13.2, the image class is conspicuously absent. In the end, the web browser only needs a byte array, and the image class does not add any value as long as you are not performing any transformations.

The downside is that line 29 now hardcodes the image type. A dynamic declaration of the image type or fetching the image type from a different field in the datastore entity would be more elegant in production code.

Reading from the datastore, transforming, and then feeding the output directly to your visitors should not be your first choice. It should be done only when the transformation depends on recent user input and is a high-priority task. In all other cases, performance improves if you can postpone transformations to be executed in background processes such as the Task Queue and cron tasks, as discussed in Chapter 12, "Running Background Work with the Task Queue API and Cron." The remainder of this chapter violates this advice in order to show simple examples.

In real-world applications, it is recommended to receive the input from the user and then use Task Queue to transform image. The result from the transformation can be stored in the Blobstore or in the datastore if it is very small. As a result, they can be retrieved later from the storage already in the required format.

Writing to User Output

The basics of writing to user output are already shown in Listing 13.3. Because the App Engine handles images as single byte arrays and not streams, you can write an image to the output in two lines of code.

The following code snippet assumes you have an image stored in a byte array. It also assumes that the type of the image is a PNG.

```
response.setContentType("image/png");

response.getOutputStream().write(data.getBytes());
```

If you forget to set the content type, the browser does not know it should display an image. Instead, it may display some raw data. An interesting thing is that if you do provide an image content type, but the wrong one, most browsers forgive you and display the image anyway.

Given the code in Listing 13.4, many browsers allow you to send a JPEG image despite the first line. This works because the byte array containing the image data starts with a standardized sequence of bytes that indicates the image format.

If you don't know the format in which your images are stored, you can create the content type dynamically with the following trick:

```
String contentType = "image/" + image.getFormat().toString().toLowerCase();
```

It is better to keep control over your image formats, though. In general, JPEG is most efficient for photographs. PNG is more efficient and provides higher-quality for images containing text and simple line drawings.

Reading from a File

In some cases, images don't come from the user input or the datastore, where the datastore is indirectly user input. You may want to transform default images you delivered with your web application.

Listing 13.4 shows you how to read images from file, or more specifically, from the class path. This means that images can be in /WEB-INF/classes or within a JAR file in /WEB-INF/lib.

Listing 13.4 **Reading Images from the Resource File**

```
package com.appspot.images;

import java.io.ByteArrayOutputStream;
import java.io.IOException;
import java.io.InputStream;

import javax.servlet.ServletException;
import javax.servlet.http.HttpServlet;
import javax.servlet.http.HttpServletRequest;
import javax.servlet.http.HttpServletResponse;

import com.google.appengine.api.images.Image;
import com.google.appengine.api.images.ImagesServiceFactory;

public class ReadImageFromFileServlet extends HttpServlet {

  private static final long serialVersionUID =
      7296574226624516172L;

  protected void doGet(HttpServletRequest req,
          HttpServletResponse resp) throws ServletException,
          IOException {
    InputStream backgroundInputStream =
         this.getClass().getResourceAsStream("background.png");
    byte[] backgroundBytes =
            inputStreamToBytes(backgroundInputStream);
    Image backgroundImage =
            ImagesServiceFactory.makeImage(backgroundBytes);

    // do something with image

  }

  public byte[] inputStreamToBytes(InputStream inputStream)
          throws IOException {

    ByteArrayOutputStream byteArrayOutputStream =
        new ByteArrayOutputStream(1024);
    byte[] buffer = new byte[1024];
    int length;

    while ((length = inputStream.read(buffer)) >= 0) {
      byteArrayOutputStream.write(buffer, 0, length);
    }

    inputStream.close();
```

Listing 13.4 **Reading Images from the Resource File (Continued)**

```
    return byteArrayOutputStream.toByteArray();
  }
}
```

In practice, reading static images and using them for manipulations makes most sense when they are used for overlays. Overlays are discussed later in this chapter. The examples in the next section also read images from the file system, mostly for simplicity.

Performing Simple Manipulations

Every operation you perform on an image is executed on an external server specialized for its task. When compared to the usual possibilities with images in Java, the Image Service is somewhat limited. However, it is questionable whether more advanced operations are desirable on a cloud-computing platform like the App Engine.

The App Engine is optimized for small, short-living, atomic tasks. Anything that involves heavy processing quickly adds to the usage of your CPU quota. The current image processing quota do not seem limiting at all.

Creating Thumbnails of Large Images

Listing 13.5 provides a full code example reading an image from file, transforming it by resizing to 100 × 500, and outputting it to the browser that requested this servlet. The next examples reuse most of this code, except the transformation.

Listing 13.5 **Resizing Images from the File System and Serving Them to the Browser**

```
package com.appspot.images;

import java.io.ByteArrayOutputStream;
import java.io.IOException;
import java.io.InputStream;
import java.io.OutputStream;

import javax.servlet.ServletException;
import javax.servlet.http.HttpServlet;
import javax.servlet.http.HttpServletRequest;
import javax.servlet.http.HttpServletResponse;

import com.google.appengine.api.images.Image;
import com.google.appengine.api.images.ImagesService;
import com.google.appengine.api.images.ImagesServiceFactory;
import com.google.appengine.api.images.Transform;
import com.google.appengine.api.images.ImagesService.OutputEncoding;

public class ResizeImageServlet extends HttpServlet {
```

(Continues)

Listing 13.5 **Resizing Images from the File System and Serving Them to the Browser (Continued)**

```

  private static final long serialVersionUID =
      -8616065571872910090L;

  protected void doGet(HttpServletRequest request,
          HttpServletResponse response) throws ServletException,
          IOException {

    InputStream backgroundInputStream =
            this.getClass().getResourceAsStream("background.png");
    byte[] backgroundBytes =
            inputStreamToBytes(backgroundInputStream);
    Image image = ImagesServiceFactory.makeImage(backgroundBytes);


    Transform transform = ImagesServiceFactory.makeResize(
                    100, 500);

    ImagesService imageService = ImagesServiceFactory
                    .getImagesService();
    image = imageService.applyTransform(transform, image,
            OutputEncoding.PNG);

    response.setContentType("image/png");

    OutputStream outputStream = response.getOutputStream();

    outputStream.write(image.getImageData());
    outputStream.close();
  }

  public byte[] inputStreamToBytes(InputStream inputStream)
          throws IOException {

    ByteArrayOutputStream byteArrayOutputStream =
        new ByteArrayOutputStream(1024);
    byte[] buffer = new byte[1024];
    int length;

    while ((length = inputStream.read(buffer)) >= 0) {
      byteArrayOutputStream.write(buffer, 0, length);
    }

    inputStream.close();
    return byteArrayOutputStream.toByteArray();
  }
}
```

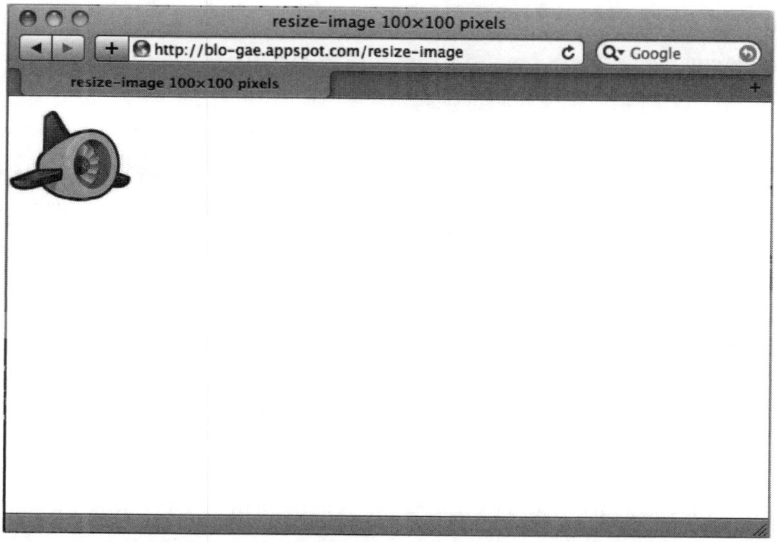

Figure 13.1 The resulting resized image loaded in the browser.

The code in Listing 13.6 leads to the screen output in Figure 13.1. It may surprise you that the resulting image is 100 × 100, although the code requested a format of 100 × 500.

As it turns out, the transformer preserves the aspect ratio and returns the biggest possible image that fits within the given boundaries. In this case, the aspect ratio is 1:1, so it is best not to use the available height to prevent stretching the image to unnatural proportions.

You have no control over the resizing algorithm. It is up to Google whether it uses nearest neighbor, bilinear, bicubic, or something completely different. If you have very specific quality requirements for the resulting images, you should consider alternatives to server-side manipulation on the Google App Engine.

Cropping Images

Specifying a transformation that crops your image requires only one change. Lines 35 and 36 in Listing 13.5 change as follows:

```
Transform transform =
    ImagesServiceFactory.makeCrop(0.1, 0.1, 0.9, 0.9);
```

This transformation cuts away 10 percent on all sides. In fact, this means it cuts away 36 percent of the image size. The values provided are left-X, top-Y, right-X, and bottom-Y, as long as left-X is less than right-X and top-Y is less than bottom-Y. All values are between 0.0 and 1.0.

The biggest difference between this and the resize transformation is that cropping requires float or double values. If you want to crop to a specific number of pixels, you need to calculate well. There are no guarantees of an exact outcome, though.

Rotating Images

The following code shows how to rotate images clockwise. The method allows degree values 90, 180, and 270. An input of 0 or 360 is pointless, of course.

```
Transform transform = ImagesServiceFactory.makeRotate(90);
```

These fixed rotations are best suited to correct the orientation of photos taken upside-down or in portrait mode. The App Engine does not solve for smaller corrections, such as an image scan that needs a 2-degree correction.

Flipping Images

Finally, the App Engine allows you to *flip* images, or *mirror* them, as it was once called. The following code snippet performs a horizontal flip and then a vertical flip.

```
Transform transform = ImagesServiceFactory.makeHorizontalFlip();

Transform transform = ImagesServiceFactory.makeVerticalFlip();
```

Flipping images may help to create a mirror effect, like a reflection on the surface of water. To accomplish this, you need to apply other transformations as well. Other transformations might be applied on the client side, or you can use techniques explained in the next section.

Performing Advanced Manipulations

One of the most common manipulations you'll see on a website's images is copyright notices placed over the images. With a bit more effort than the previous manipulations, the Google App Engine Image Manipulation API allows you to write text over images. Listing 13.6 contains code that demonstrates the basic principle.

Listing 13.6 **Using Composite Images to Write Overlay Text**

```
package com.appspot.images;

import java.io.ByteArrayOutputStream;
import java.io.IOException;
import java.io.InputStream;
import java.io.OutputStream;
import java.util.ArrayList;
import java.util.List;

import javax.servlet.ServletException;
import javax.servlet.http.HttpServlet;
import javax.servlet.http.HttpServletRequest;
import javax.servlet.http.HttpServletResponse;

import com.google.appengine.api.images.Composite;
```

Listing 13.6 **Using Composite Images to Write Overlay Text (Continued)**

```
import com.google.appengine.api.images.Image;
import com.google.appengine.api.images.ImagesService;
import com.google.appengine.api.images.ImagesServiceFactory;
import com.google.appengine.api.images.Composite.Anchor;

public class CompositeImageServlet extends HttpServlet {

  private static final long serialVersionUID =
      9107100571002086737L;

  protected void doGet(HttpServletRequest req,
          HttpServletResponse resp) throws ServletException,
          IOException {
    InputStream backgroundInputStream =
        this.getClass().getResourceAsStream("background.png");
    byte[] backgroundBytes =
        inputStreamToBytes(backgroundInputStream);
    Image backgroundImage =
        ImagesServiceFactory.makeImage(backgroundBytes);
    Composite backgroundComposite =
        ImagesServiceFactory.makeComposite(backgroundImage, 0, 0,
                1.0f, Anchor.TOP_LEFT);

    InputStream overlayInputStream =
      this.getClass().getResourceAsStream("overlay.png");
    byte[] overlayBytes = inputStreamToBytes(overlayInputStream);
    ImagesService imageService =
      ImagesServiceFactory.getImagesService();
    Image overlayImage =
      ImagesServiceFactory.makeImage(overlayBytes);
    Composite overlayComposite =
      ImagesServiceFactory.makeComposite(
              overlayImage, 0, 120, 0.5f, Anchor.TOP_LEFT);

    List<Composite> list = new ArrayList<Composite>();
    list.add(backgroundComposite);
    list.add(overlayComposite);

    Image result = imageService.composite(list, 1500, 1500,
            Long.parseLong("FF00FF00", 16));
    resp.setContentType("image/png");

    OutputStream outputStream =  resp.getOutputStream();

   outputStream.write(result.getImageData());
```

(Continues)

Listing 13.6 **Using Composite Images to Write Overlay Text (Continued)**

```
61      outputStream.close();
62
63    }
64
65    public byte[] inputStreamToBytes(InputStream inputStream)
66            throws IOException {
67
68      ByteArrayOutputStream byteArrayOutputStream =
69        new ByteArrayOutputStream(1024);
70      byte[] buffer = new byte[1024];
71      int length;
72
73      while ((length = inputStream.read(buffer)) >= 0) {
74        byteArrayOutputStream.write(buffer, 0, length);
75      }
76
77      inputStream.close();
78      return byteArrayOutputStream.toByteArray();
79    }
80 }
```

First, lines 29 through 37 and 39 through 48 load two image files. Of course, the first image could also have been read from the datastore or from user input. Both images are used as input for the composite class. The second image has an opacity of 0.5, which means you should see an image behind this second image.

Next, the composite images are added to a list. The composite images might be a different type of collection, but make sure you are using a deterministic implementation here. For example, if you use a `HashSet` instead of an `ArrayList`, the text disappears *under* the image instead of *over* it approximately half of the time.

Finally, the resulting image is created. In the example, the size of the result is overly large to show that you can specify a background color. The background color is a long value indicating alpha-red-green-blue (ARGB) format. Alpha is roughly the same as opacity.

The value provided to `Long.parseLong()` is similar to the way you specify colors in CSS. #00FF00 means green. Adding the alpha channel and starting with FF means you are providing an opacity of 1.0.

Instead of using `Long.parseLong()`, you could try to provide 0xFF00FF00 as input, but remember that Java recognizes only signed integers and longs. 0xFF00FF00 is a negative number and results in an exception.

Figure 13.2 shows the image resulting from this code example in a browser screen.

The example uses a fixed transparent PNG file containing the text "DRAFT" and overlay. The App Engine does not provide a native mechanism to write variable text. You could invent your own using 26 PNGs or using sprites and many crop transformations. But you're better off without it.

Figure 13.2 The resulting composite image loaded in the browser.

The current version of the local App Engine development environment leads to strange results with the transparent PNG. This might be a temporary bug at the time of writing or an Apple-specific problem. The App Engine instances on production process the transparent PNGs just as expected!

Summary

This chapter explained how to work with the App Engine mechanisms to manipulate images. The chapter first discussed whether you want to manipulate images on the App Engine at all. When you are dealing with uploaded images from anonymous end users, there is at least one very good reason to perform one or more manipulations: to prove you actually received an image file and not some harmful other file.

The chapter started with basic input and output of images, regardless of the manipulations. Then it demonstrated simple manipulations that can be expressed as one-liners. Finally, the chapter demonstrated the most advanced manipulation: a text overlay that can be used to watermark images with a copyright notice. The last example dealt with multiple images, opacities, and background colors in ARGB format.

The main point made in this chapter is to use the Image API sparingly, and if you do use it, do it in task queues when possible, as presented in Chapter 12.

Chapter 14

Optimizing Performance Using the Memory Cache

Memory caches optimize performance by reusing earlier results instead of repeating execution of heavy workloads. This chapter starts by showing that Google App Engine's low-level memory cache (memcache) API is relatively simple to use. Then the chapter explains that implementing a full caching strategy is less simple because of some pitfalls when implementing the serializable interface and because caches need to be maintained. At the end of the chapter, the JCache API (Java Specification Request [JSR] 107) is discussed as an alternative to Google's low-level memcache API.

Using the Cache API for Basic Purposes

Google provides two APIs for memory caching (or memcache): the low-level API and the JSR 107 JCache API. The JSR 107 JCache API is discussed at the end of this chapter.

The low-level API is simple to use and sufficient to implement anything you could reasonably ask of a cache. There are a few things to keep in mind, though.

Considering the Pitfalls of a Cache

The memcache service is unreliable by nature. If the cache is full, it throws out items. In case of system failure or scheduled maintenance, the cache may be flushed. There are no backups of caches. Good practice is to set timeouts to force yourself to deal with unavailable items in cache.

If you think this unreliable nature should prevent you from using the memcache service, then perhaps you should think about a quote made in a popular Disney movie:

> You can always trust the untrustworthy because you can always trust that they will be untrustworthy. It's the trustworthy you can't trust.
>
> —Captain Jack Sparrow in *Pirates of the Caribbean*

The performance improvements you can get using memcache is worth the trouble of checking that the content is actually available and incidentally fetching it again. It is even a good thing to use a cache mechanism knowing the limited reliability, because it forces you to use defensive programming mechanisms.

In its simplest form, defensive programming means avoiding some bad practices. Some blog posts on the Internet advocate using memcache as a locking mechanism or as a way to transport larger chunks of data to a queued task. Even though this technique works in many cases, it should be considered bad practice because it is unreliable and carries a real risk of data loss. Using APIs for other purposes than those they were designed for is bad practice in general.

Another thing to keep in mind is the execution time of a call to the memcache service. Although memcaching should be faster than querying the datastore, it isn't entirely free. Even a simple use case making a single call to memcache may take roughly 45 milliseconds because memcache is an external service. When you have multiple instances of your App Engine application, they share the same cache. In addition to the network traffic required to call the service, objects need to be serialized and deserialized in order to be transferred. Later sections in this chapter discuss object serialization.

Using memory cache is not a silver bullet, and it should be used carefully. First write your servlets without cache, measure performance, and then add caching only where necessary. These considerations are part of your caching strategy and are discussed in the following section.

Caching String Values

The most basic use of a memory cache is a *pattern*. In this pattern, code checks whether the cache contains a specific value. If it does, it uses this value. If the cache does not contain the value, the code generates a new value, taking a performance hit, stores it in the cache, and continues working with the value.

Listing 14.1 shows this pattern using the low-level memcache API. The example differs from a real-world application in two ways: generating a new value doesn't actually take time, and the value isn't used in a real way. It demonstrates the API without too much clutter and overhead, though.

Listing 14.1 **Caching a Simple String for 2 Minutes**

```
package com.appspot.cache;

import com.google.appengine.api.memcache.Expiration;
import com.google.appengine.api.memcache.MemcacheService;
import com.google.appengine.api.memcache.MemcacheServiceFactory;

import javax.servlet.ServletException;
import javax.servlet.http.HttpServlet;
import javax.servlet.http.HttpServletRequest;
import javax.servlet.http.HttpServletResponse;
```

Listing 14.1 **Caching a Simple String for 2 Minutes (Continued)**

```

import java.io.IOException;
import java.util.Date;

public class SimpleCacheServlet extends HttpServlet {

  private static final long serialVersionUID = 1211642763887796727L;

  public void doGet(HttpServletRequest request,
                    HttpServletResponse response)
      throws ServletException, IOException {

    MemcacheService cache = MemcacheServiceFactory
        .getMemcacheService();

    String cacheKey = request.getRequestURI() + "." + "article";
    String result;

    if (!cache.contains(cacheKey)) {

      result = "Loaded into cache at " + (new Date());
      cache.put(cacheKey, result, Expiration.byDeltaSeconds(120));
    } else {

      result = "FROM CACHE: " + cache.get(cacheKey);
    }

    response.getWriter().write(result);
  }
}
```

The most important thing to notice in this example is the generation of a cache key. The call to `request.getRequestURI()` returns the current path of the URL. In this version of the `web.xml`, the path is `/simple-cache`. By adding a postfix, the cache key becomes `/simple-cache.article`. You may ask two questions: Why use the URI path? And why do you need the postfix?

This is just a design choice. The low-level memcache API allows you to use any other cache key: readable, obfuscated, hashed, randomized, or democratically chosen by your website visitors.

The cache key proposed in Listing 14.1 is chosen to be readable and flexible. The readability helps when you want to invalidate the cache after an update of content. This is discussed in the section "Maintaining a Cache" later in this chapter. Using the `RequestURI` path is flexible, because a servlet may live under multiple paths, serving different content under different paths. Finally, adding the postfix allows multiple caches tied to the same URL.

Line 29 checks whether there is a value stored under the cache key. You could also implement a strategy whereby you make sure never to store `null` as a value in the cache. In that case, line 29 could be avoided: you could directly fetch the cache value itself, as line 35 does, and check whether a `null` value was returned.

Implementing a Caching Strategy

So far, using the low-level memcache API does not seem too complicated. And the good news is: that won't change. However, using the memcache service by itself doesn't make much sense if you don't look at the bigger picture.

A typical web application contains multiple layers of cache. In a typical web application, caching starts in the database. Object-relational mapping (ORM) tools on top of that usually contain their own caching mechanism. On the App Engine, you should assume that the datastore does not contain a caching mechanism; however, I do not know the exact inner workings of the datastore.

Both in the App Engine and in typical non–App Engine web applications, you have object caching mechanisms within the application. You can use them to cache results from the datastore directly, to cache objects after processing takes place, to cache snippets of the resulting page, or to cache entire pages.

Typical non–App Engine web applications employ an external page caching mechanism using Varnish, Apache mod_cache, or Squid as a reverse proxy in front of the web application. App Engine seems to have a similar mechanism built in to the *frontend* servers. See Chapter 3, "Understanding the Anatomy of a Google App Engine Application," for more details on the frontend servers.

But caching doesn't stop there. The HTTP protocol (RFC 2616, a must-read for every web developer) is designed for scalability using caches all over the Internet. HTTP headers are used to control these caches.

Before reaching the browser, a web page may be cached by a proxy server. This is particularly interesting when multiple employees of the same company use your App Engine application. If they work through a central proxy, the proxy can reduce the load on the App Engine by reusing earlier results.

The last level of cache is the browser. Depending on the HTTP headers, it can reduce the load on the App Engine if it decides that a page does not need refreshing.

Reducing App Engine Load Using ETag Headers

Let's explore browser and proxy caches. The connection to the memory cache will become clear when you see the code example in Listing 14.2.

Listing 14.2 **Using a Browser Cache with *ETag* Headers**

```
package com.appspot.cache;

import com.google.appengine.api.memcache.Expiration;
import com.google.appengine.api.memcache.MemcacheService;
import com.google.appengine.api.memcache.MemcacheServiceFactory;

```

Listing 14.2 **Using a Browser Cache with *ETag* Headers (Continued)**

```
import javax.servlet.ServletException;
import javax.servlet.http.HttpServlet;
import javax.servlet.http.HttpServletRequest;
import javax.servlet.http.HttpServletResponse;
import java.io.IOException;
import java.util.Date;

public class ETagCacheServlet extends HttpServlet {
  private static final long serialVersionUID = 4308584640538822293L;

  public void doGet(HttpServletRequest request,
                    HttpServletResponse response)
      throws ServletException, IOException {

        MemcacheService cache = MemcacheServiceFactory
        .getMemcacheService();

    String cacheKey = request.getRequestURI() + "." + "etag";
    String result;

    if (!cache.contains(cacheKey) ||
        !cache.get(cacheKey).equals(request
            .getHeader("If-None-Match"))) {

      String etag = Long.toString(System.currentTimeMillis());
      response.setHeader("ETag", etag);
      cache.put(cacheKey, etag);

      result = "Loaded into cache at " + (new Date());
      response.getWriter().write(result);

    } else {

      response.setStatus(304);
    }
  }
}
```

Most developers know how to use the `Expires` HTTP header. Some developers use `META` fields in their HTML page instead of the HTTP header. While an `Expires` header reduces the load on the server, it becomes hard to update resources once they are loaded by a browser or caching proxy. Depending on the expiry time, your visitors are stuck with an old version.

For caching static resources such as CSS and JavaScript files, some developers choose to modify the file names and include a version number. This way, the HTML page tells the browser to load a different resource file. The old version may remain in the cache for a while before it expires or is thrown out because it is not used much.

> **Caution**
>
> Instead of changing the file name, some developers add a query string to the URL of a CSS or JavaScript file. This is *bad practice*. Many proxy caches do not cache URLs containing query strings. An open source proxy server called *Squid* is one of these servers. Despite its quirky behavior, Squid is still a frequently used product. As a result, using query strings renders a lot of caching useless.

For static resources, there are ways to work with the `Expires` header. However, for dynamic resources, it is painful to use. The problem is that it is hard to predict when the next update will occur.

If you provide a `Last-Modified` header, browsers and proxies can send an `If-Modified-Since` on subsequent requests, allowing the server to respond with an HTTP status code `304` (not modified).

`Last-Modified` works better for static resources than for dynamic resources. Dynamic resources change frequently for various reasons.

A more appropriate solution for caching is the use of an `ETag` header. `ETags` can contain hashes or timestamps. Proxies and (most) browsers send the provided tags back in an `If-None-Match` tag, expecting a `304` or a new page.

This is the point where the low-level memcache API comes back into play. Listing 14.2 shows how you can use the API to cache `ETag` values and see if they have changed.

In this code example, the old value remains in the cache until either the cache is cleaned or another servlet explicitly removes this `ETag` from the cache. Line 33 puts the value in the cache without setting an expiry time and date.

Make sure you do not store `null` values in the cache to prevent `NullPointerExceptions` on line 28. If you do store `null` values, modify line 28 to include an extra check. If you do not store `null` values, the double `||` operator on line 27 makes sure lines 28 and 29 are never executed.

Even though this works, it is bad practice. In fact, it is best to always provide an expiry date and time that are in the near future. You should not entirely rely on other cache invalidation mechanisms because a `delete` operation on the memory cache may also fail. The performance penalty of these regular cache timeouts is unavoidable.

This code example is not realistic because it only checks for `ETags` and does not use the memory cache when no `ETag` is provided.

> **Caution**
>
> A few years ago, `ETags` were used mostly by proxies and not as much by browsers. The value of `ETags` slowly grows because of the increasing support by browsers. Keep in mind that not all browsers support `ETags`, though. For example, Apple's Safari does not support them. You may consider providing `Last-Modified` headers as well and checking for `If-Modified-Since` headers in addition to using `ETags` if you expect a large number of Safari users to visit your site.

Working with Fine-Grained Cache

The examples so far show you how to cache string values. Caching string values basically means that you can cache both full pages and page fragments. In many cases, caching full pages and page fragments is perfect: it is simple and straightforward, and the overhead to process the cache result and return it to the website visitor is reduced to an absolute minimum.

This approach falls short, though, in at least two situations. First, if you have multiple views of the same data, you need to retrieve the data for every view. This is not a big problem when you have only an HTML view and an RSS view. But the problem grows larger with every view you add.

Suppose you also have a feed in Atom Syndication Format, two variants of RSS (RDF Site Summary and Really Simple Syndication), one for the IPhone, one for Android, one for the Blackberry, and a few specific XML feeds for rich Internet applications built in Flex, JavaFX, and Silverlight. With this many views, you have a much bigger problem, and you need to learn how to use fewer views.

The second situation is if your pages are highly personalized and every visitor has his or her own version of the page. Learning to limit your views is still good advice here, but you can't always do so.

In such cases, you should not cache the resulting page or its fragments. You should cache the model data behind the page, which is needed to create different views. You can store model data in the form of plain old Java objects as long as they implement serializable.

Implementing Serializable

Some books say it is simple to implement serializable. Just add `implements Serializable` and provide a `serialVersionUID` value in the class. Although this is not entirely wrong, it is also not entirely true. At least it is not the whole truth.

The truth is that you should implement serializable only when you really know what you are doing. A full explanation of serializing objects is beyond the scope of this book. You can read books like Joshua Bloch's *Effective Java, Second Edition* (Addison-Wesley, Upper Saddle River, NJ) if you want to know all.

This book just provides a summary of points that deserve attention when using serializable objects for caching purposes.

First, implementing serializable introduces maintenance issues you should take care of. A serialized version of an object instance represents the internal state of an object. Private members are stored exactly as they appear in the class. Getters and setters are omitted.

This means that if you're making the slightest change to the class, even if it does not affect the interface, you can break compatibility with serialized objects of earlier versions of the class.

When you translate this to caching, updating your application may result in lots of errors unless you clear the entire cache. Both clearing the cache and handling errors are discussed later in this chapter. More elegant is to preserve backwards compatibility when updating your application.

Second, the integrity of your object instances may be violated if you don't take precautions. Usually you instantiate objects using constructors, getters, and setters. This allows you to call validating code and return errors if the input results in inconsistent states. The Java object serialization mechanism allows you to provide custom serializers and deserializers, but it takes additional effort to use them.

Third, you should consider both performance and efficiency. This chapter mentioned earlier that the memcache service runs on remote servers. Serializing and deserializing objects takes time, and so does sending them over a network. This should be relatively trivial if it weren't for the fact that it is very easy to make mistakes here.

Serializing an object also means serializing every object it refers to. An object you refer to could accidentally refer to a very large tree of objects if you don't pay attention. Such mistakes can be avoided by using the `transient` keyword in front of a field declaration.

Caching Query Results in Raw Entity Format

Usually, when working with relational databases using JDBC, you get `ResultSets` that maintain a connection to the database while reading the results. Therefore, you cannot serialize a `ResultSet` to cache.

With the App Engine datastore, however, you're in luck! Datastore results are serializable. Both the list and iterator collections as well as the entity instances can be serialized and sent to the memcache service.

In this case, you should trust Google to preserve backwards compatibility with earlier versions of the API when there is an update. Hopefully, Google updates its API less frequently than an average App Engine user updates the inner workings of a web application.

Considering the code style in the rest of this book, if you require fine-grained caching to support multiple views on the same data, it is advisable to store datastore entity objects directly.

> **Caution**
>
> Using fine-grained caching, it may be tempting to also cache user session data for a specific user in the memory cache. You should avoid doing so because the memory cache is not optimized for security. This chapter warns against using the cache for purposes other than caching. A cache is not a user session.

Maintaining a Cache

If you ask an average user of a mediocre content management system (CMS) to define the word *cache*, he or she might say it is a mechanism to delay publication of content. This average user knows nothing about performance optimization and shouldn't have to. The user only knows the cache as the mechanism that gets blamed when he or she publishes an article and it takes 5 minutes to appear online.

Sound familiar? And do you agree that this is unnecessary and unacceptable by all means? If you design your caching strategy well, the problem can be solved.

Invalidating Cache Items

It is relatively simple to invalidate a specific cache item as long as you know the cache key. The example in Listing 14.1 used the path from the URL as the basis for the cache key followed by a simple postfix. Listing 14.3 shows you how to invalidate such a specific cache from another servlet using the predictable cache keys.

Listing 14.3 **Invalidating a Single Cache Item**

```
package com.appspot.cache;

import com.google.appengine.api.memcache.MemcacheService;
import com.google.appengine.api.memcache.MemcacheServiceFactory;

import javax.servlet.ServletException;
import javax.servlet.http.HttpServlet;
import javax.servlet.http.HttpServletRequest;
import javax.servlet.http.HttpServletResponse;
import java.io.IOException;

public class InvalidateCacheServlet extends HttpServlet {

  private static final long serialVersionUID =
      -3977589077951744418L;

  public void doGet(HttpServletRequest request,
                    HttpServletResponse response)
      throws ServletException, IOException {

    MemcacheService cache = MemcacheServiceFactory
        .getMemcacheService();

    cache.delete("/simple-cache.article");

    response.getWriter().write("Cache invalidated - /simple-cache");
  }
}
```

The code in this example invalidates the cache by throwing away the old one. A more sophisticated implementation could also pregenerate a new value for the cache and store it under the same key. Depending on the organization of the code, there are multiple ways to accomplish that. The simplest way is to schedule a task in the Task Queue that invokes a URL already known from the cache key.

There are cases in which you need to invalidate multiple cache items at once. The hard part is to manage the relationships between cache items that invalidate when another item is modified. If you are inclined to invent a very clever mechanism to deal with these relationships, then you should reconsider your caching strategy.

Choosing the right granularity and knowing the priorities is the answer to keeping the system simple. For example, when you publish an article, it should be visible on the homepage right away.

It should also appear in lists of related items under some other articles. Under most circumstances, the lists of related items can wait for a few minutes, though. If you have stricter requirements on updating related items, the right granularity in combination with a tagging mechanism can also help you out here in a simple way.

Clearing the Cache

Let's go back to the example of our average user using a mediocre CMS, waiting 5 minutes for every new publication to appear online. Despite the flaws of the CMS, sometimes there are emergencies when publication of content cannot wait for 5 minutes. Or there are radical system updates that render the current cache content useless. In such cases, the usual remedy is to clear the cache.

Although you should avoid designing a system that needs to clear the cache frequently, it is good to have an escape option just in case you need it. It takes little code to clear the cache, as shown in Listing 14.4.

Listing 14.4 **Clearing the Full Cache**

```
package com.appspot.cache;

import com.google.appengine.api.memcache.MemcacheService;
import com.google.appengine.api.memcache.MemcacheServiceFactory;

import javax.servlet.ServletException;
import javax.servlet.http.HttpServlet;
import javax.servlet.http.HttpServletRequest;
import javax.servlet.http.HttpServletResponse;
import java.io.IOException;

public class ClearCacheServlet extends HttpServlet {

  private static final long serialVersionUID =
      -3977589077951744418L;

  public void doGet(HttpServletRequest request,
                    HttpServletResponse response)
      throws ServletException, IOException {

    MemcacheService cache = MemcacheServiceFactory
```

Listing 14.4 **Clearing the Full Cache (Continued)**

```
            .getMemcacheService();

        cache.clearAll();

        response.getWriter().write("Cleared cache");
    }
}
```

Unlike in the example code, it would be wise to limit access to this servlet to administrators. On a web application with many visitors, clearing the full cache may result in a large performance hit for a lot of users.

Using Other Cache Utility Methods

In addition to the basic operations presented in the code examples in this chapter, there are some utility functions you practically cannot live without when using the memcache for real-world applications.

Putting and Getting Multiple Values

From Listing 14.2 you saw that you need to retrieve multiple values from the cache in order to process even the simplest request. In this example, you need at least the `ETag` and `Last-Modified` values. If these do not match the request headers, you later need the actual content of a page.

To retrieve the `ETag` and `Last-Modified` values from the cache in a single request, you can use the `getAll()` method, providing a collection of cache keys. For the full usage, see Google's online JavaDoc reference.

Registering Error Handlers

The `MemcacheService` class provides a method called `setErrorHandler`. By default, the error handler is set to the `LogAndContinueHandler`, which lets cache errors pass silently and lets them be treated as a cache miss. In most cases, this is what you want.

There are two other alternatives, though. The first alternative is the standard class `StrictErrorHandler`, which throws a `MemcacheServiceException` for every error.

The second alternative is to provide your own implementation of the `ErrorHandler` interface. All you need to do is to implement two methods: `handleDeserializationError` and `handleServiceError`. Considering the discussion of object serialization in this chapter, you may be interested in providing alternative actions when deserialization fails.

Incrementing Values

Another operation that may be useful is the `increment` method. It is especially handy for updating computed counters, such as a comment count. This method works only for cache values in the form of byte, short, integer, or long or for strings that can be parsed as a long.

Incrementing counters on the datastore may slow down your application unnecessarily. To speed things up, you could maintain two counters: a reliable counter in the datastore that you update on a scheduled basis and a second, less reliable counter in memcache that is always up to date. You should be aware, however, that you may lose the second counter. You can use the increment operator with a line similar to the following:

```
cache.increment("my-counter-key", 1);
```

Of course, this line does not take into account the more reliable counter periodically being updated on the datastore.

Using JSR 107 as an Alternative API

You probably have noticed the preference for the low-level APIs over the more standard compliant alternatives. In other cases, performance and control are the main reasons for the preference. There are additional reasons to prefer the low-level API: at the time of writing, the status of JSR 107 is inactive, and it has been since 2001.

Google's support for the API could be a first step to a revival of the standardization process. If this is the case, a 2001 standard could use an update using features introduced in Java 5 and 6. Anticipating such an update, this book should not spend too much time on the old API.

Summary

This chapter discussed Google's memcache service and its low-level API for the App Engine. The chapter showed that, by itself, the API is relatively easy to use. However, it also explained that the bigger picture may be more complicated. It provided pointers of how memcache fits in a larger caching strategy that also uses proxies and browser caches. Then it worked out the details of the strategy, discussing how the appropriate granularity of your caching in memcache depends on your application. The chapter contained some warnings on implementing the serializable interface. When you need fine-grained caching, it is preferable to cache datastore entities directly. The chapter ended with some maintenance and utility methods. Although Google also provides an alternative API supporting JSR 107, the low-level API is preferable.

Chapter 15

Retrieving External Data Using URL Fetch

The App Engine does not allow you to set up your own socket connections to the outside world. It does allow you to perform HTTP requests on other servers, though. This chapter starts by showing that the basic URL connections in the Java language can also work on the Google App Engine. Then it shows how you can get more control over your HTTP connection using the low-level API. There is example code for how to post forms, handle exceptions, and fetch URLs asynchronously. The chapter ends with a discussion of how to reach web services, and it provides a few disclaimers on connection security.

Reading URLs Using GET Requests

The simplest use case of the URL Fetch API is to read data from another web server. In terms of HTTP, this means sending a `GET` request and reading the data returned by the server. The App Engine provides two APIs: the standard URL API and the low-level API.

When you reuse libraries and frameworks on the App Engine, some will work and some will require modification, depending mostly on whether or not the APIs they use are on Google's JRE (Java Runtime Environment) class white list. The full white list can be found at http://code.google.com/appengine/docs/java/jrewhitelist.html.

These libraries may use classes that connect to the outside world or classes that spawn their own threads. Later in this chapter, you'll learn that the App Engine helps you out with the single-threaded model when it comes to fetching URLs, which does require the low-level API.

Some libraries and frameworks create connections to the outside world, have no knowledge of the App Engine–specific APIs, and nevertheless work! The reason they work is that Google provides support for some standard APIs.

Using the Standard URL Fetch API

Google supports the `URL` and `URLConnection` classes from the standard Java API. The remainder of this chapter also refers to these classes as the *standard URL Fetch API*.

Listing 15.1 shows the use of the URL class and directly opening an InputStream from this class. This code loads a Really Simple Syndication (RSS) feed from a news site and passes it to the client as is.

Listing 15.1 **Retrieving Data Using the Standard URL Fetch API**

```
package com.appspot.urlfetch;

import javax.servlet.ServletException;
import javax.servlet.http.HttpServlet;
import javax.servlet.http.HttpServletRequest;
import javax.servlet.http.HttpServletResponse;
import java.io.IOException;
import java.io.InputStream;
import java.io.OutputStream;
import java.net.URL;

public class SimpleURLServlet extends HttpServlet {

  private static final long serialVersionUID = 5618163722864625730L;

  public void doGet(HttpServletRequest request,
                    HttpServletResponse response)
      throws ServletException, IOException {

    URL url  = new URL(
    "http://www.nu.nl/feeds/rss/algemeen.rss");

    InputStream inputStream = url.openStream();
    inputStreamToOutputStream(inputStream,
        response.getOutputStream());
  }

  public void inputStreamToOutputStream(InputStream inputStream,
                                        OutputStream outputStream)
          throws IOException {

    byte[] buffer = new byte[1024];
    int length;

    while ((length = inputStream.read(buffer)) >= 0) {
      outputStream.write(buffer, 0, length);
    }

    inputStream.close();
  }
}
```

Lines 28 through 40 read the `InputStream` as if the content were returned in a streaming format. In reality, as the low-level API examples will point out later, underneath, the Google APIs fetch one large byte array. In such cases, `InputStream` adds more overhead instead of helping efficient processing of larger files.

If you want to do more sophisticated HTTP requests, like `POST`, `PUT`, and `DELETE`, you can use the `URLConnection` class just as you would outside the App Engine.

Using the Low-Level URL Fetch API

Given the wide adoption of the standard URL Fetch API, there are good arguments to keep using them on the App Engine. When you start using the low-level API, you still need the `URL` class to specify the address of the request, so parts of the class loading overhead arguments made in other chapters are not valid here.

Still, the remainder of this chapter chooses the low-level API over the standard APIs because they offer a bit more control and a bit less overhead; the standard URL Fetch API is sufficiently documented elsewhere; and, last but not least, the low-level API provides the option to execute asynchronous requests. Asynchronous requests may improve response times by executing multiple tasks or requests to backends at the same time.

Listing 15.2 provides exactly the same functionality as Listing 15.1 using the low-level API.

Listing 15.2 **Retrieving Data Using the Low-Level URL Fetch API**

```
package com.appspot.urlfetch;

import com.google.appengine.api.urlfetch.HTTPResponse;
import com.google.appengine.api.urlfetch.URLFetchService;
import com.google.appengine.api.urlfetch.URLFetchServiceFactory;

import javax.servlet.ServletException;
import javax.servlet.http.HttpServlet;
import javax.servlet.http.HttpServletRequest;
import javax.servlet.http.HttpServletResponse;
import java.io.IOException;
import java.net.URL;

public class SyncUrlFetchServlet extends HttpServlet {

  private static final long serialVersionUID = -7935354695645343971L;

  public void doGet(HttpServletRequest request,
                    HttpServletResponse response)
      throws ServletException, IOException {
    URLFetchService urlfetch = URLFetchServiceFactory
        .getURLFetchService();

```

(Continues)

Listing 15.2 **Retrieving Data Using the Low-Level URL Fetch API (Continued)**

```
        URL url   = new URL(
        "http://www.nu.nl/feeds/rss/algemeen.rss");

        HTTPResponse httpResponse = urlfetch.fetch(url);
        response.getOutputStream().write(
            httpResponse.getContent());
    }
}
```

The most noticeable difference between Listing 15.1 and Listing 15.2 is that the low-level API reads the result of the HTTP request in one piece: a byte array. This can also be written in one piece, saving a few lines of code.

Reading Results

The first two examples focus on using the standard URL Fetch API and the low-level APIs themselves and pay no attention to the interpretation of the results. Those are passed to the client as is. In most real-world scenarios, this is not what you want, though. You want to interpret data and integrate them into your own pages.

You must make a few design choices here. How you read the data depends on what kind of data you are reading. How you store the data depends on whether you are requesting URLs on the fly or whether the code is executed in a background task, either scheduled or queued.

Interpreting Results

How you interpret results depends on the format of the data you are loading. For example, if you are reading a comma-separated values (CSV) file, you may consider reading the content manually using Java's I/O APIs.

In most cases, the content you retrieve is in JavaScript Object Notation (JSON), XML, or HTML format. JSON and HTML are relatively forgiving data formats.

In the case of XML, the well-formedness and validity may be questionable. When you are fairly sure that you are receiving a well-formed and valid XML file, it is most efficient to interpret the data using a Simple API for XML (SAX) parser. If you write your handlers carefully, SAX parsers use a minimum of memory and processor resources.

When dealing with XML of questionable quality or with HTML, using a default SAX parser will not work for you. In such cases, you have two options.

If you have simple files or want to extract only a very specific part of the file, you can consider using regular expressions and parse the text yourself.

If you still prefer SAX parsing but you cannot be sure of the quality of the input, you can use a library called Tag Soup (http://ccil.org/~cowan/XML/tagsoup/). This library behaves like a standard SAX parser, with the difference that it takes broken files and tries to fix them, much like most browsers do with broken HTML.

Writing to Memory Cache

There are many reasons why you want to cache results from a URL fetch when they are reusable on subsequent requests by other users. Fetching URLs is relatively slow, there are quotas on the number of URLs you can fetch for free, and you may want to spare the resources of the server you are fetching from.

When URLs are fetched on the fly, within the context of directly handling requests of website visitors, the memory cache introduced in Chapter 14 is the most appropriate place to store the results from the URL fetch. It is most efficient to store the results after some processing takes place. When fetching URLs, you do not require the reliability offered by the datastore. If the memory cache fails, the machine can fetch the URL again. In the rare case that you cannot fetch the content of the URL a second time, you should consider the datastore.

Writing to the Datastore

For general performance, it is better to fetch URLs from tasks either scheduled or queued than it is to fetch URLs within an end user request. Doing so requires a level of predictability of which URLs should be fetched and when. If you can predict this or settle on a fixed time and date, you may want a more reliable storage than the memory cache. When executing inside a task, you can easily overcome the penalty of writing to the datastore.

Later, when reading the fetched data from the datastore, you can always introduce an additional level of memory caching to relieve the datastore. Writing to the datastore is discussed in Chapter 10, "Storing Data in the Datastore and Blobstore."

Adding Options to URL Fetch

Listing 15.2 provided only a basic mechanism to perform `GET` requests. In most cases, you want more control over your requests. This section discusses additional options you can set on the request object.

Controlling Timeouts

Regardless whether you are fetching URLs from a task or from a request by a website visitor, you always have to finish your work within the App Engine's request timeout limit. To accomplish this, it helps if you have some control over the time your URL fetch requests take to return. Sometimes it is better to have no results, explicitly find out that you don't have any, and act accordingly. If you allow a request to be killed by the App Engine timeout, there is no way to provide appropriate exception handling.

Listing 15.3 shows how to fetch the same RSS feed as in the first two examples but with a few extra options. Most important is the timeout of 0.2 minutes.

Listing 15.3 **Adding Options to URL Fetching**

```
package com.appspot.urlfetch;

import com.google.appengine.api.urlfetch.HTTPRequest;
import com.google.appengine.api.urlfetch.HTTPResponse;
import com.google.appengine.api.urlfetch.URLFetchService;
import com.google.appengine.api.urlfetch.URLFetchServiceFactory;

import javax.servlet.ServletException;
import javax.servlet.http.HttpServlet;
import javax.servlet.http.HttpServletRequest;
import javax.servlet.http.HttpServletResponse;
import java.io.IOException;
import java.net.URL;

import static com.google.appengine.api.urlfetch.FetchOptions
                                            .Builder.withDeadline;
import static com.google.appengine.api.urlfetch.HTTPMethod.GET;

public class FetchOptionsServlet extends HttpServlet {

  private static final long serialVersionUID = -7935354695645343971L;

  public void doGet(HttpServletRequest request,
                    HttpServletResponse response)
      throws ServletException, IOException {
    URLFetchService urlfetch = URLFetchServiceFactory
        .getURLFetchService();

    URL url = new URL(
        "http://www.nu.nl/feeds/rss/algemeen.rss");
    HTTPRequest httpRequest = new HTTPRequest(url, GET,
        withDeadline(0.2).doNotFollowRedirects().allowTruncate());

    //or doNotFollowRedirects().setDeadline(0.2) - mind the change
    //from 'with' to 'set'

    HTTPResponse httpResponse = urlfetch.fetch(httpRequest);
    response.getOutputStream().write(
        httpResponse.getContent());
  }
}
```

In addition to the timeout option, the example tells the request *not* to follow redirects and to truncate the result. If you want some level of certainty from which server your results come, it is better not to follow redirects and to log an error in the event of a `301` or `302`. Truncating results helps to avoid `ResultTooLargeExceptions`.

Handling Exceptions Gracefully

To this point, all examples throw their exceptions directly to the end user. Logging is taken care of by default. The user of the service is left with a meaningless error.

Listing 15.4 shows how to take more control over exception handling. The error sent to the user is not too friendly—but it is within your control. You can easily imagine how you can replace this code with a more elaborate template providing a user-friendly message.

Listing 15.4 **Handling Exceptions with Special Care**

```
package com.appspot.urlfetch;

import com.google.appengine.api.urlfetch.*;

import javax.servlet.ServletException;
import javax.servlet.http.HttpServlet;
import javax.servlet.http.HttpServletRequest;
import javax.servlet.http.HttpServletResponse;
import java.io.IOException;
import java.net.MalformedURLException;
import java.net.URL;
import java.util.logging.Level;
import java.util.logging.Logger;

import static com.google.appengine.api.urlfetch.FetchOptions.Builder
    .withDeadline;
import static com.google.appengine.api.urlfetch.HTTPMethod.GET;
import static javax.servlet.http.HttpServletResponse
    .SC_BAD_GATEWAY;
import static javax.servlet.http.HttpServletResponse
    .SC_INTERNAL_SERVER_ERROR;

public class GracefulExceptionServlet extends HttpServlet {
  private static Logger LOG =
      Logger.getLogger("GracefulExceptionServlet");
  private static final long serialVersionUID = -6206244619884O5858L;

  public void doGet(HttpServletRequest request,
                    HttpServletResponse response)
      throws ServletException, IOException {
    String result = null;
    try {
      URLFetchService urlfetch = URLFetchServiceFactory
```

(Continues)

Listing 15.4 **Handling Exceptions with Special Care (Continued)**

```
          .getURLFetchService();

      URL url = new URL(
          "http://www.nu.nl/feeds/rss/algemeen.rss");
      HTTPRequest httpRequest = new HTTPRequest(url, GET,
          withDeadline(0.2).followRedirects().allowTruncate());

      HTTPResponse httpResponse = urlfetch.fetch(httpRequest);
      result = new String(httpResponse.getContent());

    } catch (MalformedURLException e) {
      //severe: This is a programming error, not an incident
      LOG.log(Level.SEVERE, "URL cannot be parsed", e);
      result = "<error>Internal error in the application</error>";
      response.setStatus(SC_INTERNAL_SERVER_ERROR);

    } catch (ResponseTooLargeException e) {
      //severe: allowTruncate should prevent this
      LOG.log(Level.SEVERE, "Response larger than 1MB", e);
      result = "<error>Internal error in the application</error>";
      response.setStatus(SC_INTERNAL_SERVER_ERROR);

    } catch (IOException e) {
      //minor: could happen all the time!
      LOG.log(Level.WARNING, "Feed unavailable", e);
      result = "<error>External feed unavailable</error>";
      response.setStatus(SC_BAD_GATEWAY);

    } finally {

      response.getWriter().write(result);
    }
  }
}
```

This example includes the writing process at the end of the request so it can write both successful results as well as errors.

In the exception handling routines, you see that different exceptions are logged at different levels of severity to distinguish programming errors from regular failures.

The example also shows that you can use HTTP status codes to indicate the nature of the problem back to the client. Because the example usually passes an RSS feed as is, there are good arguments to return a `502` HTTP status code (bad gateway) in case of a communication failure.

Posting Form Data

Sending an HTTP `POST` request is not much harder than sending a `GET` request, with the exception of setting URL parameters. When using a `POST` request, the query string is provided separately after the connection is opened.

When using the HTTPS protocol, `POST` requests have the advantage that the query string as a payload is sent over the line in encrypted format. Using `GET` requests, all parameters are sent over the line unencrypted regardless of the HTTPS protocol.

Listing 15.5 shows how to send a `POST` request and provide a payload. It calls a simple form on the TinyURL site. This site allows you to create short aliases for longer URLs.

Listing 15.5 **Posting Form Data Using the Low-Level API**

```
package com.appspot.urlfetch;

import com.google.appengine.api.urlfetch.*;

import javax.servlet.ServletException;
import javax.servlet.http.HttpServlet;
import javax.servlet.http.HttpServletRequest;
import javax.servlet.http.HttpServletResponse;
import java.io.IOException;
import java.net.URL;
import java.net.URLEncoder;

import static com.google.appengine.api.urlfetch.HTTPMethod.*;

public class SyncUrlPostServlet extends HttpServlet {

  private static final long serialVersionUID = -7935354695645343971L;

  public void doGet(HttpServletRequest request,
                    HttpServletResponse response)
      throws ServletException, IOException {
    URLFetchService urlfetch = URLFetchServiceFactory
        .getURLFetchService();

    URL url  = new URL(
    "http://tinyurl.com/create.php");



    HTTPRequest httpRequest = new HTTPRequest(url, POST);
    httpRequest.setPayload(("url=" +
        URLEncoder.encode("http://nu.nl", "UTF-8")).getBytes());

```

(Continues)

Listing 15.5 **Posting Form Data Using the Low-Level API (Continued)**

```

    HTTPResponse httpResponse = urlfetch.fetch(httpRequest);
    response.getOutputStream().write(
        httpResponse.getContent());
  }
}
```

Perhaps this particular news site is not a good example of a long URL that needs abbreviation. The principle should be clear from this code, though. The tough part of this code is that the payload requires a byte array, but the query string is set as a string. In addition, URL parameter values should be URL encoded. The example uses UTF-8 as the encoding scheme for the byte conversion.

Fetching URLs Asynchronously

Early releases of the Google App Engine were designed using a single-threaded model. The main exception to this rule so far is the capability to add tasks to a queue and have them executed simultaneously.

Over time, Google added more and more functionality for multithreaded execution of code. With the low-level URL Fetch API, you can fetch multiple URLs simultaneously, or you can fetch a single URL and do something else while the App Engine is loading it for you.

Listing 15.6 shows how this multithreaded model works with a simple example loading a single URL and code that sleeps while the URL is loading. You can imagine that instead of sleeping, the code could also send Extensible Messaging and Presence Protocol (XMPP) messages to the owner of the website you are loading from to complain how slow the server is. Sending XMPP messages is discussed in Chapter 17.

Listing 15.6 **Fetching Responses Asynchronously**

```
package com.appspot.urlfetch;

import com.google.appengine.api.urlfetch.HTTPResponse;
import com.google.appengine.api.urlfetch.URLFetchService;
import com.google.appengine.api.urlfetch.URLFetchServiceFactory;

import javax.servlet.ServletException;
import javax.servlet.http.HttpServlet;
import javax.servlet.http.HttpServletRequest;
import javax.servlet.http.HttpServletResponse;
import java.io.IOException;
import java.net.URL;
import java.util.concurrent.ExecutionException;
import java.util.concurrent.Future;
import java.util.logging.Logger;
```

Listing 15.6 **Fetching Responses Asynchronously (Continued)**

```
16
17 public class ASyncUrlFetchServlet extends HttpServlet {
18
19   private static final long serialVersionUID = -793535469564534397L;
20
21   public void doGet(HttpServletRequest request,
22                     HttpServletResponse response)
23       throws ServletException, IOException {
24     URLFetchService urlfetch = URLFetchServiceFactory
25         .getURLFetchService();
26
27     URL url  = new URL(
28     "http://www.nu.nl/feeds/rss/algemeen.rss");
29
30     Future<HTTPResponse> future = urlfetch.fetchAsync(url);
31
32     while(!future.isDone()) {
33       try {
34         Thread.sleep(10);
35       } catch (InterruptedException e) {
36         throw new ServletException(e);
37       }
38     }
39     HTTPResponse httpResponse;
40     try {
41
42       httpResponse = future.get();
43       response.getOutputStream().write(
44         httpResponse.getContent());
45
46     } catch (InterruptedException e) {
47       throw new ServletException(e);
48     } catch (ExecutionException e) {
49       throw new ServletException(e);
50     }
51
52
53   }
54 }
```

In this code, you see that the low-level URL Fetch API returns a `Future` object. The code on line 30 can be repeated to fetch multiple (up to 10) URLs simultaneously. The `while` loop becomes a bit more complicated then. The exact setup depends on whether you want to wait for all URLs to finish loading or you want to start processing after receiving the first URL.

More information on `Future` objects can be found in Oracle's Java API documentation: http://download.oracle.com/javase/6/docs/api/java/util/concurrent/Future.html.

You can reuse the exception handlers from Listing 15.4 unchanged if you want to improve exception handling. The `Future` object does not prevent the API from throwing the same exceptions.

Consuming Web Services

Instead of receiving data, you can also use the low-level URL Fetch API to access web services running on remote machines. The only difference is that web service requests are more likely to be associated with one specific user. This reduces the possibilities for caching results. Other than that, most web services are simple HTTP requests.

Accessing RESTful Services

It would take a long text to explain how to design a Representational State Transfer (REST)ful service. There are many subtleties in the design of descriptive resources and caching strategies.

Consuming a RESTful service is a different story. Basically, it is as simple as this: you have a URL, and you can perform either a `POST`, `GET`, `PUT`, or `DELETE` on the URL. In most cases, the respective meanings of these operations on a resource are `CREATE`, `READ`, `UPDATE`, and `DELETE`.

The hardest part is client authentication. Originally, RESTful services used HTTP authentication. More recent services use protocols such as OAuth. OAuth is discussed further in Chapter 16, "Securing a Web Application Using Google Accounts, OpenID, and OAuth."

Communicating with SOAP

On the open Internet, Simple Object Access Protocol (SOAP) web services are becoming less popular. Many SOAP services are being slowly replaced with RESTful alternatives using either XML or JSON as a data format.

SOAP is still popular within company walls to connect to backend systems. Perhaps you are designing an App Engine application that needs to connect to a SOAP web service.

At the time of writing, the usual web service APIs like Axis and Metro do not work on the App Engine, but there are feature requests to correct this limitation.

In the meantime, you can send SOAP requests manually. After all, SOAP is not much more than standardized XML as the payload of an HTTP `POST` request. Creating a simple SOAP request should not be problematic after reading this chapter. Supporting the larger WS-* stack with all subtleties and security mechanisms may be a bit more challenging. though.

Considering Security

It would not be inappropriate to quote Jack Sparrow again, as Chapter 14 does in reference to the memcache. You can trust the App Engine to be untrustworthy when it comes to securing connections.

Using HTTPS

You can access servers using the HTTPS protocol. However, there is currently no mechanism to check the validity of a server certificate. The App Engine accepts self-signed certificates. This means that the App Engine may be prone to man-in-the-middle attacks. This should be given serious consideration before you start setting up critical communication channels from the App Engine.

Using Open Ports

The App Engine does not allow you to access every port using the HTTP protocol. The range of ports that is allowed is not too restrictive however. The full range is 80 to 90, 440 to 450, and 1024 to 65535.

Summary

This chapter introduced the mechanisms for fetching URLs on the Google App Engine. The chapter started with the Java standard classes `URL` and `URLConnection` that help the reusability of existing libraries and frameworks to run on the App Engine. The remainder of the chapter used the low-level API. After a simple introduction, options were added to the requests, `POST` requests were made, and exceptions were handled gracefully. Next, the chapter introduced a mechanism allowing you to fetch up to 10 URLs simultaneously in a background thread while your code may continue with other actions. The chapter ended with a discussion of how to consume web services, and it provided some security considerations.

Chapter 16

Securing a Web Application Using Google Accounts, OpenID, and OAuth

This chapter presents Google's APIs for authenticating users and authorizing access by third parties. It starts by explaining Google Accounts API then discusses the use of OpenID for external identity providers. The OAuth API, which allows your application to securely expose data to third-party applications, is demonstrated next. This chapter ends with a brief discussion of general security concerns specific to the App Engine.

Authenticating Users with Google Accounts

In most web applications, you want to be able to store data for your users. You also want to be sure that users cannot read or modify each other's data. Even when users' data is of a public nature, you want to be fairly sure that writers of that data are who they claim to be.

The level of certainty you desire depends on your application. For basic authentication, Google provides an API that allows authentication using Google Accounts. It provides only a limited level of certainty about your user's identity but allows you to be reasonably sure that the next time the user logs in, it is the same user as last time. And you can be sure that the Gmail address really belongs to this user.

Listing 16.1 demonstrates how you can check whether a user is logged in, how to create a link to log in and log out, and how to fetch an e-mail address and user ID.

Listing 16.1 **Displaying Information on the User Currently Logged In**

```
package com.appspot.security;

import com.google.appengine.api.users.User;
import com.google.appengine.api.users.UserService;
import com.google.appengine.api.users.UserServiceFactory;
```

(Continues)

Listing 16.1 **Displaying Information on the User Currently Logged In (Continued)**

```
06 import org.antlr.stringtemplate.StringTemplate;
07 import org.antlr.stringtemplate.StringTemplateGroup;
08
09 import javax.servlet.ServletException;
10 import javax.servlet.http.HttpServlet;
11 import javax.servlet.http.HttpServletRequest;
12 import javax.servlet.http.HttpServletResponse;
13 import java.io.IOException;
14
15 public class CheckUserServlet extends HttpServlet {
16   @Override
17   protected void doGet(HttpServletRequest request,
18                        HttpServletResponse response)
19       throws ServletException, IOException {
20
21     StringTemplateGroup group = new StringTemplateGroup("xhtml",
22             "WEB-INF/templates/xhtml");
23
24     UserService userService = UserServiceFactory.getUserService();
25
26     if(userService.isUserLoggedIn()) {
27       User user = userService.getCurrentUser();
28       String url = userService.createLogoutURL(
29           request.getRequestURI());
30       StringTemplate template = group.getInstanceOf("logged-in");
31       template.setAttribute("user", user);
32       template.setAttribute("url", url);
33       response.getWriter().write(template.toString());
34
35     } else {
36       String url = userService.createLoginURL(
37                request.getRequestURI());
38       StringTemplate template = group.getInstanceOf("logged-out");
39       template.setAttribute("url", url);
40       response.getWriter().write(template.toString());
41     }
42   }
43 }
```

Line 26 uses `UserService` to check whether the user is logged in. An alternative for line 26 is to read `request.getUserPrincipal()`. The advantage of `UserService` is that it provides more detail. You can also check whether the user has admin privileges.

If `isUserLoggedIn` is false, lines 36 through 40 provide the visitor with a screen containing a login URL. In a real-world example, you could do more than just display a login URL. You could have two versions of a page: one general page with basic information, nothing specific or confidential, and one personalized page containing user-specific details or modifications based on preferences. Listing 16.2 provides the HTML template for the resulting screen.

Listing 16.2 **Displaying a Login URL in HTML**

```
<html>
<body>
<h1>Not Logged In</h1>
<p><a href="$url$">Click here to log in</a></p>
</body>
</html>
```

If the user is logged in already, lines 27 through 33 of Listing 16.1 provide the visitor with a page presenting the details known to the web application. The page with details also contains a link the visitor can use to log out of the web application. Listing 16.3 shows the HTML template for presenting the user details.

Listing 16.3 **Displaying User Details and a Logout URL in HTML**

```
<html>
<body>
<h1>Logged In as $user.nickname$</h1>
<p>EMail: $user.email$</p>
<p>User ID: $user.userId$</p>
<p>Federated ID: $user.federatedIdentity$</p>
<p>Authentication Domain: $user.authDomain$</p>
<p><a href="$url$">Click here to log out</a></p>
</body>
</html>
```

The Google Accounts API works both on the development server and in production. On the development server, you can enter a fake e-mail address and no password is required. On production, you can use your own Google account to log in. The resulting screen on production is shown in Figure 16.1.

You can configure your app to accept any Google account, or you can limit the users to accounts from your own Google App domain.

If you need to store information about the user accessing your system, you should consider storing the e-mail address because it seems the most constant factor when switching between multiple authentication and authorization mechanisms.

Figure 16.1 The resulting screen after login using Google Accounts.

Authenticating Users with OpenID

You may not always want to be restricted to Google Accounts. Despite the wide availability of Gmail accounts, some people use Hotmail, Yahoo!, or an e-mail address from their own provider. These visitors may not have a Google account. You do not want to lose customers over that.

In some cases, you may require a higher authentication level. As long as you keep in mind that OpenID may not be the safest authentication protocol existing today, it may help improve security at least one step beyond the Google Accounts.

OpenID allows you to verify your user's identity with third-party external identity providers. When you do so, your web application becomes a so-called relying party.

Google simplifies the process of becoming a relying party by allowing you to configure it in your User API. Figure 16.2 shows how to modify the management interface to switch from Google Accounts to OpenID.

If you do not change your code, your web application will switch to the OpenID protocol but still use Google Accounts as the identity provider. Visitors may notice one extra step in the authentication process: they must confirm that the web application is allowed access to their e-mail address.

To switch to different identity providers, you must specify additional parameters. Listing 16.4 provides an example that uses Yahoo! accounts as the identity provider. This can be replaced by any other OpenID identity provider.

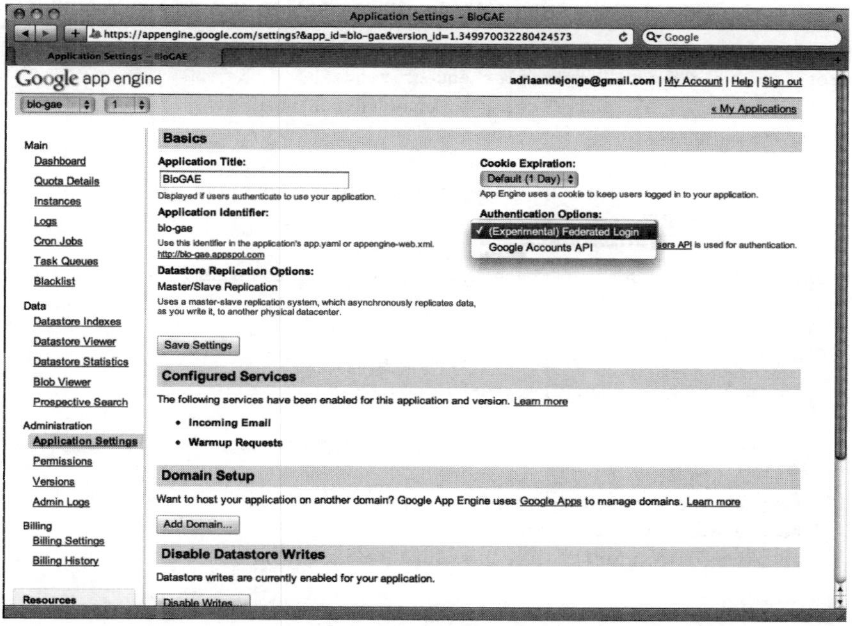

Figure 16.2 Changing the settings for login.

> **Warning**
>
> The OpenID functionality is still experimental at the time of writing. This means that the API might be subject to change.

Listing 16.4 **Logging In with a Yahoo! Account Using OpenID**

```
package com.appspot.security;

import com.google.appengine.api.users.User;
import com.google.appengine.api.users.UserService;
import com.google.appengine.api.users.UserServiceFactory;
import org.antlr.stringtemplate.StringTemplate;
import org.antlr.stringtemplate.StringTemplateGroup;

import javax.servlet.ServletException;
import javax.servlet.http.HttpServlet;
import javax.servlet.http.HttpServletRequest;
import javax.servlet.http.HttpServletResponse;
import java.io.IOException;

public class CheckFederatedServlet extends HttpServlet {
```

(Continues)

Listing 16.4 **Logging In with a Yahoo! Account Using OpenID (Continued)**

```
16    @Override
17    protected void doGet(HttpServletRequest request,
18                         HttpServletResponse response)
19        throws ServletException, IOException {
20
21      StringTemplateGroup group = new StringTemplateGroup("xhtml",
22              "WEB-INF/templates/xhtml");
23
24      UserService userService = UserServiceFactory.getUserService();
25
26      if(userService.isUserLoggedIn()) {
27        User user = userService.getCurrentUser();
28        String url = userService.createLogoutURL(
29            request.getRequestURI());
30        StringTemplate template = group.getInstanceOf("logged-in");
31
32        template.setAttribute("user", user);
33        template.setAttribute("url", url);
34        response.getWriter().write(template.toString());
35
36      } else {
37        String url = userService.createLoginURL(
38            request.getRequestURI(),
39            null,
40            "yahoo.com",
41            null);
42        StringTemplate template = group.getInstanceOf("logged-out");
43        template.setAttribute("url", url);
44        response.getWriter().write(template.toString());
45      }
46    }
47  }
```

The differences between this code and Listing 16.1 are in lines 37 through 41. The rest of the code remains unchanged. To connect with a Yahoo! account, you only need to provide yahoo.com as a federated identity parameter, as demonstrated on line 40.

When you deploy this servlet on production, the visitor is redirected to Yahoo! and, after logging in, receives a screen similar to the one displayed in Figure 16.3.

At the time of writing, the User API does not implement all OpenID features. For example, it is not yet possible to acquire more user details (attributes) from the identity provider. Judging from the availability of an `attributesRequest` parameter in the API (line 41, currently set to `null` because it does not work), this might change in later implementations.

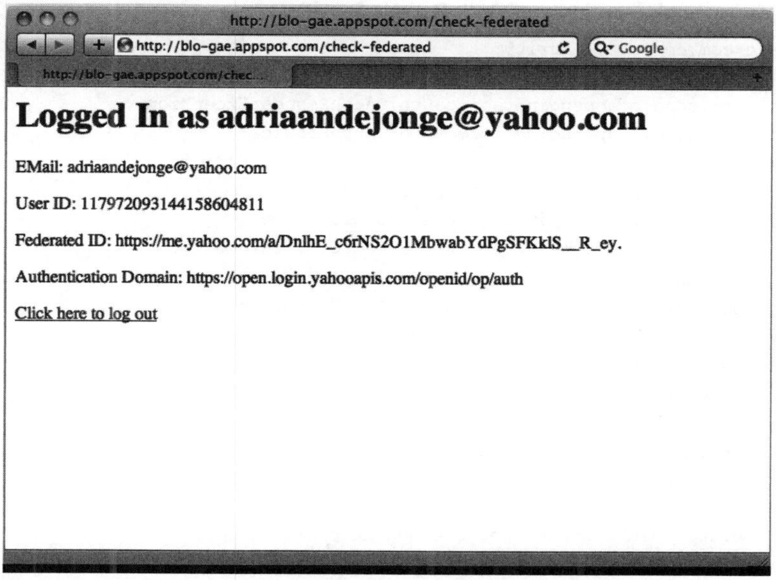

Figure 16.3 The resulting screen after login using OpenID.

Providing Access to Third Parties Using OAuth

OpenID is used to authenticate human users. OAuth can be used to grant access to machines working on behalf of a human user. In general, OAuth makes it possible to work with fine-grained authorizations, allowing users to specify exactly which data an application can or cannot access.

A common scenario is Facebook applications asking permission to post and read data from a Facebook account. Applications in the Google Marketplace that are designed to cooperate with Google Apps work in a similar way.

Your App Engine application may contain data that is valuable to other applications. Google provides an API that helps you make your data available in a secure way using OAuth.

> **Warning**
>
> The OAuth functionality is still experimental at the time of writing. This means that the API might be subject to change.

Listing 16.5 demonstrates how to check whether a data consumer is properly authorized by a user to access his data.

Listing 16.5 **Implementing an OAuth Service Provider**

```
01 package com.appspot.security;
02
03 import com.google.appengine.api.oauth.OAuthRequestException;
04 import com.google.appengine.api.oauth.OAuthService;
05 import com.google.appengine.api.oauth.OAuthServiceFactory;
06 import com.google.appengine.api.users.User;
07 import com.google.appengine.api.users.UserService;
08 import com.google.appengine.api.users.UserServiceFactory;
09 import org.antlr.stringtemplate.StringTemplate;
10 import org.antlr.stringtemplate.StringTemplateGroup;
11
12 import javax.servlet.ServletException;
13 import javax.servlet.http.HttpServlet;
14 import javax.servlet.http.HttpServletRequest;
15 import javax.servlet.http.HttpServletResponse;
16 import java.io.IOException;
17
18 public class CheckOAuthServlet extends HttpServlet {
19   @Override
20   protected void doGet(HttpServletRequest request,
21                        HttpServletResponse response)
22       throws ServletException, IOException {
23
24     StringTemplateGroup group = new StringTemplateGroup("xhtml",
25             "WEB-INF/templates/xhtml");
26
27     OAuthService oauthService = OAuthServiceFactory
28         .getOAuthService();
29
30     try {
31       User user = oauthService.getCurrentUser();
32       StringTemplate template = group.getInstanceOf("oauth");
33       template.setAttribute("user", user);
34       response.getWriter().write(template.toString());
35
36     } catch (OAuthRequestException e) {
37       response.setStatus(401);
38     }
39   }
40 }
```

Line 31 retrieves the user on behalf of whom the consumer is fetching data. The full authorization process is handled under the hood by Google using the following URLs (replace *app-id* with your own application identifier):

https://app-id.appspot.com/_ah/OAuthGetRequestToken
https://app-id.appspot.com/_ah/OAuthAuthorizeToken
https://app-id.appspot.com/_ah/OAuthGetAccessToken

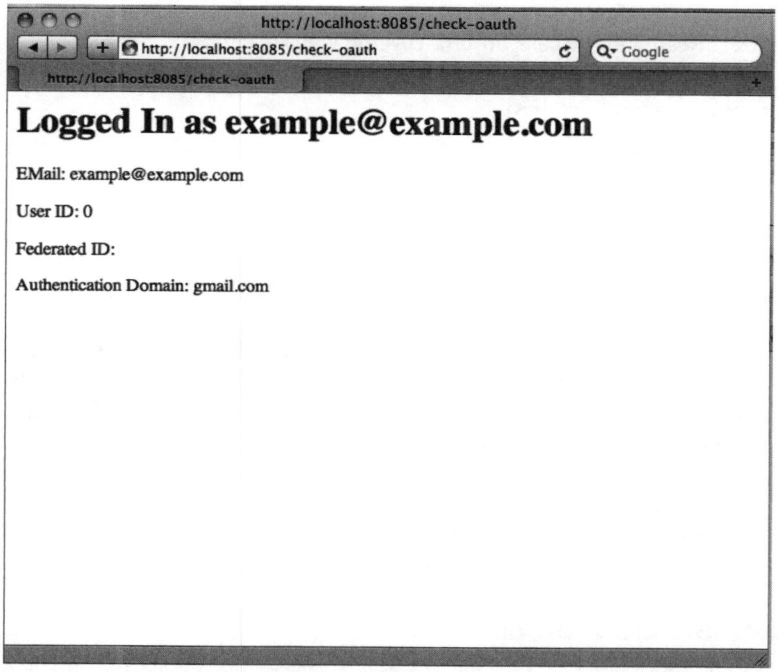

Figure 16.4 The resulting screen for OAuth in the development environment.

You need not worry about their implementation. Using `OAuthService`, you can check whether the authorization process has taken place. In Figure 16.4, you can see the result of this code in the development environment. In production, you need a consumer API to test the OAuth process.

OAuth is a subject that may require more explanation beyond the scope of this book. You can find more information on the OAuth website at http://oauth.net/.

Securing URLs in web.xml

Up to this point, you have seen code that checks whether a user has logged in. This allows hybrid scenarios in which the application can serve both users who have logged in and users who have not yet logged in. You can also enforce authentication before the user reaches the servlet by modifying web.xml.

Enforcing Authentication

In some cases, you want to restrict access to URLs on a more central level and make sure users who have not logged in cannot access them at all. Listing 16.6 demonstrates how you can modify web.xml to restrict access to do so.

Listing 16.6 **Restricting Access on URL Level in web.xml**

```
01 <security-constraint>
02   <web-resource-collection>
03     <url-pattern>/my-url/*</url-pattern>
04   </web-resource-collection>
05   <auth-constraint>
06     <role-name>*</role-name>
07   </auth-constraint>
08 </security-constraint>
```

On line 6, the role-name is `*`, meaning both admin and normal users can access the web application. If you want to restrict access to admin level, you can replace the `*` with the word `admin`. This way of access control is used in Chapter 12 for scheduling tasks and assuring tasks are scheduled only by the system or by an administrator. The URL restriction prevents the resources from being manipulated by anonymous users or users without admin privileges.

You can add other Google Accounts to your group of administrators using the App Engine configuration dashboard under the Permissions tab.

Enforcing Secure Protocols

For data to be confidential, it must be sent over a secure line, which means the App Engine should be accessed using HTTPS instead of HTTP.

When your application runs on the *.appspot.com domain and not on a custom domain, by default, you can use both HTTP and HTTPS. You can turn off access using HTTPS in appengine-web.xml, but that does not help the security of your web application.

It makes more sense to enforce the use of HTTPS for URLs where sensitive data is exchanged. Listing 16.7 demonstrates how to enforce HTTPS for certain URLs.

Listing 16.7 **Enforcing Confidential Communication on URL Level**

```
<security-constraint>
  <web-resource-collection>
    <url-pattern>/my-url/*</url-pattern>
  </web-resource-collection>
 <user-data-constraint>
    <transport-guarantee>CONFIDENTIAL</transport-guarantee>
  </user-data-constraint>
</security-constraint>
```

> **Warning**
>
> At the time of writing, if you are using a custom domain instead of an *.appspot.com domain, you cannot use HTTPS on the domain itself. This is on the roadmap for future releases, so it will improve later on. Until then, make a clear distinction between confidential and public data and switch to the appspot.com domain when secure communication is necessary.

Security Considerations

Google Accounts, OpenID, and Secure Sockets Layer (SSL) are useless if the rest of the application is not secure. An extensive discussion of how to secure your web application is beyond the scope of this book. Detailed documentation is available on this subject: take a look at www.owasp.org for a quick start.

Google also offers useful study material on application security with Google Gruyere, which is available at http://google-gruyere.appspot.com/.

This is a brief discussion of some security considerations specific to the Google App Engine.

Validating Input

The Google App Engine datastore does not use a query language like SQL, XQuery, or SPARQL, so there is no risk of query language injection vulnerabilities.

Remain alert, though. If you search the datastore using input parameters, those parameters could still be modified to return different data. Especially if they are `GET` parameters, even using HTTPS, the data is sent to the server unencrypted and can easily be modified.

Remain cautious of the data you are storing. It could be too large, it could contain JavaScript that gets injected in pages for other users, or someone could be uploading data that you were not expecting. For example, you could get illegal software when you were expecting an image.

Configuring Multitenancy

The App Engine datastore allows you to separate data in the datastore for multiple tenants by introducing namespaces. This subject is briefly discussed in Chapter 10, "Storing Data in the Datastore and Blobstore." You could introduce different namespaces for different users or for different domains. Be cautious, though.

Namespaces work inside the datastore, in memcache, and in the Task Queue. Namespaces do *not* work in the Blobstore! This means that you should double check data written to and read from the Blobstore and connect to the datastore for additional information on the owner of the data.

It is easy to forget setting a namespace somewhere in the code. To prevent such errors, you should consider implementing namespaces as a single `Filter` configured on all URLs instead of duplicating the code through all your servlets.

Storing Personal Data

Make sure you know government regulations on storing personal data and privacy guidelines when you start using the App Engine. For example, the European Union requires that personal data be stored and processed inside the European Union.

The App Engine may store data anywhere in the world, not only in the European Union or the United States. Some countries may not have treaties concerning privacy and personal data. Make sure you know the regulations that apply to data your application is storing in those countries.

At the time of writing, the App Engine does not allow you to control the location where data is stored. There is an open issue discussing this topic. Currently, this topic refers to a governmental website on U.S.–EU Safe Harbor Benefits. You should judge for yourself whether these regulations sufficiently address your privacy concerns.

Summary

This chapter introduced the Google User API to connect with Google Accounts to authenticate users. It demonstrated the experimental feature to replace Google Accounts with OpenID identity providers. Also, the experimental OAuth API was demonstrated. This API allows third parties to access user data from your application in a secure way. The chapter ended with a brief discussion of App Engine–specific security concerns.

Chapter 17

Sending and Receiving Messages Using XMPP

In this chapter, the Google APIs for sending and receiving XMPP messages are introduced. The chapter starts with an example that sends a message to a client that has subscribed to the App Engine's XMPP address. Next, the App Engine application is configured to receive messages, subscriptions, and presences. All of these are stored in the Google App Engine datastore for further analysis.

Sending Messages Using XMPP

Google Talk uses an open standard called XMPP (Extensible Messaging and Presence Protocol), popularly known as Jabber. This is an open standard maintained by the Internet Engineering Task Force (IETF). Google is not the only party using XMPP. For example, if you have a Facebook account and an XMPP client, you can use the XMPP client to chat on Facebook. However, Facebook does not allow direct communication with Google Talk or the Google App Engine, which makes it less interesting as an example for this chapter.

Other implementations do interconnect. If you register an account on http://jabber.org, you can exchange messages with Google Talk and Google App Engine.

Applications of XMPP are not limited to chat. Although it may be fun to implement a chat robot impersonating a human being, it makes more sense to use XMPP for other purposes. You could use the protocol to notify system administrators of changes in the server status. Depending on the client, this may still be similar to chat. You could also use XMPP for machine-to-machine communication. Some message queue servers allow XMPP (like ActiveMQ) connections. In professional environments, such connections improve the integration between the App Engine and your existing company infrastructure.

XMPP is a decentralized protocol. It is not run on a proprietary central server. Instead, as an open technology, it can be run from multiple servers that interact with each other. For example, Google Talk, jabber.org, and the Google App Engine all have XMPP servers—anyone can run an XMPP server on their own domain. An XMPP account is identified in the format username@server/resource. The username and server work similarly to e-mail. The resource is used to distinguish multiple clients, for example, the Google Talk application, Gmail, and a mobile client. The full identifier is called a JID (Jabber ID).

You can send messages to a JID without specifying the exact resource. The receiving client may or may not have set preferences for which resource the messages are sent to by default.

The Google App Engine sends messages from *app-id*@appspot.com. Listing 17.1 provides an example that sends a message to adriaandejonge@gmail.com from blo-ga@appspot.com.

Listing 17.1 **Sending a Message to a Google Talk Client Using XMPP**

```
package com.appspot.xmpp;

import com.google.appengine.api.xmpp.*;

import javax.servlet.ServletException;
import javax.servlet.http.HttpServlet;
import javax.servlet.http.HttpServletRequest;
import javax.servlet.http.HttpServletResponse;
import java.io.IOException;

public class SendXMPPServlet extends HttpServlet {
  @Override
  protected void doGet(HttpServletRequest request,
                       HttpServletResponse response)
      throws ServletException, IOException {

    JID jid = new JID("adriaandejonge@gmail.com");
    String text = "hello world";
    Message message = new MessageBuilder()
        .withRecipientJids(jid)
        .withBody(text)
        .build();

    XMPPService xmppService = XMPPServiceFactory.getXMPPService();
    if(xmppService.getPresence(jid).isAvailable()) {
      SendResponse sendResponse = xmppService.sendMessage(message);
      if(sendResponse.getStatusMap().get(jid) == SendResponse
          .Status.SUCCESS) {
```

Listing 17.1 **Sending a Message to a Google Talk Client Using XMPP (Continued)**

```
29          response.getWriter().write("OK");
30        }
31        else {
32          response.getWriter().write("NOT OK");
33        }
34
35      }  else {
36        response.getWriter().write("Unavailable");
37      }
38
39    }
40 }
```

Lines 17 through 22 set up a message with the desired recipient. Line 25 checks if the recipient is currently online. If you are communicating with Google Talk and you haven't established a connection before, the XMPP service will say the recipient is not available. Before you can exchange messages, the recipient must first be invited.

Although the XMPP service allows sending invitations, it may be preferable to let the client invite the server. Once you added the app-id@appspot.com address to the recipient's Google Talk, line 25 starts returning true when the recipient is available.

Lines 27 through 35 check the outcome after sending the message. For the example, the status is written in plain text. More sophisticated implementations are imaginable.

Figure 17.1 displays the "hello world" message as it could appear in Gmail's Google Talk client.

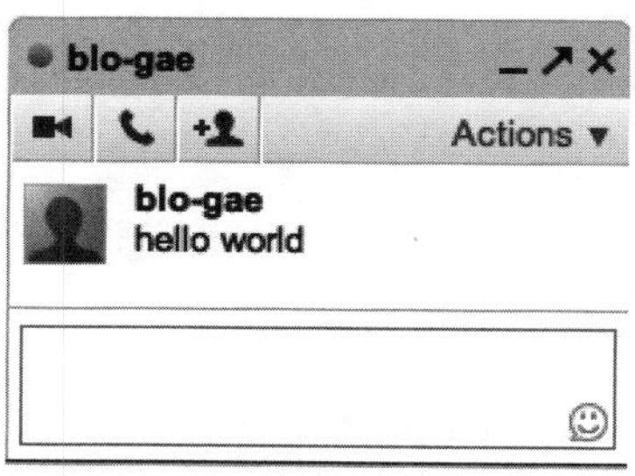

Figure 17.1 The message as it appears in Google Talk in Gmail.

Receiving Messages Using XMPP

You can receive XMPP messages by hooking up a servlet to a specific URL using web.xml, where the App Engine sends its messages to:

```
/_ah/xmpp/message/chat/
```

XMPP defines five message types: chat, error, groupchat, headline, and normal. The App Engine receives only chat messages and normal messages. Both are sent to `/_ah/xmpp/message/chat/`. The `getMessageType` method allows you to distinguish between chat messages and normal messages. Other messages are ignored.

Listing 17.2 provides an example of receiving an XMPP message and storing it to the App Engine datastore.

Listing 17.2 **Storing Received XMPP Messages in the Datastore**

```
package com.appspot.xmpp;

import com.google.appengine.api.datastore.DatastoreService;
import com.google.appengine.api.datastore.DatastoreServiceFactory;
import com.google.appengine.api.datastore.Entity;
import com.google.appengine.api.xmpp.*;

import javax.servlet.ServletException;
import javax.servlet.http.HttpServlet;
import javax.servlet.http.HttpServletRequest;
import javax.servlet.http.HttpServletResponse;
import java.io.IOException;
import java.util.Date;

public class XMPPMessageServlet extends HttpServlet {
  @Override
  protected void doPost(HttpServletRequest request,
                        HttpServletResponse response)
      throws ServletException, IOException {

    XMPPService xmppService = XMPPServiceFactory.getXMPPService();
    Message message =
        xmppService.parseMessage(request);

    DatastoreService datastoreService = DatastoreServiceFactory
        .getDatastoreService();
    Entity entity = new Entity("Message");

    StringBuilder to = new StringBuilder();
    for(JID jid : message.getRecipientJids()) {
      to.append(jid.toString());
      to.append("; ");
```

Listing 17.2 **Storing Received XMPP Messages in the Datastore (Continued)**

```
33      }
34      entity.setProperty("to", to.toString());
35
36      entity.setProperty("from", "" + message.getFromJid());
37      entity.setProperty("type", "" + message.getMessageType());
38      entity.setProperty("stanza", message.getStanza());
39      entity.setProperty("body", message.getBody());
40      entity.setProperty("xml", message.isXml());
41      entity.setProperty("created", new Date());
42
43      datastoreService.put(entity);
44    }
45 }
```

The Google XMPP API simplifies reading the XMPP message from the HTTP request by parsing it into a `Message` object, as demonstrated in lines 22 and 23.

Lines 29 through 41 copy the content of the message into a datastore entity.

To receive messages on the App Engine, you must modify appengine-web.xml similarly to how you did in Chapter 11, "Sending and Receiving E-Mail." Listing 17.3 shows how to configure the App Engine to pass on XMPP messages, presence notifications, and subscription notifications.

Listing 17.3 **Configuring Services in appengine-web.xml**

```
01 <inbound-services>
02      <service>xmpp_message</service>
03      <service>xmpp_presence</service>
04      <service>xmpp_subscribe</service>
05 </inbound-services>
```

If you are interested only in receiving the chat messages, you should remove lines 3 and 4. Similarly, if you are interested only in one or two of the other services, you could leave out any of the services you do not use.

After configuring appengine-web.xml and registering the servlet to listen at the right URL, you are ready to receive messages. Access control on the URL level is done by the App Engine without extra configuration requirements.

Figure 17.2 shows the datastore after receiving a few test messages. From this input, you can decide which fields you need to implement your application. For example, you may ignore the rough message provided in the `stanza` and just read the `body` attribute directly.

Google Talk allows voice and video connections to other Google Talk users. Voice and video connections cannot be sent to the App Engine. The Google Talk client says this right away when you try to send such messages. The Google Talk client does allow you to send a voicemail. The App Engine never receives a notification of an available voicemail, though.

Figure 17.2 The messages received and stored in the datastore.

Receiving Subscriptions

Much like the way you receive messages, your application can listen for updates in subscriptions. You can register a servlet to listen on the following URLs:

```
/_ah/xmpp/subscription/*/
```

where the * is replaced by one of the following four words, depending on the message:

- `subscribe`: Used when a client wants to subscribe. The App Engine accepts automatically in all cases.
- `subscribed`: Used when a client allows the App Engine to see his presence.
- `unsubscribe`: Used when a client is no longer interested in the presence of the App Engine.
- `unsubscribed`: Used when a client no longer allows the App Engine to see his presence.

Although these words are not really intuitive, they help to maintain a list of users who are connected to your application in their chat clients. Such a list is called a roster in XMPP terms.

Listing 17.4 logs (un)subscription notifications in the datastore, not explicitly maintaining a list of subscriptions. The list may be extracted from the subscription notifications, though.

Listing 17.4 Receiving Subscription Notifications

```
package com.appspot.xmpp;

import com.google.appengine.api.datastore.DatastoreService;
import com.google.appengine.api.datastore.DatastoreServiceFactory;
import com.google.appengine.api.datastore.Entity;
import com.google.appengine.api.users.User;
import com.google.appengine.api.users.UserService;
import com.google.appengine.api.users.UserServiceFactory;
import com.google.appengine.api.xmpp.*;

import javax.servlet.ServletException;
import javax.servlet.http.HttpServlet;
import javax.servlet.http.HttpServletRequest;
import javax.servlet.http.HttpServletResponse;
import java.io.IOException;
import java.util.Date;

public class XMPPSubscriptionServlet extends HttpServlet {
  @Override
  protected void doPost(HttpServletRequest request,
                        HttpServletResponse response)
      throws ServletException, IOException {


    String action = request.getRequestURI()
        .replaceAll("/_ah/xmpp/subscription/", "")
        .replaceAll("/", "");

    XMPPService xmppService = XMPPServiceFactory.getXMPPService();
    Subscription subscription =
        xmppService.parseSubscription(request);

    DatastoreService datastoreService = DatastoreServiceFactory
        .getDatastoreService();
    Entity entity = new Entity("Subscription");
    entity.setProperty("from", "" + subscription.getFromJid());
    entity.setProperty("to", "" + subscription.getToJid());
    entity.setProperty("type",
```

(Continues)

Listing 17.4 **Receiving Subscription Notifications (Continued)**

```
39           "" + subscription.getSubscriptionType());
40       entity.setProperty("stanza", subscription.getStanza());
41       entity.setProperty("created", new Date());
42       entity.setProperty("action", action);
43
44       datastoreService.put(entity);
45     }
46 }
```

Lines 25, 26, and 27 interpret the last part of the URL that the request is sent to. The servlet is configured to listen to all four possible URLs. This can be done using a wild card in the web.xml, as shown in Listing 17.5.

Lines 33 through 44 of Listing 17.4 store all available fields from the interpreted `Subscription` object.

Figure 17.3 displays the datastore administration interface after receiving a number of subscription messages.

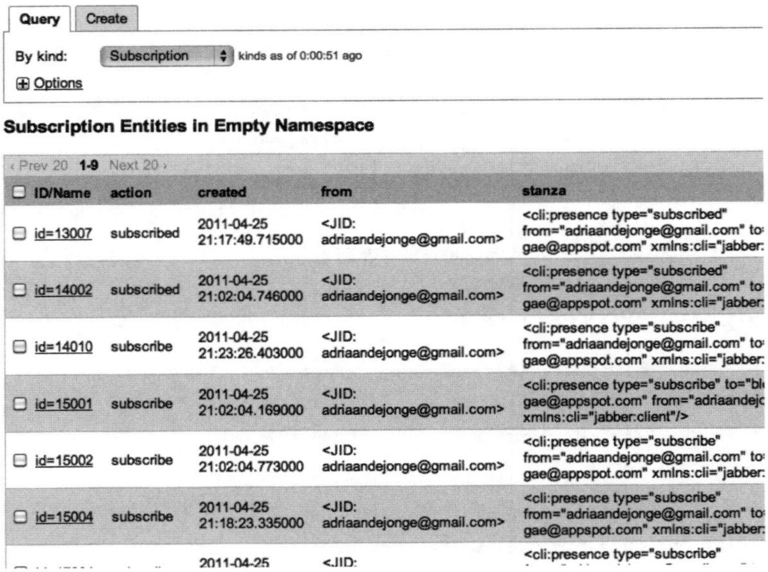

Figure 17.3 The subscriptions received and stored in the datastore.

Listing 17.5 **Configuring URLs with a Wild Card in web.xml**

```
<servlet>
  <servlet-name>XMPPSubscriptionServlet</servlet-name>
    <servlet-class>
      com.appspot.xmpp.XMPPSubscriptionServlet
    </servlet-class>
  </servlet>
  <servlet-mapping>
    <servlet-name>XMPPSubscriptionServlet</servlet-name>
    <url-pattern>/_ah/xmpp/subscription/*</url-pattern>
</servlet-mapping>
```

The screen is the result of adding and removing the appspot address from Google Talk a couple of times. It seems as if Google Talk does not explicitly `unsubscribe` when you remove or block a user. You do see `unavailable` followed by `probe` in Figure 17.3 on blocking and `available` followed by `probe` on unblocking. Receiving this pattern is not a solid proof that you are being blocked, though.

The action attribute extracted from the URL is the same as the subscription type attribute extracted from the request. Using just one of these is sufficient. In this example, one servlet listens to all four URLs. The URL is most useful if you want different servlets to handle the actions differently.

Receiving Presence

For some applications, you want to track explicitly whether or not a user is available right now. Consider implementing an online service desk whereby you connect online users to a varying number of employees available to answer calls. When no employee is available, you may need to put the customer on hold for a while.

You can track presence by listening on the following URL:

```
/_ah/xmpp/presence/*/
```

The wild card in the URL may be replaced with the values `available` or `unavailable` when the recipient goes online or offline. Note that when a recipient is "away," he or she is still "available." `Probe` is received when the recipient wants to know the server's current presence.

Listing 17.6 shows a servlet that stores all available fields in presence requests in the App Engine datastore.

Listing 17.6 **Storing XMPP Presence Notifications in the Datastore**

```
package com.appspot.xmpp;

import com.google.appengine.api.datastore.DatastoreService;
import com.google.appengine.api.datastore.DatastoreServiceFactory;
import com.google.appengine.api.datastore.Entity;
```

(Continues)

Listing 17.6 **Storing XMPP Presence Notifications in the Datastore (Continued)**

```
06 import com.google.appengine.api.xmpp.Presence;
07 import com.google.appengine.api.xmpp.Subscription;
08 import com.google.appengine.api.xmpp.XMPPService;
09 import com.google.appengine.api.xmpp.XMPPServiceFactory;
10
11 import javax.servlet.ServletException;
12 import javax.servlet.http.HttpServlet;
13 import javax.servlet.http.HttpServletRequest;
14 import javax.servlet.http.HttpServletResponse;
15 import java.io.IOException;
16 import java.util.Date;
17
18 public class XMPPPresenceServlet extends HttpServlet {
19   @Override
20   protected void doPost(HttpServletRequest request,
21                         HttpServletResponse response)
22       throws ServletException, IOException {
23
24
25     String action = request.getRequestURI()
26         .replaceAll("/_ah/xmpp/presence/", "")
27         .replaceAll("/", "");
28
29     XMPPService xmppService = XMPPServiceFactory.getXMPPService();
30     Presence presence =
31         xmppService.parsePresence(request);
32
33     DatastoreService datastoreService = DatastoreServiceFactory
34         .getDatastoreService();
35     Entity entity = new Entity("Presence");
36     entity.setProperty("from", "" + presence.getFromJid());
37     entity.setProperty("to", "" + presence.getToJid());
38     entity.setProperty("type","" + presence.getPresenceType());
39     entity.setProperty("stanza", presence.getStanza());
40     entity.setProperty("show", "" + presence.getPresenceShow());
41     entity.setProperty("status", presence.getStatus());
42     entity.setProperty("available", presence.isAvailable());
43     entity.setProperty("created", new Date());
44     entity.setProperty("action", action);
45
46     datastoreService.put(entity);
47   }
48 }
```

Similar to Listing 17.4, lines 25, 26, and 27 determine whether an available, unavailable, or probe request was received. Lines 33 through 46 store all available fields in a datastore entity.

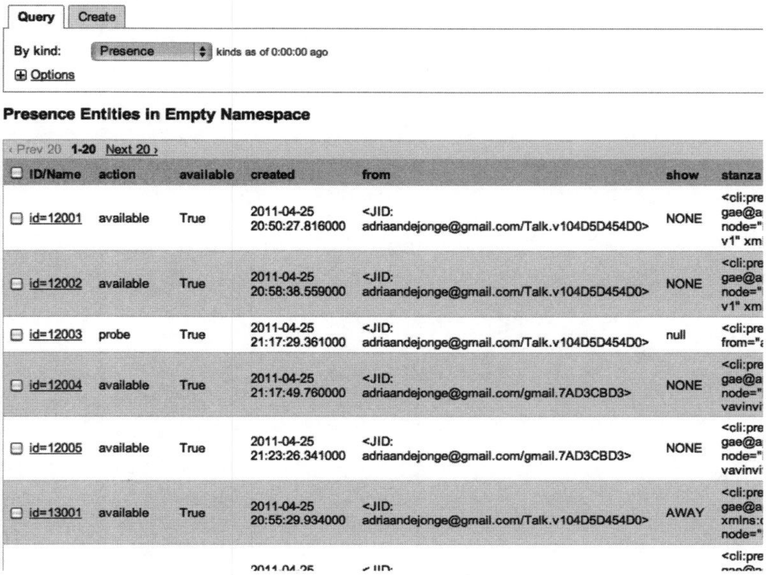

Figure 17.4 The presences received and stored in the datastore.

Figure 17.4 shows the datastore admin interface after receiving a number of presence notifications.

If you compare this figure with Figures 17.2 and 17.3, you notice that the number of presence notifications is higher than the other two. You should consider whether you really need the presence notifications before implementing them. If you can do without them, it helps you save valuable resources.

A full in-depth explanation of XMPP is beyond the scope of this book. More information on XMPP can be found at the following website: http://xmpp.org/.

Summary

This chapter started by demonstrating how to send messages using the XMPP protocol. It is important to invite the App Engine's XMPP address from the client before sending messages. After that, a servlet is configured to receive messages, which involves configuration in both web.xml and appengine-web.xml. First, the servlet needs to listen to the right URL. Then, the App Engine needs to be told to pass messages to this servlet. Receiving notifications for subscription and presence works similarly. Handling subscriptions, you should expect the number of subscriptions to exceed the unsubscriptions. Because the App Engine accepts all connections, you should control access in a different way if you want to restrict access. Finally, this chapter explained how receiving presence notifications is both powerful and resource consuming. Use it only when you really need to.

PART V

Application Deployment

Chapter 18

Improving the Development Process

This chapter discusses the development process from a customer point of view, focusing on commercial Internet projects rather than in-company software development. It discusses common developer activities in terms of their benefit to customers and to revenue. Next, the development process is discussed in terms of end user functionality, and then we look briefly at quality measurement. The chapter ends with a reevaluation of what is important to developers in terms of productivity.

Optimizing the Development Process for the Internet

Developing applications for the Internet is different from developing software targeted at a single company and its employees. If you have been doing company-specific development, you may not be used to competing with other developers who may also be targeting your market.

As an example, in a typical development project, the end users may or may not like the user interface you created. Whether they do or not, they usually have no choice but to get used to it. If the user interface is unfriendly enough, a manager might ask you to redesign it or, worse, might have to arrange a training course to teach employees to use it. None of these scenarios is ideal.

Cloud computing might change the way managers think about their company's applications. Cloud computing gives employees the option to buy their own IT solutions without consulting the internal IT department—the old days of unfriendly IT departments may be numbered, and competitive development has begun.

Developing applications for the Internet is the same as opening a shop and selling products or services. Even if you do not think of your product as a shop, it is. Your customers can leave your site any time and switch to the site of a competing product. You need to monitor constantly how many customers stay and how many leave so you can optimize your site to attract and keep customers.

Some software developers despise thinking commercially. They may acknowledge that marketing attracts customers and earns revenue, but they tend to dislike it and ignore it. Developers might think that customers cannot see through marketing tricks and cannot distinguish good software from inferior products. They tend to overlook that what is good software to them may not be what their customer is looking for.

Thinking Like a Project Manager

Usually, project managers have a simplified view of how an application works. In the simplest model, they see their end result as a product of scope, time, and cost. This model holds that only two of those three can be constant, so when the client asks for a fixed-time, fixed-budget project, the scope is automatically considered variable.

In more elaborate models, scope is further divided over functional requirements, non-functional requirements, and quality. The fundamental concept does not change, however. The project model is still reasoned from a "scarcity" mind set in which less tangible aspects like quality suffer because managers consider such trade-offs as cutting back on software quality in order to reduce cost or beat a deadline.

This book is not primarily for project managers. It is for developers, and that allows us to take a more sophisticated worldview.

The central question in this chapter is: How can we improve the development process to deliver the most value for the end customer? The answer is to focus on the right things and choose the right balance!

Reducing Overhead

All activities that do not directly contribute to your end goal can be classified as overhead. Not all overhead is unnecessary, but when improving your development process, you need to distinguish overhead from production.

Knowing Your End Goal

The key step in distinguishing between overhead and production is to know exactly what your *end goal* is. Then you can determine if your activities contribute directly, indirectly, or not at all to that goal.

A common mistake made by software developers is to pursue long-term goals. For now, though it sounds a bit shortsighted, let's assume that pursuing long-term goals is *wrong*.

A proper end goal is to make profit as quickly as possible. To make profit, you need to attract customers, persuade them to spend money, and satisfy them enough to get them to come back and spend more money later.

Profit can take care of your long-term goals when the time comes.

Making profit depends not only on high revenue but also on low cost. This is one of the strongest features of the Google App Engine pricing model. When you do not have many visitors, you do not pay much money. If you manage to minimize development costs, you can bring products to the market with negligible investments. And as long as you have a sound earning model, you can easily pay for Google's increasing charges when your number of visitors grows.

Cutting Away Unnecessary Activities

What kind of overhead can you cut from your development cycle? Depending on your requirements and situation, you could consider the following examples:

- **Test-driven development: Unit testing 100 percent of your code.** Only part of your code contains interesting algorithms that break the software if an error is introduced. A large part of website code is simple plumbing that passes variables from datastores into view templates. There is not much to test other than for typos in variables. Unit testing all the code makes more sense when you use a script language than when you program in a compiled programming language.
- **Dependency injection with interfaces.** Although dependency injection provides an elegant mechanism to separate concerns and keep code loosely coupled, in many cases, this loose coupling is just overengineering beyond the actual requirements.
- **Data transfer objects.** Many Java courses have taught using data transfer objects to ensure static typing and correct naming. Some people advocate using these objects for separation of concerns and validity checks. In many simple applications, you may as well transfer your data using a `HashMap` or a similar structure. When passing variables to a view template, static typing does not add value if the view template itself does not observe static typing.
- **Integration with the main system.** Many organizations have one or more central systems. A common pitfall is to connect each and every application with the central system without considering the actual benefits of doing so. As a result, there are so many connections that the application landscape becomes hard to manage. If you consider the costs and advantages before you connect, you may conclude that some systems can function independently.
- **Architecture.** Some organizations spend a lot of time on large documents, thinking in a more fundamental way about the application landscape. In their focus on following principles and adhering to mission statements, they work toward a fictive point on the horizon and model systems in a way that abstracts away from the actual technology. Many of these documents are not understood by the rest of the organization, including developers, and remain no more than an academic exercise that ends up in a desktop drawer. A pragmatic approach to architecture is preferable.
- **Detailed design.** Organizations sometimes hire technical designers to write detailed documents on how the software should be written. This can be useful for offshoring projects, but for many projects, development reveals that things work a little differently in practice than on paper. In many cases, writing the software with just a high-level design works better than writing software according to a detailed design.

- **JavaDoc.** Automated API documentation using JavaDoc is particularly useful for public APIs. Documenting your own private code should be done in a simple and efficient way, however. Obligatory JavaDoc often leads to a lot of useless text that confuses more than it clarifies. Writing readable code is often the best documentation strategy.

In some situations, these activities are very helpful. In the context of the Google App Engine, though, you should ask yourself whether you actually need them.

A clear warning sign that an activity is unnecessary is when you tend not to pay attention to it unless someone else explicitly asks you to. Take test-driven development (TDD), for example. You might know an eager colleague who watched a presentation, completed training, or read a book on TDD. He test-drives very conscientiously himself, claims great successes, and convinces others that TDD is important. Together they produce lots of useless code.

In many cases, only 10 percent of your code is complex enough to justify TDD. When it's justified, please use it! Just be wary of tools that measure the percentage of your code that is covered with unit tests assuming that you aim for 100 percent coverage instead of 10 percent. Using such tools under this false assumption may result in thousands of lines of junk code you need to maintain.

You can ask yourself six questions about any activity that you suspect not to be helpful:

- Do I want it myself, or did someone ask me to include it?
- What problem does it solve?
- Is it applicable in this situation?
- What are the alternative solutions?
- What is the risk of *not* doing this activity?
- Is it possible to do it only *part* of the time?

Answering these questions will clarify whether or not an activity is necessary and will streamline your work. You can stop feeling guilty about ignoring certain activities if you don't need them and they don't help the customer anyway. You can stop listening to other people who read a book and tell you to do unnatural stuff. Make your own judgment calls. The same holds for anything you read in *this* book!

Improving Functionality

When you want to improve functionality, you usually have a long list of customer requirements; some items are highly detailed functional requirements and others are features the customer wishes to have. Customers might also have pointed out some technical issues with a current release. This section provides some pointers on how to make sure all wishes are handled in a customer-friendly way.

Setting Priorities

Customers don't always know exactly what they want. They do want to make sure they get *everything* they asked for, on time and within budget, though. Combine this with a developer who lacks focus on customer needs, and you have a disaster waiting to happen.

The key to satisfying the customer's need is to prioritize each requirement. Only a single feature can have priority 1, a single feature can have priority 2, and so on, so you have as many priorities as you have features. The customer *must* be involved in setting the priorities, and the end goal is an important steering factor in making these choices.

Never let yourself be lured into a plan that only separates *must haves* from *should haves* and *could haves*—an approach called MoSCoW (must haves, should haves, could haves, won't haves). It involves the risk of a monolithic project, with customers classifying too many requirements as must have. By numerically prioritizing each feature, you can always choose what should be in the next release and what should wait for a later release.

Planning Iterations

What you need to improve functionality in a linear and predictable way is an iterative project. In the first iteration, you need to plan the absolute minimum amount of work that realizes your top priorities essential to achieving the first step toward your end goal.

A first iteration is a bare-bones, no-nonsense, do-the-simplest-thing-that-could-possibly-work effort. If the priorities are right, this approach should be sufficient to have a fully functional application that can be deployed on production. Whether or not you actually deploy your first iteration to production depends mostly on commercial considerations. The important thing is that the end user can already start doing real work on the software released in the first iteration. By doing real work, the end user can give you informed input for the following iterations. Your challenge is to translate this feedback into better software without forgetting the rest of your project planning.

Projects for the Internet do not necessarily have a beginning and an end, but your iterations do. There are potentially endless iterations after the initial release of your software. An Internet application is *never* finished. The Internet is ever improving, and so is competition. There is no such thing as a perfect project. Requirements and insights are continuously changing.

Distinguishing Iterations from Increments

It is common to confuse iterative development with incremental development. While iterative development is meant to continually improve and expand existing software, incremental development only expands software.

In other words, in a typical incremental development project, the manager discourages developers from touching the code they built earlier. In typical iterative development projects, the manager does the opposite: encourages developers to further improve the code they built earlier in response to user feedback on the previous iteration.

In most cases, incremental development is just another way of saying the development is done in phases. Phases may be helpful in old-fashioned business projects. If you call your process iterative, make sure you do it the right way: improve continually and learn from feedback.

Practicing Experiment-Driven Development

The best way to help your customer is to practice experiment-driven development. In its simplest form, experiment-driven development means developing an application very quickly, without design, user research, or customer interviews. You bring it to the market and find out how people respond to it. If the response is positive, you continue to improve it. If the response is negative, you throw it away!

A more conservative form of experiment-driven development is A/B testing. You serve at least two different versions of a page to randomly selected users and measure the effect on your conversion rate. Conversion is the percentage of visitors who spend money on your website.

Tools like Google Analytics allow you to model a *funnel* for measuring conversion. In most cases, websites have many different entry points and a single (or a very small number of) checkout point where the customer pays for products or services.

Google Website Optimizer is a part of Google Analytics that allows A/B testing and measuring. To attribute changes in conversion to the exact cause, you need to change a single parameter at a time. The Website Optimizer also allows you to make multiple changes. Make sure you have enough experience with A/B testing before you start doing it.

Making Changes Gradually

In general, regardless of whether you are A/B testing or simply making improvements, try to make just one change at a time. Look at how Facebook slowly evolves. Major overhauls tend to scare some existing customers away. Adding new features gradually is both friendly to the user and manageable in terms of project management. It is the way the Internet works!

Measuring Quality

What is the definition of quality? It depends on who you ask. To your customer, quality may mean something entirely different from what it means to developers. For some, quality may be different aspects of reliability: fault tolerance, recoverability, degradation scenarios in case of errors. To others, quality may be different aspects of usability: learnability, clarity, attractiveness, user friendliness. Yet others may focus on efficiency or maintainability. There is even an International Standards Organization (ISO) model for software quality called Quint2.

Quality is such a broad subject that you may easily lose focus. Perhaps you are used to spending most of your energy on one aspect of a project, but your current customer is asking for attention on a completely different aspect. Again, the key is to know what is most important in your specific situation.

Are you measuring the right things for quality? For example, you may be using a product like Sonar to investigate whether source code adheres to certain standards and whether your code is fully covered by unit tests. If you really want to measure this, Sonar is a great product. But does it help you attract customers and increase revenue?

You have probably heard that anything you measure *will* improve. Of course, quality will not improve just by measuring it. Measuring quality requires you to focus on specific aspects of your program, such as speed, accuracy, and ease of use. During the next improvement cycles, you are likely to spend most of your energy on the qualities your measurements focus on. It follows that to improve the right aspects of your program, you need to measure the right qualities: the aspects your *customers* value.

You will find it useful to spend time on profiling, logging, and measuring conversion rates. With those measures, you can improve performance, reliability, and usability. These are the quality attributes most likely to attract customers quickly.

Optimizing Developer Productivity

There is another side to the customer-centric model: developer productivity. A happy developer is a productive developer. The question is: What makes you, as a developer, happy?

Performing Rituals

Some developers like to follow rituals that do not directly contribute to the customer. If it makes a developer feel happier about his or her work, and feeling happy makes the developer three to five times more productive, then why not keep the rituals?

As an example of such a ritual, consider a developer who likes version control systems and checking in atomic commits with software such as Subversion or Git. Especially when working on a single-developer project, version control does not directly improve anything noticeable for the customer. Checking in code can provide a feeling of productivity, though.

As long as the productivity increase outweighs the amount of extra work—and there may be other benefits—there is no harm in following rituals.

Using New Programming Languages

Not all technology adds value for the end customer, but it may improve developer productivity. This is good as long as the productivity does not harm the customer value. For example, developers have been switching to new Java Virtual Machine (JVM) languages over the past several years: Scala, Clojure, Groovy, and others.

The end user won't notice a new programming language. The developer will. The challenge of learning a new language and the ability to do more with less code may be exciting enough to boost productivity. At least for a while.

Be cautious with frameworks and libraries, though, especially frontend frameworks, which sometimes do more harm than good.

Managing Time and Surroundings

In many ways, writing software is similar to writing any other texts: documentation, articles, or books. Your productivity depends on your level of concentration. For some, productivity means waking up at 5.30 a.m. and writing a lot of code before driving to work.

For others, productivity means staying up late and working until 2 a.m. before falling asleep. For those who prefer normal hours, productivity may increase by working at other locations: trains, at home, or outside.

Productivity may also depend on your surroundings. Some people can tune out disturbances, and others lose their concentration with the slightest distraction. Some people play Mozart as they work, and others pound out their code to the industrial metal sounds of Rammstein. Whatever your preferences, try to ensure your environment is conducive to your work. The potential productivity gain can sometimes be astonishing!

Summary

This chapter began by explaining why Internet projects require developers to focus on the commercial aspects of their applications, like profit, revenue, and cost cutting. It discussed measuring the quality attributes that are important to your customer. Your improvement efforts tend to focus on the aspects you are measuring, so if revenue is your goal, then you should measure conversion rather than code coverage. Quality should be noticeable by the end user, and your product should have the quality attributes the customer asks for, not just those that are important to you. The chapter ended with a discussion of productivity. Gains in developer productivity may be large enough to allow some extra overhead that does not directly accomplish end user goals.

Chapter 19

Assuring Quality Using Measuring Tools

This chapter provides an alternative approach to quality assurance, focusing on end user quality attributes rather than following cliché processes. The chapter starts with a discussion of fixing issues directly after a production release. It continues with a clear definition of the word *usability* as an introduction to a more hands-on approach to assuring quality. The Capabilities API is introduced; it helps you prevent server errors—a better approach than having to respond to errors after they occur. The App Engine logging capabilities are introduced as a means to make improvements based on feedback. This chapter covers the App Engine's AppStats mechanism, which continuously profiles calls to App Engine services on production. Finally, this chapter discusses quality assurance mechanisms that run outside the App Engine. Google provides Google Analytics to track user actions in production.

Testing on a Production Environment

There is no better test than production! The suggestion of testing on production might offend some people who believe you must have a separate test environment, a dedicated acceptance environment that should be 100 percent equal to production. And this process works very well—on paper at least.

In practice, on what day do you find the most bugs in the shortest period of time? The first day in production!

Putting the Added Value of Testing in Perspective

For a number of reasons, testers sometimes fail to find errors that are blatantly obvious in production environments. Testers are good at finding common flaws and corner cases, but the practical needs of a real-world user may pose challenges a tester will not encounter or cannot duplicate in an acceptance environment. Real-world users in real-world environments therefore provide the most practical test—and that doesn't happen until production.

Also, an acceptance environment is not the same as a production environment. They are supposed to be equal, but they never are. Even if the hardware and software is comparable (which is unusual because of the costs involved), there is no constant load of other users influencing the system. And even if there are tricks to simulate or reroute real-world traffic, do the costs justify their use?

Performing a Sanity Check

Of course, you should still test in a test environment. Perform a sanity check to see if everything works to an acceptable level. The point is that you should not assume that your product is 100 percent perfect when it is released on production. It is wiser to expect a number of flaws after the release and set up a process whereby you can respond to them quickly.

To know what an acceptable level of quality is before you go live, you must be able to distinguish between flaws that affect just a few customers and flaws that affect *many* customers. In addition, you need to know the impact of an error. Loss of critical data is unacceptable even for a few customers.

The question is whether or not your application actually handles critical data.

Minimizing Damage from Failures

To minimize possible damage from failures on production, you should write your code to *fail fast* after catching an exception. Some programs do not know what to do with an exception. They log it, ignore it, and continue working with a broken application. That is like driving a car with a red warning light flashing in the dashboard. Although the car may run, you risk damaging it.

There are multiple exception handling strategies that do work the right way. Whether you use checked exceptions, unchecked exceptions, exceptions caught as early as possible, or exceptions caught as late as possible, make sure you choose a clear strategy and implement it consistently.

What you should do with an exception is present it to your visitor in the nicest possible way. Perhaps you should consult a marketing expert on how to formulate friendly error messages. You could even offer a contact form with the error message, allowing the user to enter complaints, feedback, or suggestions to help resolve the issue.

Even better is when you can prevent exceptions from happening by checking dependencies before performing actions. This chapter introduces the Capabilities API to help you check the status of the App Engine's services.

It is crucial to fix any error that is not a result of a temporary system outage. To do this, you need to monitor your server's log files and release patches often. This chapter demonstrates how to work efficiently with App Engine logs.

Finally, you should make sure you can always roll your application back to an old version. Chapter 4, "Data Modeling for the Google App Engine Datastore," provides some pointers on how to make sure your data model remains backwards compatible.

Thinking Differently about Usability

Usability does not mean that you have a good-looking site. Usability means that your application "knows" what users want and helps them do it as efficiently as possible. Some designers spend so much time on the looks of a website that they forget to offer something useful to the user. Users do not visit sites because of their visual appeal. Or do they?

Choosing Functionality over Appearance

Why do you choose Google's search engine over Bing? Bing has nice background pictures! Google has a better reach and more relevance, and it is faster and simpler. Bing does not perform poorly in those areas—it just doesn't perform well enough to beat Google.

Why do you choose Facebook over Google Buzz? Again: reach, relevance, simplicity. The key point is that Facebook seems to know what you like.

Why do you choose Amazon over Barnes & Noble? Because Amazon knows what you want! It suggests books you might like, and it even corrects your spelling errors.

Google, Facebook, and Amazon are pretty big compared to an average App Engine application, but you can learn from these successful sites.

On a news site, for example, the top five most read articles can be a pretty good indicator of what other visitors may like to read. On a content site, tagging may provide a simple way to navigate the visitor to related or similar content, especially if the tags are presented in a user-friendly way: "Other readers of this article also liked...." In an application, a "Recently Opened" menu helps the user quickly navigate back to the last items he or she edited. Using an "Add to Favorites" button can help achieve similar improvements in navigation speed.

Saving the user a lot of clicks does not need to be complicated.

Optimizing Usability by Analyzing Analytics

The quality of your application can be measured by its ability to do what the user wants with a minimum of user actions. The lack of quality can be measured by the percentage of users who leave the application because it did not help them.

Later in this chapter, Google Analytics is introduced as a tool to measure conversion rates. It also shows how much time users spend on the site and which click paths they choose to navigate through the site.

Software developers know how to use profiling tools to optimize the performance of their source code. A profiler indicates which parts of the code consume the most processor time or system memory.

If you think of Google Analytics as yet another profiling tool, targeted at optimizing actions performed by users rather than by the machine, it can provide a lot of pointers for improving the efficiency of your web application.

Checking Availability with the Capabilities API

Most applications are written with the mind-set of "how to get things working." The "how to break things" mind-set usually follows during testing. When getting things to work, you usually assume that services like the datastore are available.

But what do you do during maintenance of the datastore or when it is otherwise unavailable? You hope the period of unavailability is limited, but even the most well-known cloud service providers may have bad luck and be unavailable for a day.

You must be able to detect when a server is unavailable so you can start alternative scenarios proactively instead of running into exceptions too late in an interaction. Listing 19.1 demonstrates the use of the Capabilities API by creating a simple page communicating the current status of the App Engine services.

Listing 19.1 Fetching the Status of App Engine Services

```
package com.appspot.capabilities;

import com.google.appengine.api.capabilities.CapabilitiesService;
import com.google.appengine.api.capabilities.
    CapabilitiesServiceFactory;
import com.google.appengine.api.capabilities.Capability;
import com.google.appengine.api.capabilities.CapabilityState;
import org.antlr.stringtemplate.StringTemplate;
import org.antlr.stringtemplate.StringTemplateGroup;

import javax.servlet.ServletException;
import javax.servlet.http.HttpServlet;
import javax.servlet.http.HttpServletRequest;
import javax.servlet.http.HttpServletResponse;
import java.io.IOException;
import java.util.Collection;
import java.util.HashMap;
import java.util.Map;

public class CapabilitiesServlet extends HttpServlet {

  protected void doGet(HttpServletRequest request,
                       HttpServletResponse response)
      throws ServletException, IOException {
    long start = System.currentTimeMillis();

    CapabilitiesService service =
        CapabilitiesServiceFactory.getCapabilitiesService();

    StringTemplateGroup group = new StringTemplateGroup("xhtml",
        "WEB-INF/templates/xhtml");
    StringTemplate template = group.getInstanceOf("capabilities");
    Map<String, CapabilityState> statusMap =
        new HashMap<String, CapabilityState>();
    statusMap.put("blobstore",
        service.getStatus(Capability.BLOBSTORE));
```

Listing 19.1 **Fetching the Status of App Engine Services (Continued)**

```
37      statusMap.put("datastore",
38          service.getStatus(Capability.DATASTORE));
39      statusMap.put("datastorewrite",
40          service.getStatus(Capability.DATASTORE_WRITE));
41      statusMap.put("images",
42          service.getStatus(Capability.IMAGES));
43      statusMap.put("mail",
44          service.getStatus(Capability.MAIL));
45      statusMap.put("memcache",
46          service.getStatus(Capability.MEMCACHE));
47      statusMap.put("taskqueue",
48          service.getStatus(Capability.TASKQUEUE));
49      statusMap.put("urlfetch",
50          service.getStatus(Capability.URL_FETCH));
51      statusMap.put("xmpp",
52          service.getStatus(Capability.XMPP));
53      template.setAttributes(statusMap);
54
55      Collection<CapabilityState> states = statusMap.values();
56      StringBuilder result = new StringBuilder();
57      for(CapabilityState state : states) {
58        if("ENABLED".equals(state.toString())) {
59          result.append(result.length() > 0 ? " " : "");
60          result.append(state.getCapability().getName());
61        }
62      }
63      template.setAttribute("gaestatus",
64          result.length() <= 0 ? "OK" : "DOWN: " + result);
65
66      template.setAttribute("loadtime",
67              "" + (System.currentTimeMillis() - start));
68
69      response.getWriter().write(template.toString());
70
71    }
72 }
```

Lines 27 through 53 use the Capabilities Service to ask the `CapabilityState` of each App Engine backend. The results are put in a `HashMap` for later use in the HTML template.

Lines 55 through 64 loop through the `Map` to investigate whether one or more services are out of order. If not, the status is set to `OK`. Otherwise, the status is `DOWN`, followed by the service's name. The resulting status is used later in this chapter: it is a custom input parameter for Google Analytics.

Listing 19.2 contains a simple HTML template presenting the status of all App Engine services.

Listing 19.2 **Displaying Capabilities in HTML**

```
<html>
<head>
<title>Test Capabilities</title>
$analytics()$
</head>
<body>
<p>Capabilities</p>
<ul>
<li>BLOBSTORE: $blobstore.status$ - $blobstore.scheduledDate$</li>
<li>DATASTORE: $datastore.status$ - $datastore.scheduledDate$</li>
<li>DATASTORE_WRITE: $datastorewrite.status$
    - $datastorewrite.scheduledDate$</li>
<li>IMAGES: $images.status$ - $images.scheduledDate$</li>
<li>MAIL: $mail.status$ - $mail.scheduledDate$</li>
<li>MEMCACHE: $memcache.status$ - $memcache.scheduledDate$</li>
<li>TASKQUEUE: $taskqueue.status$ - $taskqueue.scheduledDate$</li>
<li>URL_FETCH: $urlfetch.status$ - $urlfetch.scheduledDate$</li>
<li>XMPP: $xmpp.status$ - $xmpp.scheduledDate$</li>
</ul>
</body>
</html>
```

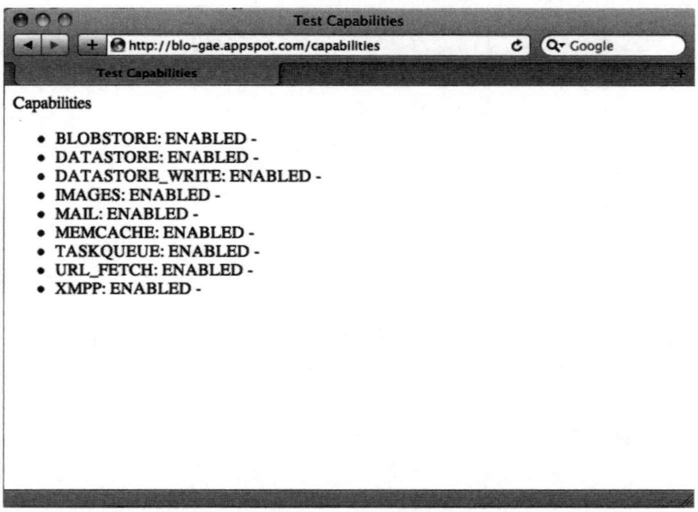

Figure 19.1 Resulting screen showing current server statuses using the Capabilities API.

Line 4 refers to an external template containing a Google Analytics script, presented later in this chapter.

Lines 9 through 18 present the status for each service, followed by a date of maintenance. The maintenance dates are mostly empty. If they are set, they allow the application to warn the user in advance of downtime.

Figure 19.1 presents the resulting screen in a browser.

Logging Unexpected Behavior

The sooner issues are fixed in production, the better the quality of your product. To fix issues in production, you must be able to investigate where problems occur and what causes them. In other words, you need logging.

On the App Engine, you cannot set up a secure shell connection and type a command like `tail -f` to follow a live log file. You can open an admin interface on http://appengine.google.com and see log messages online, though.

If your application writes to the `System.out` stream, then the App Engine turns your messages into the log statements on INFO level. Similarly, anything you write to `System.err` is logged on WARNING level by the App Engine. A more fine-grained level of control is possible using `java.util.logging` classes.

Listing 19.3 demonstrates how to use the standard Java `Logger` class to write messages to the App Engine management interface.

Listing 19.3 Logging Messages to the Admin Interface

```
package com.appspot.capabilities;

import org.antlr.stringtemplate.StringTemplate;
import org.antlr.stringtemplate.StringTemplateGroup;

import javax.servlet.ServletException;
import javax.servlet.http.HttpServlet;
import javax.servlet.http.HttpServletRequest;
import javax.servlet.http.HttpServletResponse;
import java.io.IOException;
import java.util.logging.Level;
import java.util.logging.Logger;

public class LogServlet extends HttpServlet {

  protected void doGet(HttpServletRequest request,
                       HttpServletResponse response)
      throws ServletException, IOException {

    long start = System.currentTimeMillis();
    Logger logger = Logger.getLogger(this.getClass().getName());
    logger.fine("fine");
```

(Continues)

Listing 19.3 **Logging Messages to the Admin Interface (Continued)**

```
23      logger.info("info");
24      logger.severe("severe");
25      logger.warning("warning");
26      try {
27        // FAIL on purpose
28        (new String[1])[2].toLowerCase();
29      } catch(Exception e) {
30        logger.log(Level.SEVERE, "Failed 'unexpectedly'", e);
31      }
32
33
34
35      StringTemplateGroup group = new StringTemplateGroup("xhtml",
36          "WEB-INF/templates/xhtml");
37      StringTemplate template = group.getInstanceOf("hello-world");
38
39      template.setAttribute("loadtime",
40          "" + (System.currentTimeMillis() - start));
41      template.setAttribute("gaestatus", "OK");
42      response.getWriter().write(template.toString());
43
44    }
45 }
```

Lines 22 through 25 demonstrate the use of convenience methods. Using this notation requires the least amount of code to record a simple message on the right log level.

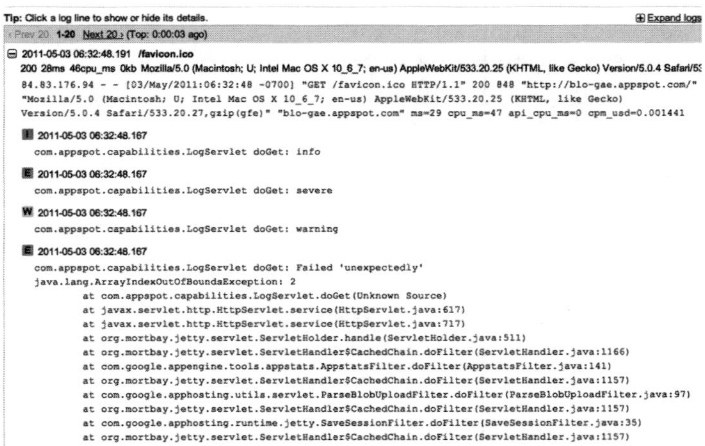

Figure 19.2 Test Log messages shown in the Admin interface.

Lines 26 through 31 cause an exception (on purpose) to demonstrate how to record a full stack trace in the log file. There is no convenience method allowing you to pass `Throwable` implementations. Line 30 shows the full notation for logging, setting the log level, and passing an `Exception`.

Figure 19.2 shows the resulting screen in the admin interface. The log messages are grouped into a single request, which makes them easier to separate from other logging messages than you are used to in classic log files.

The admin interface allows you to filter on the basis of the severity of the message. You can also configure this in your `logging.properties`. Directly after a release, you should be interested in more fine-grained logging. When your release has proven stable in production, you want to raise the log level to make sure you do not overlook the more serious error messages.

Profiling Continuously on Production

Java profiling tools are not used as much as they should be. Using a profiling tool, you can easily discover which parts of your application take most of your resources. Those are the parts where you should start your performance optimization efforts.

Profiling tools help you focus on the right problems. They prevent you from spending lots of time optimizing code that does not really need optimization.

This book encourages you to install profiling tools on your local machine and investigate your code. The App Engine development server may complicate the installation of such tools. If you cannot profile the development environment, you can always profile independent modules and libraries outside the development environment with any profiling tool.

In addition, the App Engine helps you profile your code on production. The scope of the profiling information is somewhat limited but nonetheless useful.

Google provides a module called AppStats, which monitors all your calls to Google Services, which is interesting, because calls to Google Services are the slowest parts of your code (that is, of course, unless you implement inefficient algorithms or useless libraries and frameworks). It is also interesting because calls to Google Services are an important factor in your quota and payments.

Note that AppStats also costs a little bit of your quota, so after thorough investigation, it is better to turn off AppStats when you no longer need the tool.

You can implement AppStats by configuring a filter in your web.xml. This filter makes sure that every remote procedure call (RPC) is logged in memcache. Google saves the latest 1000 requests. Listing 19.4 demonstrates how to modify web.xml.

Listing 19.4 **Configuring AppStats**

```
<servlet>
  <servlet-name>appstats</servlet-name>
  <servlet-class>
    com.google.appengine.tools.appstats.AppstatsServlet
```

(Continues)

Listing 19.4 **Configuring AppStats (Continued)**

```
05      </servlet-class>
06    </servlet>
07    <servlet-mapping>
08      <servlet-name>appstats</servlet-name>
09      <url-pattern>/appstats/*</url-pattern>
10    </servlet-mapping>
11    <filter>
12      <filter-name>appstats</filter-name>
13      <filter-class>
14        com.google.appengine.tools.appstats.AppstatsFilter
15      </filter-class>
16    </filter>
17    <filter-mapping>
18      <filter-name>appstats</filter-name>
19      <url-pattern>/*</url-pattern>
20    </filter-mapping>
```

After configuring AppStats in your web.xml and running some tests with your application code, you can view the results on the URL configured on line 9. Figure 19.3 shows a screen with AppStats.

The screen displays both the number of RPCs to each service and their response times. With this combination, you can invent a strategy to reduce the number of calls. Reducing

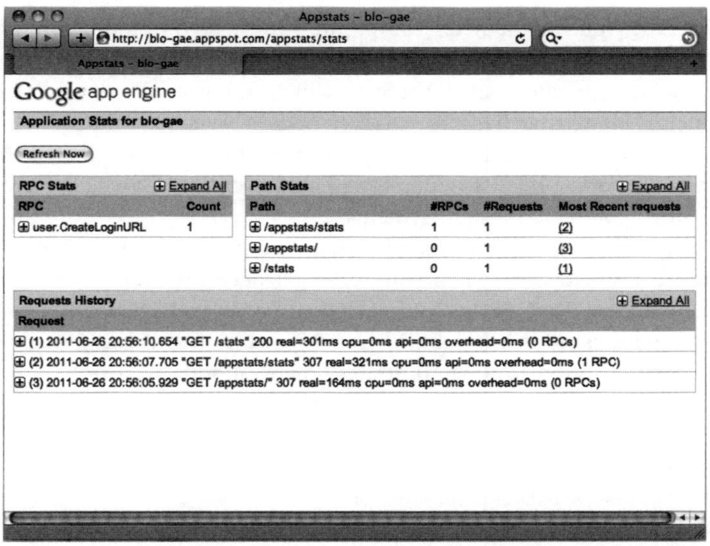

Figure 19.3 Screen generated by the AppStats application.

the numbers may help reduce the costs of running your application. Reducing the response times improves the performance for your end users, which may lead to increasing revenue.

One of the simplest and most effective ways to reduce the number of RPCs is to implement a proper caching strategy. Chapter 14, "Optimizing Performance Using the Memory Cache," elaborates on this subject.

Measuring User Response to Your Interface

The best way to find out what an average user thinks of your application is to sit next to him or her and ask open questions as the user clicks through the application. On the open Internet, that is almost impossible. If you have the budget, a usability test with a reference group is the closest thing to sitting next to your actual end user.

Another, less personal, way to find out what your customer thinks is to measure all of his or her actions, such as the click path, the time spent on the site, whether or not the user makes a purchase, and perhaps other variables you think are relevant.

This way of measuring is based on statistics. You try to get the best possible view of what your visitors are doing on your site and where potential problems are on your site. You can also measure how changes on your site affect user behavior, positively or negatively.

Google Analytics is one of the tools available to do this. If you haven't used Analytics for a few years, you may only remember it as a simple statistics tool, similar to other tools on the market. If you haven't looked at Google Analytics for a while, it is worth looking at again.

Google Analytics has evolved into a complete programming platform for site analytics. It provides APIs for inputting, viewing, and exporting statistics. The possibilities are countless.

Listing 19.5 provides a simple example JavaScript adding an analytics counter to your application. It sets the server-side load time as an additional parameter if it is available, and it allows registration of system outages using the Capabilities API (used in Listing 19.1).

Listing 19.5 **Scripting Google Analytics**

```
<script type="text/javascript">

  var _gaq = _gaq || [];
  _gaq.push(['_setAccount', 'UA-XXXXXX-X']);
  _gaq.push(['_trackPageview']);
  $if(loadtime)$
  _gaq.push(['_trackEvent', 'Load', 'Page Load Time',
    'Page Load Time', $loadtime$]);
  $endif$
  $if(gaestatus)$
  _gaq.push(['_trackEvent', 'Status', 'GAE Status', '$gaestatus$']);
```

(Continues)

Listing 19.5 **Scripting Google Analytics (Continued)**

```
12   $endif$
13
14   (function() {
15     var ga = document.createElement('script');
16     ga.type = 'text/javascript';
17     ga.async = true;
18     ga.src = ('https:' == document.location.protocol?
19                         'https://ssl' : 'http://www')
20             + '.google-analytics.com/ga.js';
21     var s = document.getElementsByTagName('script')[0];
22     s.parentNode.insertBefore(ga, s);
23   })();
24 </script>
```

Line 4 contains the analytics identifier. You need to replace it with your own identifier.

Lines 6 through 9 set the page load time, and lines 10, 11, and 12 set the server status if available.

Lines 14 through 23 are unchanged from the original Google script. Line breaks have been added to make the code readable.

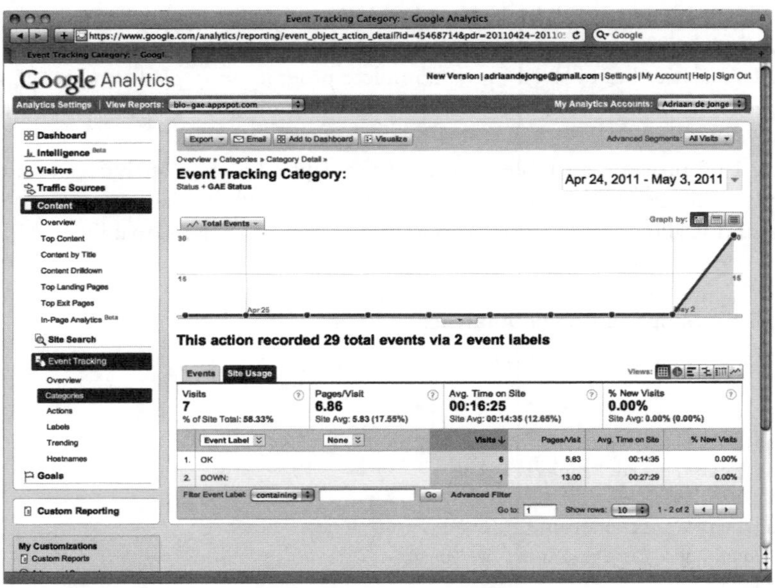

Figure 19.4 An example screen for Google Analytics.

Figure 19.4 shows the Analytics interface showing statistics for the server uptime variable. This is not real data: the downtime is simulated. As a result, the statistics show that users stay longer when the system is down. It would be surprising to see that in real-world data.

Introducing all features of Google Analytics is beyond the scope of this book. Analytics is a tool that helps track campaigns, measure conversion in multistep funnels toward a clear end goal, and discover correlations between certain parameters and resulting revenue.

You are encouraged to use Google Analytics for your application and use your curiosity to get the most information out of it.

Summary

This chapter emphasized that testing is not sufficient to find all deficits in a software product. It suggested using the somewhat unorthodox approach of allowing a short period right after a production release to fix possible flaws.

This chapter considered usability as a measure of fitness for purpose rather than a statement on the appearance of an application. If an application helps its users perform tasks in a minimum amount of time, with minimal effort, and without a learning curve, an application is more usable than one that only looks good.

The chapter explained how the Capabilities API is used to detect availability of services. If you know a service is unavailable, you can prevent exceptions and provide a friendly message to users early in their interaction rather than later in the process.

The App Engine admin interface was demonstrated, showing how it allows access to log messages in a fine-grained way. Right after a production release, fine-grained messages are important to optimizing the application and fixing early problems. Once the early flaws are corrected, the errors should be filtered by severity, allowing the more substantial errors to stand out.

Finally, this chapter explained how Google Analytics is more than just another statistics tool. It has grown into a full programming platform for measuring user actions on web applications. Curiosity and some programming skills are the key ingredients to optimizing a web application to fit user preferences.

Chapter 20

Selling Your Application

This chapter provides a high-level overview of ways to promote your application and improve sales. It starts by advising you to hire professional sales people if you can afford to. If you can't, the remainder of the chapter discusses promotional techniques that don't require much marketing knowledge. Finally, the chapter describes Google's facility for handling payments once you have converted your visitors into customers.

Determining How to Approach Sales

If you are developing your application for a large company, you should leave the selling of your product to the people who do it best: your marketing and sales departments. Team up with them, and give them a say in your App Engine application development. Even if you don't like their suggestions, keep an open mind and try to compromise: their ideas may help your application reach a broader audience.

Chances are, you do not have the luxury of dedicated sales professionals to market your product. If you work for yourself or for a smaller company, you are the target audience of this chapter. This chapter provides basic advice on promoting your application with minimal resources.

Note that I do not have a background in sales or marketing: this chapter therefore approaches sales from a technical perspective. It provides an overview of technical tools available to help promote your application. Any nontechnical advice in this chapter is opinion and should be disregarded if your sales professionals have better advice.

Once you generate sufficient revenues on your own, don't make the mistake of becoming overly confident in your marketing skills. Chances are good that you can be even more successful if you use the right resources. Once you can afford it, invest in a professional marketing or sales consultant and set a sales strategy to further expand your market.

Knowing Your Audience

It is impossible to write a generic recipe for promoting your App Engine application that works in every situation for every audience. For example, compare selling an online game for 5-year-old children to selling a productivity tool for Java developers.

You must find out the needs and desires of your target audience. What problems do they encounter regularly that your tool can solve? What sites do they visit? How much are they willing to spend on a solution? Are they willing to recommend your App Engine application to their friends? How can you build a relationship with your customers? How can you walk the extra mile to exceed their expectations?

Do you have a single uniform audience or multiple, diverse customer groups? Have you considered white-labeling your App Engine application and offering it under multiple brands, each optimized and targeted to a specific audience?

Is it possible to form a reference group of people who are representative of your audience? Are they willing to review applications and ideas, providing input and feedback to help you tailor your offering to users' needs?

An approach used in many companies is to invent fictive *personas*. A persona is an imaginary person with a name, a description of stereotypical characteristics, and a mood board with drawings, pictures, and trademarks. Using two or three personas to characterize your audience helps you design your application to fit your customers' needs and communicate your marketing strategy efficiently. Imagining a real person also helps your own thought process when you are tuning your application for your audience.

Reaching Your Audience

Once you know your audience, you should have a general idea of the sites they visit. You must create a presence on these sites, which can provide your first entry point to reach potential customers. Several strategies are available to do so, each with varying costs and effort.

Making the News

The best way to get promoted is to offer something so revolutionary or radically different that it is worth a news story. If published on the right sites, using a catchy title, a significant audience is confronted with your offer. If your application is mentioned in a headline on a well-known news site, you can be sure to attract new visitors.

Larger companies use press releases to get the attention of news sites. Smaller companies and the self-employed can do the same. Write a story about your application, submit it to your contacts (you can find advice on the Internet about expanding your professional network), and use your creativity to grab the attention of news site editors.

You can search Google for sites allowing you to post your press release. Make sure your web site has sufficient follow-up on the news story to convert curious readers into customers.

Writing Articles

Not every new feature or application is stunning news. Not stunning can still be interesting, though. If you have innovative concepts in your App Engine application, you can write about them or ask others to write about them. Use the concept to entice readers to start using your application or at least to find out more about it. When writing your article, introduce the concept in an independent and objective way. For example, a few positive and sincere notes about a competitor may work to your advantage because readers recognize honesty. *Biased or commercial stories are unlikely to get published.*

Make sure you get your article published on a large website with a lot of daily visitors. An example of a website containing many articles on software development is IBM developerWorks. Keep in mind that IBM is mainly interested in selling its own products and providing objective technical insight. It is not a site for commercial advertisements.

Blogging

Publishing on larger websites is not always feasible. Your article must be selected by the site's editors, and the selection process sometimes takes several months. Some sites are not even open to outside contributions.

On the Internet, however, anyone can publish anything, any time, by opening a personal weblog. You can set up a basic weblog with your own domain and customized styling in less than an hour using simple tools like Blogger or Wordpress. Figure 20.1 displays an example of the weblog management interface of Blogger.

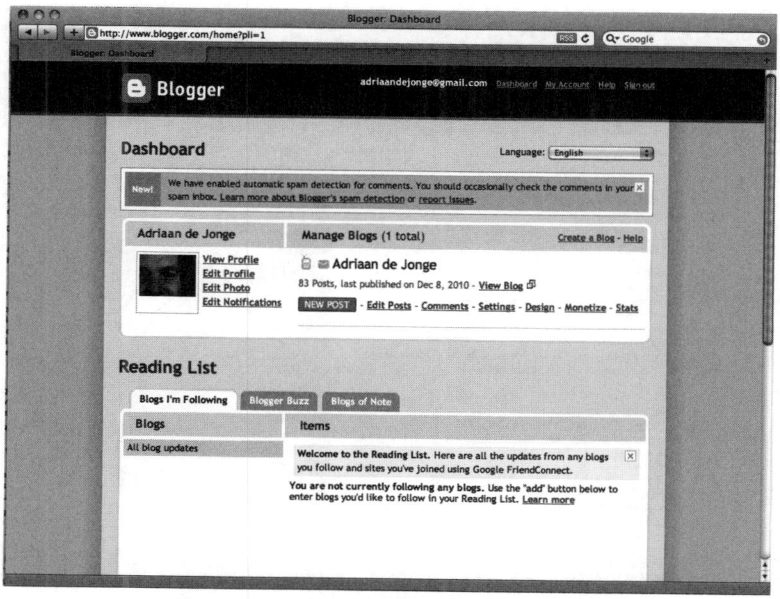

Figure 20.1 Managing a blog on Blogger.

If you blog regularly, your posts are picked up by Google and appear in relevant searches. In some cases, Google gives recent posts a higher ranking in the search results.

You can encourage your visitors to add your blog to their Really Simple Syndication (RSS) reader. That way, you increase the chance that the visitor returns to your site.

Another bonus feature of a weblog is that it allows you to publicly respond to other blog posts on the Internet. By notifying the author of the original post, sometimes you can initiate a public dialog, drawing the readers from the other blog to your site.

Writing on Twitter

It is challenging to write something stimulating or provocative in Twitter's limit of 140 characters, but people have proven it is possible to collect huge numbers of visitors just by typing short messages that draw attention.

Messages on Twitter regarding your App Engine application are unlikely to attract new followers. You have a better chance of attracting followers with thought-provoking messages not directly mentioning your product. Once people start following your Tweets, they also receive your messages that do directly mention your product. Figure 20.2 displays Twitter messages regarding Google App Engine, demonstrating how easy it is to pick up anonymous posters writing on specific subjects.

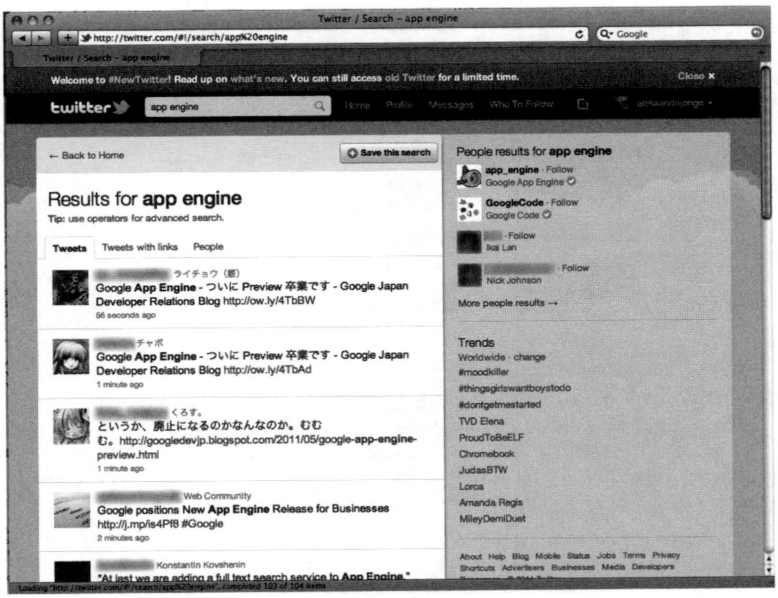

Figure 20.2 Gaining a following on Twitter.

Many active Twitter users collect their news using custom searches. If you know common search keys, you can use them to reach an audience beyond your own followers.

Responding to other people's Tweets is also a way to draw attention. If you capture their interest, their followers may check out your profile and start following you.

Despite all these efforts, the real key to success is in the quality of your messages. Generating a steady stream of messages that constantly persuades new visitors to keep following you is a real talent.

Publishing Facebook Pages

Companies, products, celebrities, and fictional characters are not allowed to have a regular Facebook page. Facebook allows you to create pages for such entities. A page can contain most of the same items a regular user has, but instead of becoming friends, a visitor "Likes" the page in order to subscribe to it. Figure 20.3 shows the automatically created Facebook page for the Google App Engine.

Messages posted to the page are displayed in the user's news feed. The challenge is to avoid flooding the user with useless, boring, and irrelevant commercial messages. Instead, you should post small numbers of entertaining items, seemingly unrelated to your App Engine application, attracting the user to visit your site and remember your brand. Don't be too eager to sell. That may scare potential customers away.

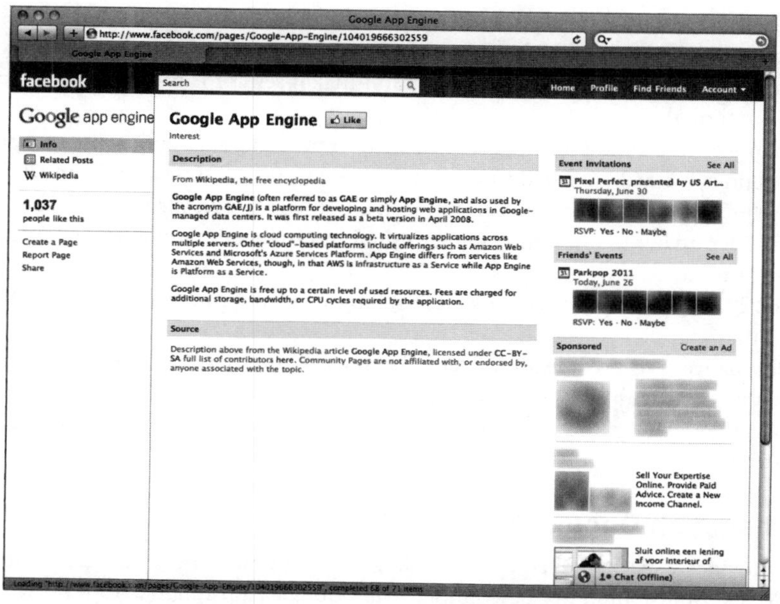

Figure 20.3 Creating a page on Facebook Pages.

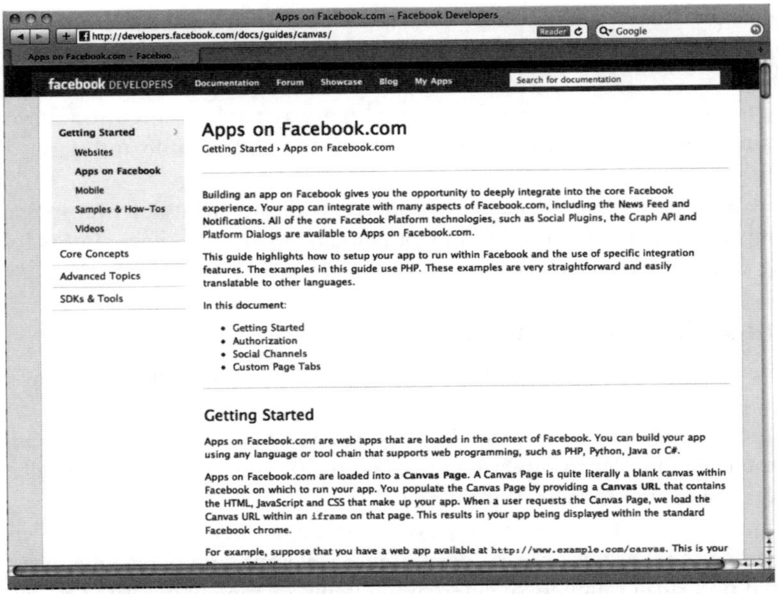

Figure 20.4 Getting started with Facebook Apps.

Connecting through Facebook Apps

With a little creativity, your application may become a Facebook App. This means connecting with the user's Facebook profile, integrating with pictures, messages, videos, and friends. It is important that this integration makes sense for the purpose of your application, though.

Your application should encourage users to recommend your application to their friends. Some incentive is usually needed to encourage users to spread the word. Rewarding accomplishments with a credible scoring mechanism may get results at minimal costs. You could consider giving the monthly winner significant influence in the feature list planned for the next release.

Figure 20.4 displays the Facebook page telling you how to create your own Facebook applications.

An alternative is to provide a monetary incentive. Customers bringing in new customers could be rewarded with (for example) a 10 percent discount for every new customer they bring in. If they manage to provide more than 10 customers, perhaps they could even be allowed to use your services for free.

Advertising on Google Apps Marketplace

Google provides a specialized App Store selling web applications that integrate with Google Apps. Google Apps should not be confused with Google App Engine. Apps is the name for Google's online office suite, providing a word processor, spreadsheet, and presentation tool all through a browser interface.

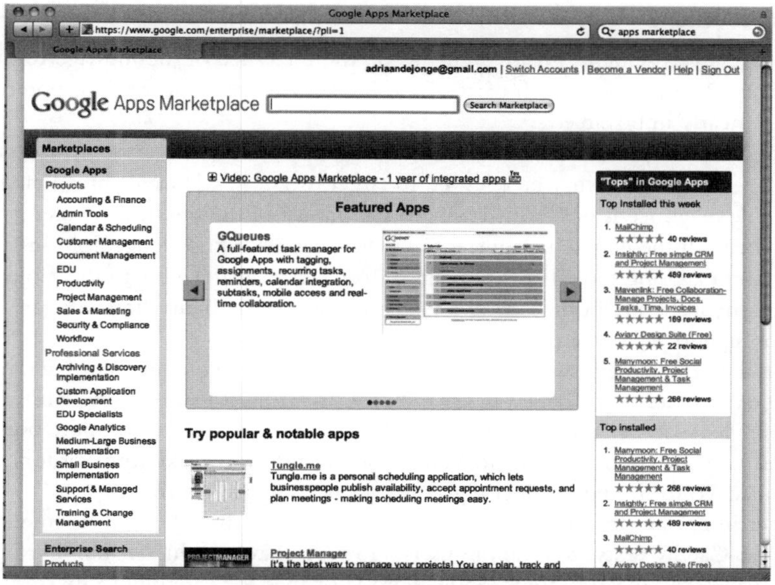

Figure 20.5 Google Apps Marketplace.

The marketing of Google Apps is mainly targeted at companies. The slogan "Going Google" means replacing Microsoft Office with Google's online suite. The main advantage is that Google Apps is not tied to a single workstation or platform. It is ideally suited for working from multiple locations, and it even allows editing a single document with multiple users at the same time. Figure 20.5 shows a screenshot the Google Apps Marketplace.

You can integrate your application with Google Apps using the technology introduced in Chapter 16, "Securing a Web Application Using Google Accounts, OpenID, and OAuth." Using a combination of OpenID and OAuth, you can request access to part of the content of a user's Google Apps. To simplify communication with Apps, Google provides the Google Data (GData) library on multiple platforms, including Java. Demonstrating GData is beyond the scope of this book. You can find introductory articles on Google's website.

The purpose of integrating with Google Apps greatly depends on your application. If your application processes even the most basic dates, Google Calendar may be an interesting platform to target.

To announce your application on Google Apps Marketplace, you must comply with Google's conditions. Part of the deal is that Google receives 20 percent of your revenue generated through the Marketplace. Because of that, you are required to use Google Checkout as your payment provider.

A small but useful feature of Google Apps Marketplace is *suggestions*. Visitors unable to find applications to meet their needs can post requests on a board. Other visitors can vote for existing suggestions to increase their popularity. A quick glance at the most popular feature requests can be inspiring for your next application release cycle.

Using AdWords

The value of advertisements greatly depends on the relevance of the message to the user who reads it. Determining which parts of the Internet are relevant for your potential audience is nearly impossible.

Google AdWords provides out-of-the box machinery to serve advertisements to the exact users to whom they may be relevant. To target users, Google uses a broad range of methods. The relevance is not limited only to the subject of the site that the user is visiting at that moment. If the engine recognizes the user, it has prior knowledge from his or her browsing history. Using some heuristics, this history can be matched with the subjects of the advertisements. Only in the case of a match is the advertisement shown. Figure 20.6 displays the signup page where you can start using Google Ads.

To optimize the benefit of AdWords, you should analyze the conversion rate. You can use Google Analytics, as described in Chapter 19, "Assuring Quality Using Measuring Tools." Google Analytics and Google AdWords can be connected to compute both the conversion rate and revenue from AdWords. The revenue you make from visitors you gain from AdWords should far outweigh the cost of using AdWords.

Another important factor to get the most out of AdWords is the advertisement text you provide. Catchy texts attract more users. However, having a higher number of visitors does not necessarily mean more revenue. Word your message carefully to make sure you attract visitors interested in your application rather than visitors who are only curious to find out what your advertisement meant.

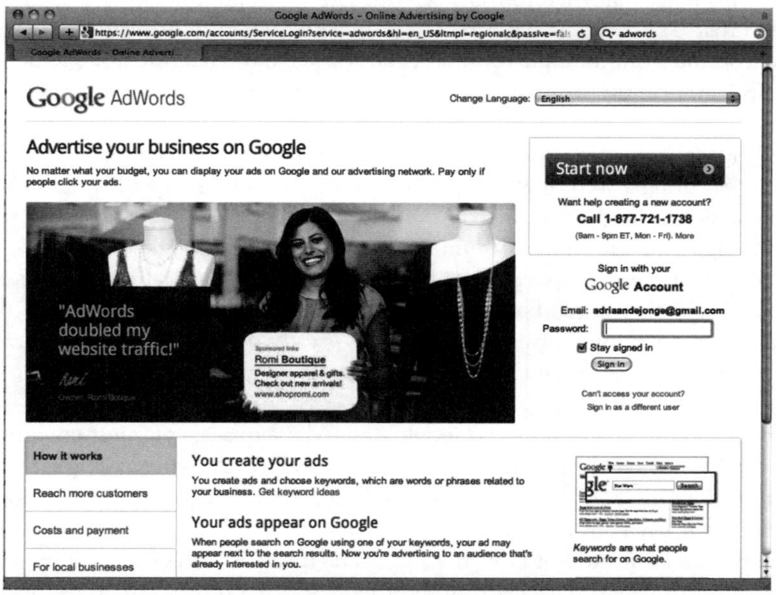

Figure 20.6 Google AdWords.

Optimizing Your App for Search Engines

The section on blogging already mentioned the Google search engine as a source of potential customers. Even better is to attract visitors directly to your application's website through searches. There are some common pitfalls that undermine your position in Google results. A few simple best practices help you avoid these pitfalls.

Your application should use clean, human-readable URLs. Google prefers descriptive URLs containing the most important keywords over computer-generated IDs. URLs using only paths are preferable over URL `GET` parameters if you want to achieve higher rankings.

Meaningful hierarchical structures are preferred over large, flat collections of content. To index a page, there must be a link. Websites using nested index pages as a hierarchy referring to logically separated sets of content documents get better ranks.

Readable, clean HTML that does not rely on JavaScript for a basic view gets better results than JavaScript-dependent pages. See Chapter 8, "Adding Static Interactions Using JavaScript," for a more detailed explanation.

Last but not least, for a Google visitor to find a specific page, the term he or she is searching on must be in the text of the document he or she wants to find. In other words, for a page to be found in Google, it needs unique, relevant, and descriptive texts discussing the subjects that users search on. Search engine optimization (SEO) texts must be authentic and genuine to do well in Google. Using tricks to generate or steal texts may lead to punishments with lower rankings if Google finds out.

Using Social Bookmarking Sites

A few years ago, just before the Facebook hype really took off, a lot of people were sharing links using tools like Digg, Del.icio.us, Slashdot, and RedDit. Even though their popularity declined a little due to Facebook, these social bookmarking and voting tools still generate lots of traffic if your site is highlighted as a popular resource.

AddThis.com is a site providing a simple JavaScript to add a set of buttons anywhere you like. These buttons refer to Facebook, Digg, Del.icio.us, Slashdot, and RedDit. Adding such button bars makes it easier for your users to share a page from your site.

Keep in mind that AddThis.com is an additional client-side script that may affect the load time of your application. Depending on the services you'd like to promote, you can perhaps offer a more efficient implementation if you write the scripts displaying the social buttons instead of using AddThis.com. Or you can start with AddThis.com and replace it with your own implementation as soon as you have time.

Attracting Customers Using Mobile App Stores

Google Apps Marketplace is not the only centralized online software store. There is also the Google AppStore for Android, Apple's iTunes, Nokia's Ovi Store, Microsoft Windows Phone Marketplace, and BlackBerry AppWorld. These are all places where you can sell mobile applications related to your App Engine application.

Depending on the functionality of your application, you can consider developing a mobile alternative interface. This serves multiple purposes. First of all, you help your customer by providing extra ways to access your application. Second, you may attract additional customers coming in through the mobile app stores.

However, if a mobile application does not fit in your application's strategy, there is a good chance that the development and maintenance costs are prohibitive for using additional interfaces as a marketing tool. The way you market your App Engine application greatly depends on your audience and the application domain.

Converting Prospects into Paying Customers

So far, we have focused on attracting customers to your website. Once they are there, you need to lead them from the entrance page to the step where they pay for an application they selected. As explained in Chapter 19, the percentage of users who complete the full process from entering to paying is called your conversion rate. In addition, you have conversion rates for each step in the process. If you want to optimize your revenue, you should optimize your conversion rates.

Your goal is to convince the customer as quickly as possible of the following things:

1. He or she has a problem that needs fixing or a need that must be fulfilled.
2. Your App Engine application fixes the problem or fulfills the need in a unique, outstanding way.
3. He or she should buy your application right now!

How you do this depends on your application. Some companies provide pages with lots of text and details to convince their customers. Other companies present their application in no more than three keywords together with visuals like icons and drawings.

You can choose to offer demonstration movies, screenshots, 30-day trials, free editions with limited functionality, or any variant of any of these themes. If you offer free samples of your application, make sure your application invites the user to upgrade to the paid edition. Nagging customers is not always the best invitation.

Handling the Payment Process

Receiving payments from credit cards and bank accounts in a safe and reliable way requires specialized knowledge and a well-organized backend to handle all possible details, exceptions, and legal issues.

Most websites outsource their payment process to a payment service provider (PSP). PSPs take most of the work and details off your hands. However, even after payments have been handled, you should take great care that paying customers receive the services they paid for. Refer to Chapter 16 for more information on security concerns when handling an important transaction.

Earlier in this chapter, Google Apps Marketplace was mentioned as a way to promote your application. The Apps Marketplace requires you to use Google Checkout as your PSP.

When you rely on Google for the rest of your application's infrastructure, you can justify also relying on Google Checkout for handling your payments.

If you do not use the Apps Marketplace, you may consider Amazon Payments, PayPal, or similar services. Your decision may depend on transaction costs, service level agreements, and possible legal issues in the countries you are targeting.

Summary

This chapter introduced the subject of selling your application. Marketing and selling applications requires different skills than developing software applications. The chapter suggested hiring marketing professionals to improve your sales if you can afford to. If not, you can use some of your technical skills to attract the attention of potential customers.

Next, this chapter suggested practical ways to attract customers, including publishing news items, articles, blog posts, and Twitter messages. In addition, it suggested creating a presence on Facebook in more than one way. Google offers the Apps Marketplace, AdWords, and its own search engine to help you promote your application. Other tools that may attract additional customers are social bookmarking sites or app stores targeted at mobile applications related to your App Engine application.

Once you attract visitors to your website, you must convince them to buy your App Engine application. There is no silver bullet for closing sales, but this chapter provided some pointers on what you should pay attention to.

Finally, you need to choose how you handle payments. If you choose the Google infrastructure, then Google Checkout is a logical choice. There are alternatives to consider if you are not bound to Google Apps Marketplace.

Index

Numbers

A

B

D

E

F

K

L

M

N

O

P

Q

R

S

U

V

W

X

Y

Addison
Wesley
REGISTER
THIS PRODUCT
informit.com/register